Touring Atlas of South Africa

and

Botswana · Mozambique · Namibia · Zimbabwe

CONTENTS

South Africa : Main Map pages and Key 2-3

Cape Town, Clanwilliam and Swellendam 4
Knysna, Oudtshoorn and Beaufort West 5
Port Elizabeth, Graaff-Reinet and Grahamstown 6
East London, King William's Town and Umtata 7
Namaqualand and Alexander Bay 8
Upington, Kenhardt and Calvinia 9
Prieska, Griquatown and Carnarvon 10
Bloemfontein, Kimberley and Middelburg 11
Lesotho, Harrismith and Umtata 12
Durban, Ulundi and Port Edward 13
Namib Desert, Ai-Ais and Fish River Canyon Park 14
Kgalagadi Transfrontier Park and Karasburg 15
Kalahari Desert and Kuruman 16
Mafikeng, Vryburg and Welkom 17
Gauteng, Ermelo and Harrismith 18
Swaziland, Nelspruit and Ulundi 19
Gaborone, Palapye and Mokopane (Potgietersrus) 20
Polokwane (Pietersburg) and Kruger National Park 21

South Africa : Areas of Interest in detail and Key 22-23

The Cape Peninsula 24-25
Stellenbosch, Paarl and Franschhoek Vineyards 26-27
Wine Region of the Western Cape 28-29
Western Cape 30-31
The Wilderness 32-33
Tsitsikamma National Park 34-35
Port Elizabeth and East London 36-37
KwaZulu-Natal's South Coast 38-39
KwaZulu-Natal's North Coast 40-41
uKhahlamba-Drakensberg Park 42-43
Kruger National Park 44-45
Pilanesberg and Magaliesberg Region 46-47
The Witwatersrand 48-49

City and Administrative Centres and Key 50

Cape Town and The Waterfront 51
Pretoria 52
Johannesburg 53
Bloemfontein and Environs 54
Durban and Environs 55
Pietermaritzburg and Ulundi 56
East London, King William's Town and Bisho 57
Port Elizabeth and Environs 58
Kimberley and Environs 59
Mafikeng and Environs 60
Nelspruit and Environs 61
Polokwane (Pietersburg) and Environs 62

Neighbouring Countries and Key 63

Namibia 64-65
Windhoek – Namibia 66
Etosha National Park – Namibia 67
Botswana 68
Gaborone and Okavango Delta – Botswana 69
Zimbabwe – Victoria Falls and Hwange National Park 70-71
Harare and Bulawayo – Zimbabwe 72
Nyanga National Park and Great Zimbabwe 73
Mozambique 74
Maputo and Beira – Mozambique 75

SUNBIRD PUBLISHING

First published 2000
6 8 10 9 7

Publisher Dick Wilkins
Cartographer & Designer John Hall
Production Manager Andrew de Kock
Reproduced by Unifoto (Pty) Ltd, Cape Town
Printed and bound by Tien Wah Press (Pte) Ltd, Singapore

ISBN 0 624 03846 7

PHOTOGRAPHIC CREDITS

Cover: Giant's Castle, uKhahlamba-Drakensberg Park – Roger de la Harpe

Page 7 – Roger de la Harpe
Page 8 – Pat de la Harpe
Page 13 – D. Allen / Photo Access
Page 37 – G. Whittal / Gallo Images
Page 39 – Roger de la Harpe
Page 41 – W. Knirr / Photo Access
Page 67 – F. Savigny / Cape Photo Library
Page 73 – D. Allen / Photo Access
Page 74 – P. Wagner / Photo Access

Please note that where town names have changed we have included the previous name in brackets as road signs may still show the old name.

Scale 1 : 1 500 000

FOR THE MAPS IN THE MAIN MAP SECTION

0 15 30 45 60 75 km

0 10 20 30 40 miles

KEY

Motorway
National road
Main road
Secondary road
Route numbers — N7, R43, R302
Other route numbers — B1, 208, D620
Toll route — T
Distances in kilometres — 6
Mountain pass — Hex River
Railway
International boundary
Provincial boundary
Nature reserve — Kirstenbosch N.R.
River, marsh and dam
City with built-up area
City or major town
Administrative town/city
Secondary town
Small town
Large village
Village
Small village or station
International airport
Secondary airport
Rest camp/holiday resort
Border crossing — Vioolsdrif
Place of interest — Picnic area
Battle site
Monument
Cave
Waterfall — Augrabies Falls
Hot spring
Page continuation number (outside map border) — 15

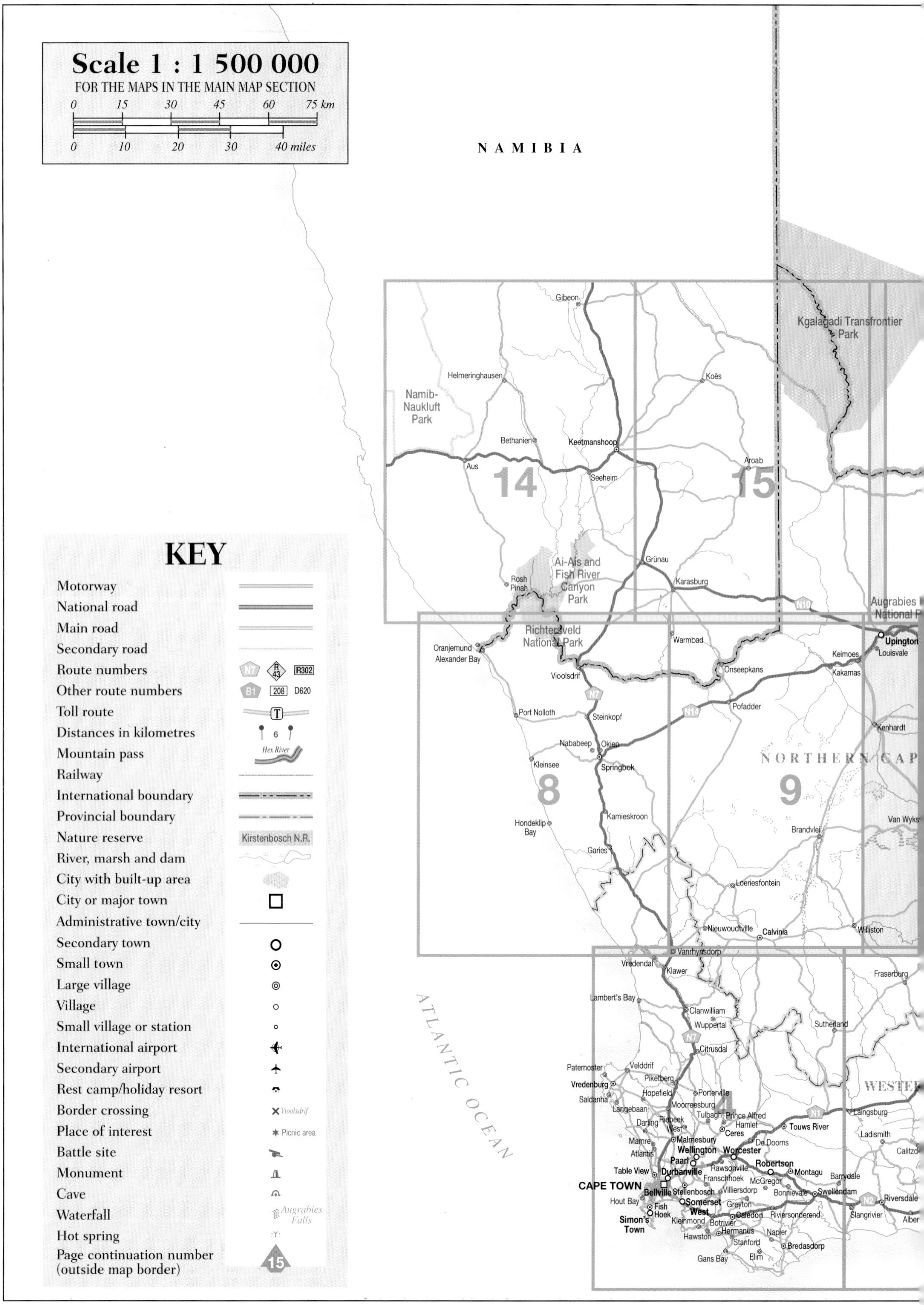

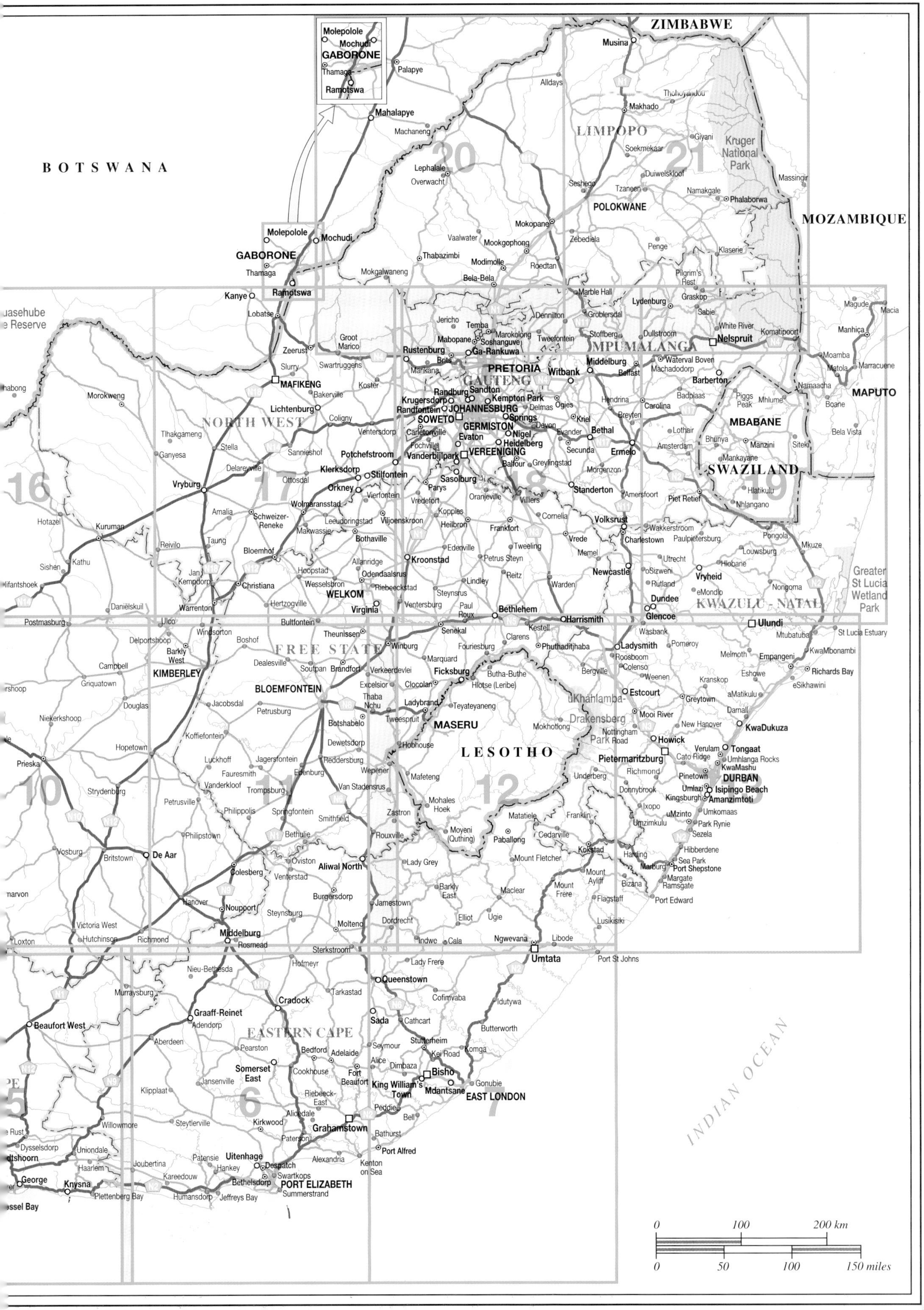
ZIMBABWE
BOTSWANA
MOZAMBIQUE
LIMPOPO
MPUMALANGA
GAUTENG
NORTH WEST
FREE STATE
KWAZULU - NATAL
EASTERN CAPE
LESOTHO
SWAZILAND
INDIAN OCEAN
Kruger National Park
Greater St Lucia Wetland Park
uKhahlamba-Drakensberg Park
Molepolole
Mochudi
GABORONE
Thamaga
Ramotswa
Palapye
Mahalapye
Machaneng
Lephalale
Overwacht
Musina
Alldays
Thohoyandou
Makhado
Giyani
Soekmekaar
Duiwelskloof
Seshego
Tzaneen
Namakgale
Phalaborwa
Massingir
POLOKWANE
Mokopane
Zebediela
Vaalwater
Mookgophong
Penge
Klaserie
Thabazimbi
Modimolle
Roedtan
Pilgrim's Rest
Mokgalwaneng
Bela-Bela
Marble Hall
Lydenburg
Graskop
Sabie
Kanye
Lobatse
Jericho
Temba
Dennilton
Groblersdal
Marokolong
Mabopane
Soshanguve
Tweefontein
Stoffberg
Dullstroom
White River
Nelspruit
Komatipoort
Magude
Macia
Manhiça
Groot Marico
Zeerust
Rustenburg
Ga-Rankuwa
Brits
Marikana
PRETORIA
Witbank
Middelburg
Belfast
Waterval Boven
Machadodorp
Moamba
Matola
Marracuene
MAPUTO
Slurry
Swartruggens
MAFIKENG
Koster
Bakerville
Barberton
Namaacha
Boane
Randburg
Sandton
Kempton Park
Krugersdorp
Randfontein
JOHANNESBURG
Delmas
Ogies
Hendrina
Carolina
Badplaas
Piggs Peak
Mhlume
MBABANE
Lichtenburg
Coligny
SOWETO
Springs
Kriel
Breyten
Bela Vista
Morokweng
Ventersdorp
Carletonville
GERMISTON
Evaton
Nigel
Devon
Evander
Bethal
Lothair
Bhunya
Manzini
Siteki
Tlhakgameng
Stella
Fochville
Heidelberg
Secunda
Amsterdam
Ganyesa
Sannieshof
Potchefstroom
Vanderbijlpark
VEREENIGING
Balfour
Greylingstad
Ermelo
Mankayane
Delareyville
Klerksdorp
Stilfontein
Morgenzon
Vryburg
Ottosdal
Orkney
Sasolburg
Parys
Standerton
Hlatikulu
Wolmaransstad
Vierfontein
Vredefort
Oranjeville
Villiers
Amersfoort
Piet Retief
Nhlangano
Hotazel
Amalia
Schweizer-Reneke
Leeudoringstad
Viljoenskroon
Kopples
Heilbron
Cornelia
Volksrust
Wakkerstroom
Kuruman
Makwassie
Frankfort
Charlestown
Paulpietersburg
Pongola
Mkuze
Taung
Bothaville
Edenville
Tweeling
Vrede
Louwsburg
Reivilo
Bloemhof
Kroonstad
Memel
Sishen
Kathu
Jan Kempdorp
Hoopstad
Allanridge
Petrus Steyn
Utrecht
Hlobane
Odendaalsrus
Newcastle
oSizweni
Vryheid
Christiana
Wesselsbron
Riebeeckstad
Lindley
Reitz
Rutland
Nongoma
WELKOM
Steynsrus
Warden
eMondlo
Daniëlskuil
Warrenton
Hertzogville
Virginia
Ventersburg
Paul Roux
Bethlehem
Dundee
Glencoe
Postmasburg
Ulco
Bultfontein
Theunissen
Senekal
Kestell
Harrismith
Ulundi
Windsorton
Clarens
Wasbank
Mtubatuba
St Lucia Estuary
Delportshoop
Boshof
Winburg
Fouriesburg
Phuthaditjhaba
Ladysmith
Pomeroy
Barkly West
Marquard
Roosboom
KwaMbonambi
Campbell
KIMBERLEY
Dealesville
Soutpan
Brandfort
Verkeerdevlei
Ficksburg
Butha-Buthe
Bergville
Colenso
Melmoth
Empangeni
Richards Bay
Griquatown
Excelsior
Clocolan
Hlotse (Leribe)
Weenen
Kranskop
Eshowe
eSikhawini
BLOEMFONTEIN
Thaba Nchu
Estcourt
Douglas
Jacobsdal
Petrusburg
Ladybrand
Teyateyaneng
Greytown
aMatikulu
Tweespruit
MASERU
Mooi River
Darnall
Niekerkshoop
Botshabelo
Mokhotlong
Nottingham Road
New Hanover
KwaDukuza
Koffiefontein
Dewetsdorp
Howick
Hopetown
Hobhouse
Verulam
Tongaat
Jagersfontein
Reddersburg
Pietermaritzburg
Cato Ridge
Umhlanga Rocks
KwaMashu
Prieska
Luckhoff
Fauresmith
Edenburg
Wepener
Richmond
Pinetown
DURBAN
Vanderkloof
Trompsburg
Mafeteng
Underberg
Donnybrook
Umlazi
Isipingo Beach
Kingsburgh
Amanzimtoti
Strydenburg
Van Stadensrus
Mohales Hoek
Petrusville
Philippolis
Springfontein
Smithfield
Zastron
Matatiele
Franklin
Ixopo
uMzinto
Umkomaas
Umzimkulu
Park Rynie
Sezela
Philipstown
Bethulie
Rouxville
Moyeni (Quthing)
Paballong
Cedarville
Kokstad
Hibberdene
Vosburg
Britstown
De Aar
Ovistion
Aliwal North
Lady Grey
Mount Fletcher
Harding
Sea Park
Port Shepstone
Marburg
Margate
Ramsgate
Colesberg
Venterstad
Barkly East
Mount Ayliff
Bizana
Mount Frere
Maclear
Flagstaff
Port Edward
Hanover
Burgersdorp
Jamestown
Noupoort
Steynsburg
Elliot
Ugie
Lusikisiki
Victoria West
Hutchinson
Molteno
Dordrecht
Middelburg
Richmond
Loxton
Rosmead
Indwe
Cala
Ngwevana
Libode
Sterkstroom
Umtata
Port St Johns
Hofmeyr
Lady Frere
Nieu-Bethesda
Queenstown
Murraysburg
Tarkastad
Cofimvaba
Cradock
Idutywa
Graaff-Reinet
Adendorp
Beaufort West
Sada
Cathcart
Aberdeen
Butterworth
Stutterheim
Pearston
Bedford
Adelaide
Seymour
Kei Road
Komga
Somerset East
Cookhouse
Fort Beaufort
Alice
Dimbaza
Bisho
Gonubie
Jansenville
Riebeeck-East
King William's Town
Mdantsane
EAST LONDON
Klipplaat
Alicedale
Peddie
Willowmore
Steytlerville
Kirkwood
Grahamstown
Bell
Paterson
Bathurst
Rust
Dysselsdorp
Uniondale
Port Alfred
Oudtshoorn
Joubertina
Patensie
Uitenhage
Alexandria
Kenton on Sea
Haarlem
Hankey
Despatch
George
Knysna
Kareedouw
Swartkops
Bethelsdorp
PORT ELIZABETH
Summerstrand
Plettenberg Bay
Humansdorp
Jeffreys Bay
Mossel Bay
Kgalagadi Transfrontier Park / Mabuasehube Game Reserve
N1
N2
N3
N4
N6
N9
N10
N11
N12
N14
N17
5
6
7
10
11
12
16
17
18
19
20
21
0
100
200 km
0
50
100
150 miles

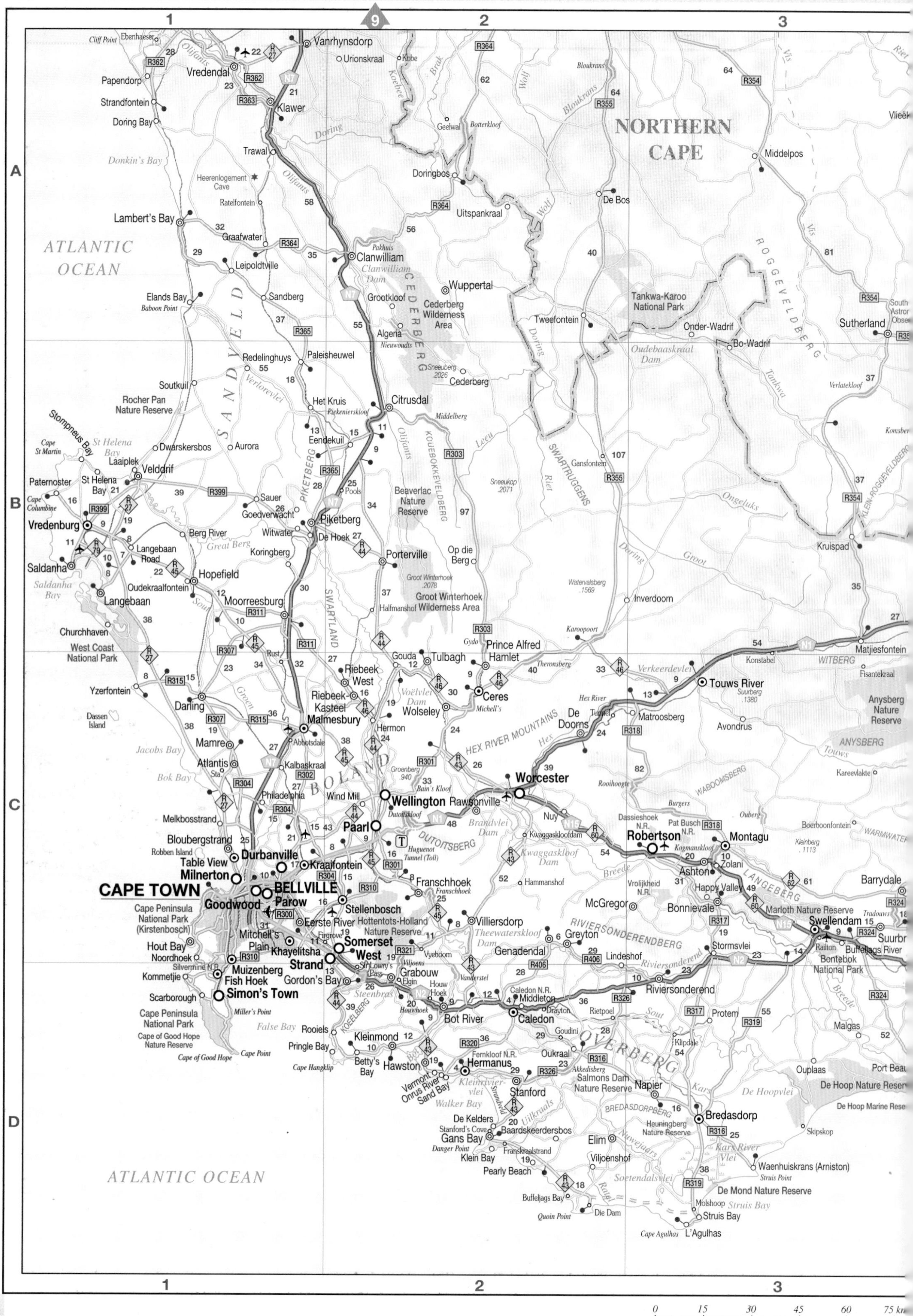
1
2
3
9
A
B
C
D
ATLANTIC OCEAN
NORTHERN CAPE
Cliff Point
Ebenhaeser
Vanrhynsdorp
Urionskraal
Kobe
Vredendal
Papendorp
Strandfontein
Klawer
Doring Bay
Donkin's Bay
Trawal
Heerenlogement Cave
Ratelfontein
Lambert's Bay
Graafwater
Leipoldtville
Clanwilliam
Clanwilliam Dam
Pakhuis
Elands Bay
Baboon Point
Sandberg
Grootkloof
Wuppertal
Cederberg Wilderness Area
CEDERBERG
Algeria
Nieuwoudts
Redelinghuys
Paleisheuwel
Soutkuil
Sneeuberg 2026
Cederberg
Rocher Pan Nature Reserve
SANDVELD
Het Kruis
Piekenierskloof
Citrusdal
Middelberg
Eendekuil
Stompneus Bay
Cape St Martin
St Helena Bay
Dwarskersbos
Aurora
Laaiplek
Velddrif
Paternoster
St Helena Bay
Cape Columbine
Vredenburg
Sauer
Goedverwacht
Piketberg
PIKETBERG
Witwater
De Hoek
Porterville
Berg River
Great Berg
Koringberg
Saldanha
Saldanha Bay
Langebaan Road
Hopefield
Oudekraalfontein
Langebaan
Moorreesburg
Beaverlac Nature Reserve
KOUEBOKKEVELDBERG
Op die Berg
Groot Winterhoek 2078
Groot Winterhoek Wilderness Area
Halfmanshof
SWARTLAND
Churchhaven
West Coast National Park
Rust
Gouda
Tulbagh
Prince Alfred Hamlet
Gydo
Riebeek-West
Riebeek-Kasteel
Voëlvlei Dam
Ceres
Michell's
Wolseley
Yzerfontein
Darling
Dassen Island
Malmesbury
Abbotsdale
Hermon
Mamre
Jacobs Bay
Atlantis
Kalbaskraal
BOLAND
Groenberg 940
Bain's Kloof
Bok Bay
Philadelphia
Wind Mill
Wellington
Rawsonville
Worcester
Melkbosstrand
Paarl
Dutoitskloof
Brandvlei Dam
Bloubergstrand
Robben Island
Table View
Durbanville
Kraaifontein
Huguenot Tunnel (Toll)
DUTOITSBERG
Milnerton
CAPE TOWN
BELLVILLE
Parow
Goodwood
Franschhoek
Stellenbosch
Cape Peninsula National Park (Kirstenbosch)
Eerste River
Hottentots-Holland Nature Reserve
Villiersdorp
Hout Bay
Noordhoek
Mitchell's Plain
Khayelitsha
Firgrove
Somerset West
Theewaterskloof Dam
Silvermine N.R.
Muizenberg
Fish Hoek
Kommetjie
Strand
Gordon's Bay
Sir Lowry's Pass
Viljoens
Vyeboom
Grabouw
Elgin
Vanderstel
Houw Hoek
Scarborough
Simon's Town
Steenbras
KOGELBERG
Houwhoek
Bot River
Cape Peninsula National Park
Miller's Point
False Bay
Rooiels
Cape of Good Hope Nature Reserve
Cape Point
Cape of Good Hope
Pringle Bay
Kleinmond
Cape Hangklip
Betty's Bay
Hawston
Vermont
Onrus River
Sand Bay
Hermanus
Fernkloof N.R.
Kleinriviervlei
Walker Bay
Stanford
De Kelders
Stanford's Cove
Gans Bay
Danger Point
Baardskeerdersbos
Franskraalstrand
Klein Bay
Pearly Beach
Buffeljags Bay
Quoin Point
Die Dam
Geelwal
Botterkloof
Doringbos
Uitspankraal
Bloukrans
Wolf
De Bos
Tankwa-Karoo National Park
Tweefontein
Onder-Wadrif
Bo-Wadrif
Oudebaaskraal Dam
ROGGEVELDBERG
Middelpos
Sutherland
South African Astronomical Observatory
Vlieëkraal
Verlatekloof
Komsberg
KLEIN-ROGGEVELDBERG
Kruispad
Sneeukop 2071
SWARTRUGGENS
Gansfontein
Watervalsberg 1569
Inverdoorn
Karoopoort
Theronsberg
Verkeerdevlei
Touws River
Suurberg 1380
Matjiesfontein
Konstabel
WITBERG
Fisantekraal
Anysberg Nature Reserve
ANYSBERG
Hex River
Tunnel
Matroosberg
De Doorns
HEX RIVER MOUNTAINS
Avondrus
Rooihoogte
WABOOMSBERG
Burgers
Kareevlakte
Nuy
Dassieshoek N.R.
Pat Busch N.R.
Robertson
Kogmanskloof
Montagu
Boerboonfontein
Kleinberg 1113
WARMWATERBERG
Kwaggaskloofdam
Kwaggaskloof Dam
Hammanshof
Breede
Ashton
Zolani
Vrolijkheid N.R.
Happy Valley
LANGEBERG
Barrydale
McGregor
Bonnievale
Marloth Nature Reserve
Tradouws
Swellendam
Suurbraak
Buffeljags River
Railton
Bontebok National Park
RIVIERSONDERENDBERG
Greyton
Genadendal
Lindeshof
Stormsvlei
Riviersonderend
Caledon N.R.
Middleton
Caledon
Drayton
Rietpoel
Protem
Malgas
Goudini
Oukraal
OVERBERG
Klipdale
Akkedisberg
Salmons Dam Nature Reserve
Napier
Ouplaas
Port Beaufort
De Hoop Nature Reserve
De Hoopvlei
De Hoop Marine Reserve
BREDASDORPBERG
Heuningberg Nature Reserve
Bredasdorp
Skipskop
Elim
Nuwejaars
Kars River Vlei
Viljoenshof
Waenhuiskrans (Arniston)
Struis Point
Soetendalsvlei
De Mond Nature Reserve
Molshoop
Struis Bay
Cape Agulhas
L'Agulhas
N1
N2
N7
R27
R43
R44
R45
R46
R60
R62
R300
R301
R302
R303
R304
R307
R310
R311
R315
R316
R317
R318
R319
R320
R321
R324
R326
R354
R355
R362
R363
R364
R365
R399
R406
0
15
30
45
60
75 km

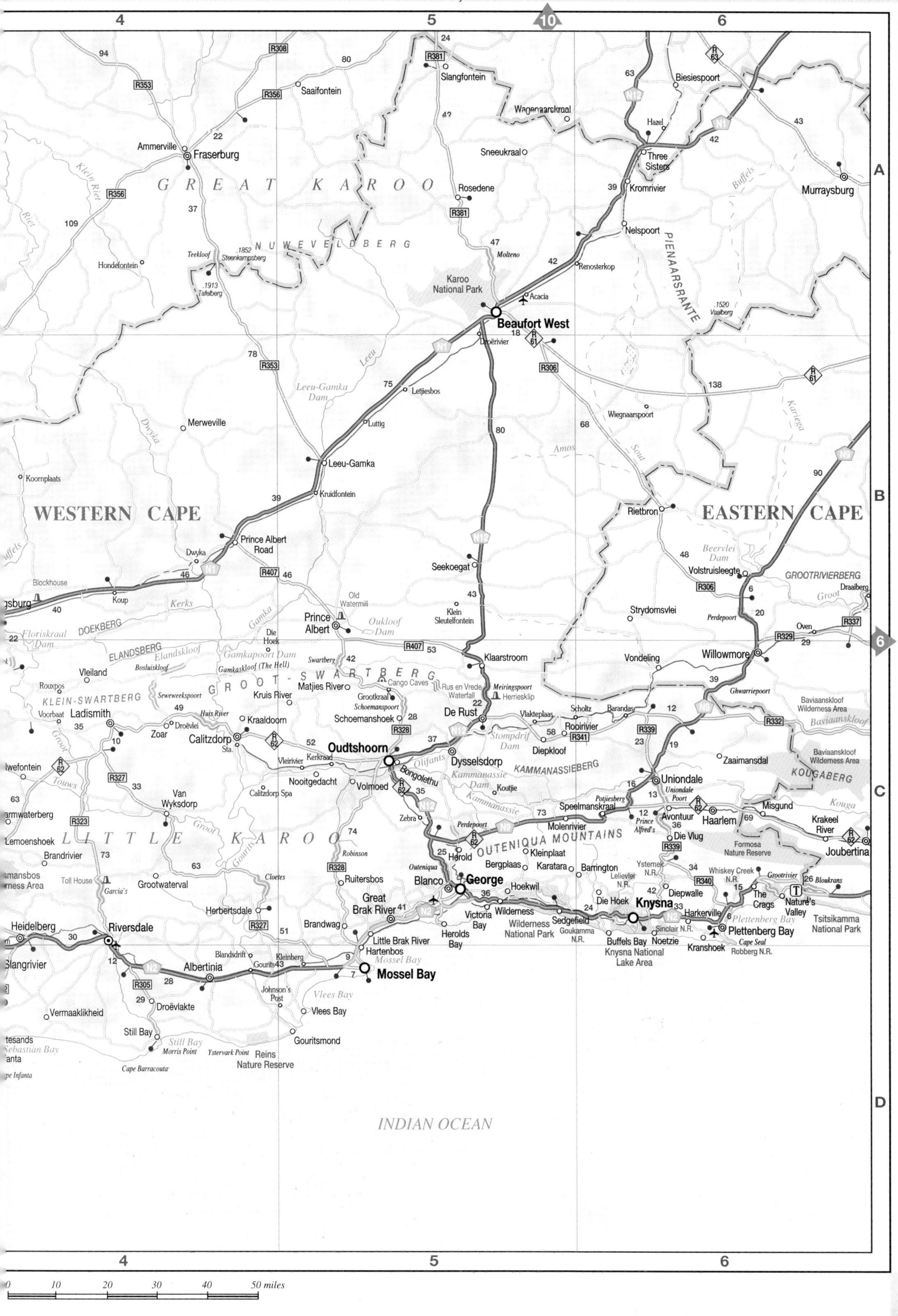
4
5
10
6
A
B
C
D
GREAT KAROO
NUWEVELDBERG
WESTERN CAPE
EASTERN CAPE
PIENAARSRANTE
LITTLE KAROO
GROOT-SWARTBERG
KLEIN-SWARTBERG
OUTENIQUA MOUNTAINS
KAMMANASSIEBERG
KOUGABERG
GROOTRIVIERBERG
ELANDSBERG
DOEKBERG
INDIAN OCEAN
Fraserburg
Ammerville
Saaifontein
Slangfontein
Wagenaarskraal
Biesiespoort
Hazel
Three Sisters
Kromrivier
Murraysburg
Sneeukraal
Rosedene
Nelspoort
Renosterkop
Molteno
Karoo National Park
Acacia
Beaufort West
Droërivier
Teekloof
1852 Steenkampsberg
1913 Tafelberg
1520 Vaalberg
Hondefontein
Leeu-Gamka Dam
Letjiesbos
Luttig
Leeu-Gamka
Merweville
Kruidfontein
Koornplaats
Wiegnaarspoort
Rietbron
Beervlei Dam
Volstruisleegte
Prince Albert Road
Dwyka
Blockhouse
Koup
Seekoegat
Klein Sleutelfontein
Old Watermill
Prince Albert
Oukloof Dam
Strydomsvlei
Draaiberg
Oven
Perdepoort
Willowmore
Vondeling
Klaarstroom
Die Hoek
Gamkapoort Dam
Gamkaskloof (The Hell)
Swartberg
Floriskraal Dam
Vleiland
Rouxpos
Voorbaat
Ladismith
Seweweekspoort
Huis River
Kruis River
Matjies River
Cango Caves
Grootkraal
Schoemanspoort
Schoemanshoek
Rus en Vrede Waterfall
Meiringspoort
Herrieskip
De Rust
Ghwarriepoort
Baviaanskloof Wilderness Area
Baviaanskloof
Vlakteplaas
Scholtz
Barandas
Rooirivier
Stompdrif Dam
Diepkloof
Zaaimansdal
Kraaldoorn
Droëvlei
Zoar
Calitzdorp
Oudtshoorn
Vleirivier
Kerkraad
Nooitgedacht
Calitzdorp Spa
Volmoed
Bongolethu
Dysselsdorp
Kammanassie Dam
Koutjie
Uniondale
Uniondale Poort
Potjiesberg
Speelmanskraal
Misgund
Kouga
Krakeel River
Joubertina
Avontuur
Prince Alfred's
Haarlem
Die Vlug
Formosa Nature Reserve
Van Wyksdorp
Zebra
Perdepoort
Molenrivier
Kleinplaat
Herold
Robinson
Ruitersbos
Outeniqua
Blanco
George
Bergplaas
Karatara
Barrington
Lelievlei N.R.
Ystervlei N.R.
Whiskey Creek N.R.
Grootrivier
Bloukrans
Nature's Valley
The Crags
Diepwalle
Hoekwil
Wilderness
Victoria Bay
Wilderness National Park
Sedgefield
Goukamma N.R.
Die Hoek
Knysna
Harkerville
Plettenberg Bay
Sinclair N.R.
Noetzie
Buffels Bay
Knysna National Lake Area
Kranshoek
Cape Seal
Robberg N.R.
Tsitsikamma National Park
Herolds Bay
Great Brak River
Little Brak River
Hartenbos
Mossel Bay
Brandwag
Herbertsdale
Cloetes
Grootwaterval
Gourits
Toll House
Garcia's
Lemoenshoek
Brandrivier
Riversdale
Heidelberg
Albertinia
Blandsdrift
Kleinberg
Johnson's Post
Vlees Bay
Droëvlakte
Vermaaklikheid
Still Bay
Morris Point
Ystervark Point
Reins Nature Reserve
Gouritsmond
Cape Barracouta
N1
N2
N9
N12
R61
R62
R63
R306
R308
R323
R327
R328
R329
R332
R337
R339
R340
R341
R353
R356
R381
R407
0
10
20
30
40
50 miles

PORT ELIZABETH, GRAAFF-REINET and GRAHAMSTOWN

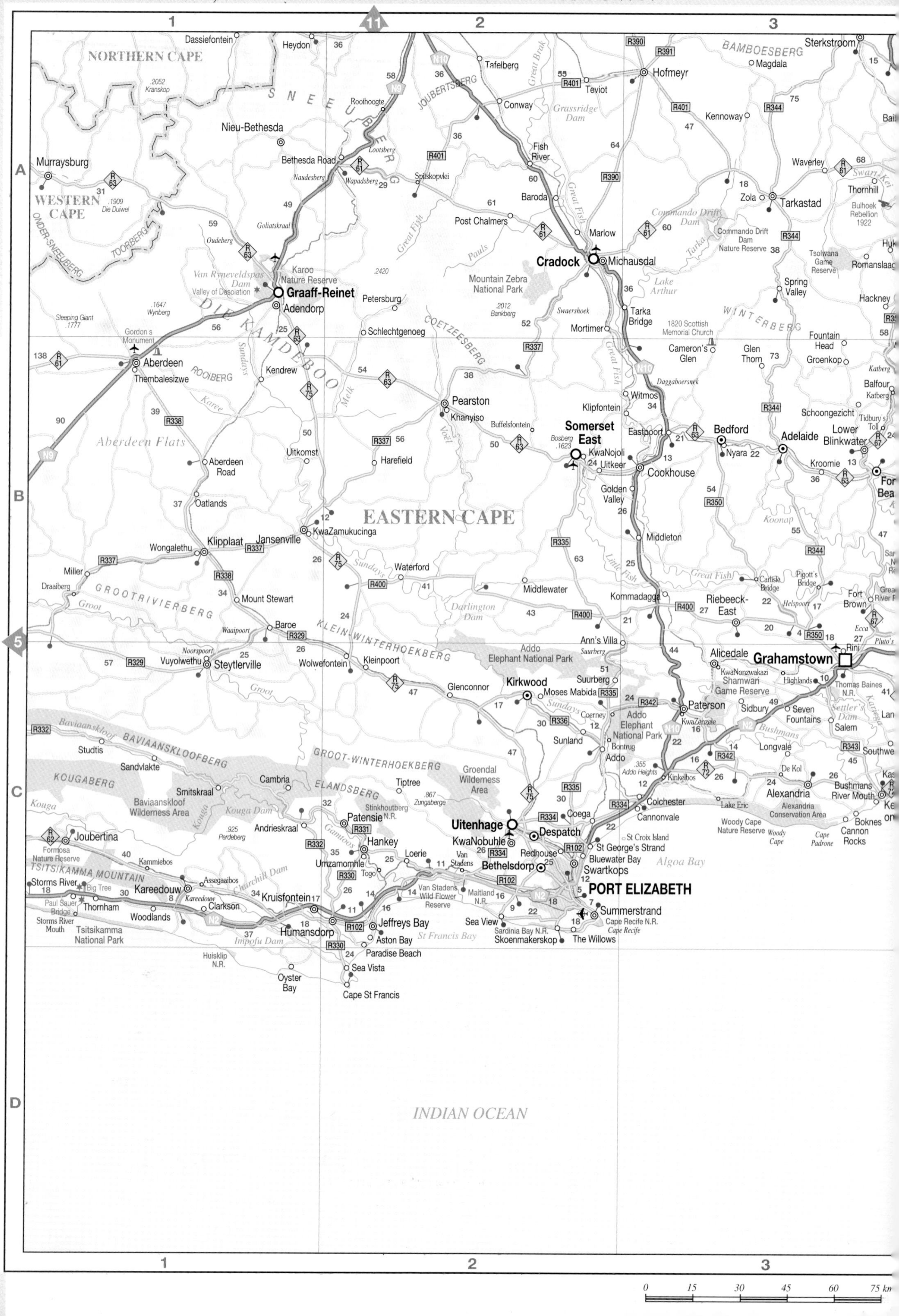

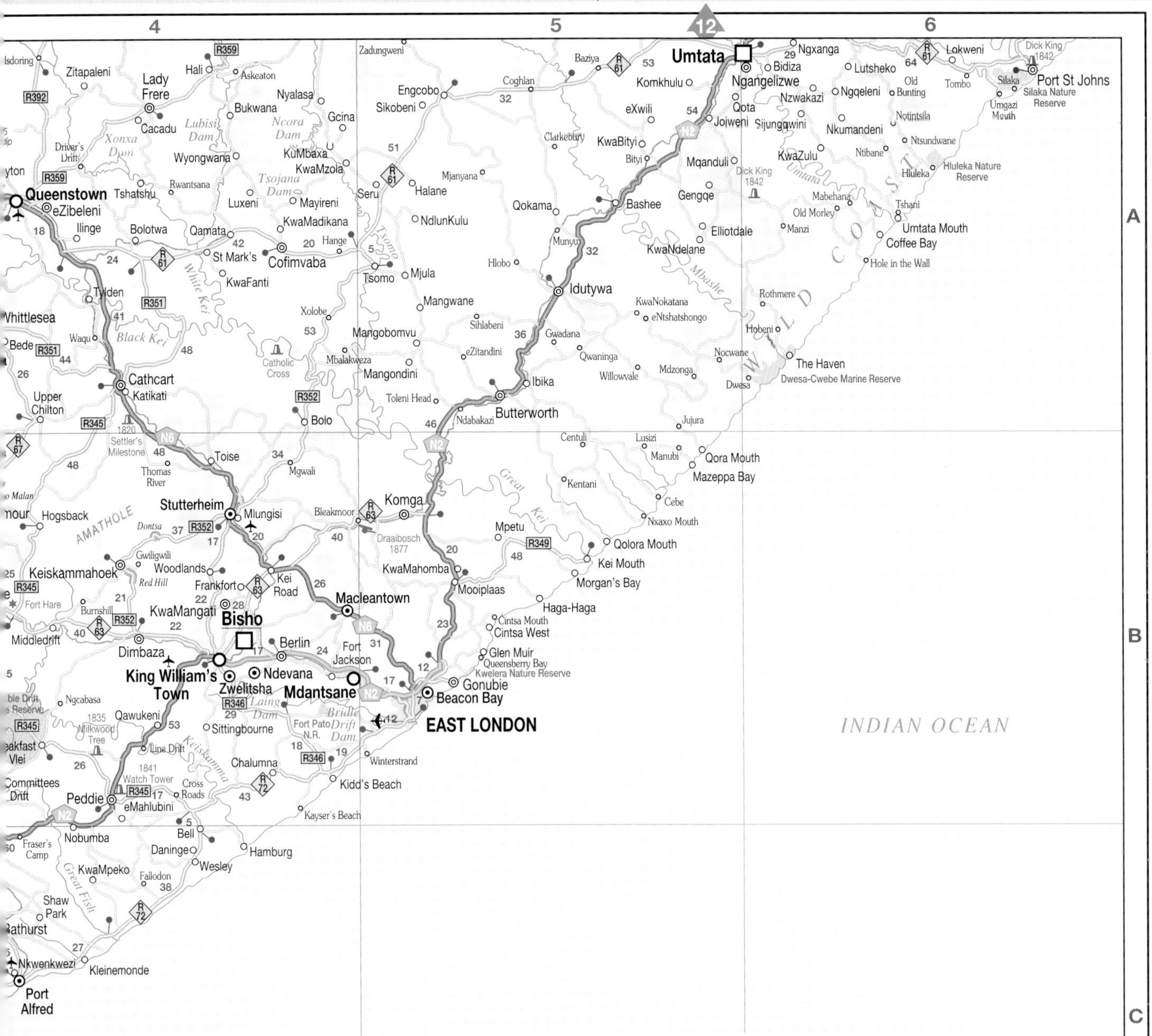

Mountain Zebra National Park near Cradock

0 10 20 30 40 50 miles

NAMAQUALAND and ALEXANDER BAY

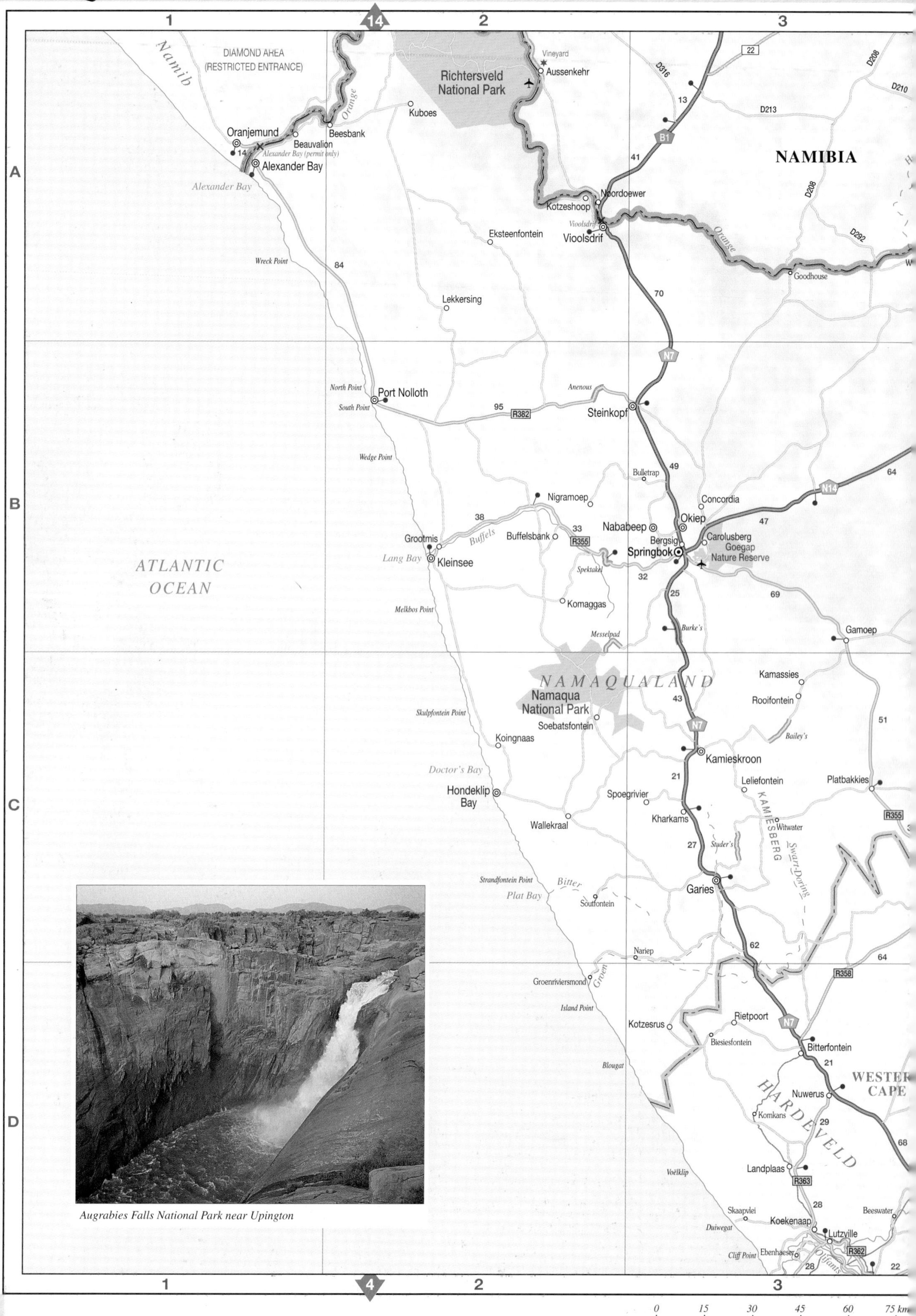

Augrabies Falls National Park near Upington

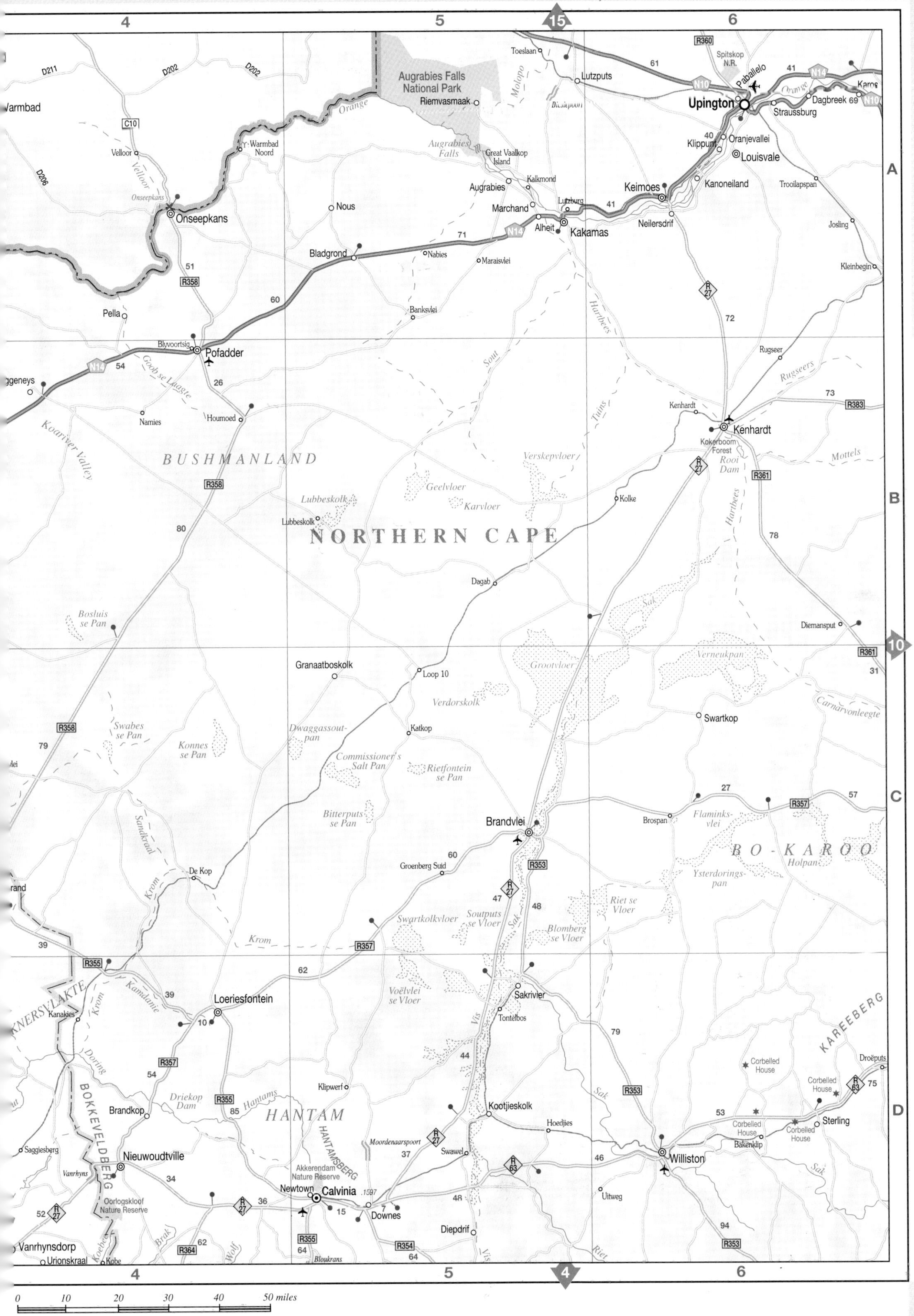
Augrabies Falls National Park
Riemvasmaak
Upington
Paballelo
Spitskop N.R.
Lutzputs
Toeslaan
Dagbreek
Straussburg
Klippunt
Oranjevallei
Louisvale
Kanoneiland
Trooilapspan
Keimoes
Neilersdrif
Josling
Kleinbegin
Warmbad
Warmbad Noord
Velloor
Onseepkans
Nous
Augrabies
Great Vaalkop Island
Kalkmond
Marchand
Lutzburg
Alheit
Kakamas
Bladgrond
Nabies
Maraisvlei
Banksvlei
Pella
Blyvoortsig
Pofadder
Namies
Houmoed
Rugseer
Kenhardt
Kokerboom Forest
Rooi Dam
BUSHMANLAND
NORTHERN CAPE
Geelvloer
Karvloer
Verskepvloer
Lubbeskolk
Kolke
Dagab
Bosluis se Pan
Diemansput
Grootvloer
Verneukpan
Granaatboskolk
Loop 10
Verdorskolk
Swartkop
Carnarvonleegte
Swabes se Pan
Konnes se Pan
Dwaggassout-pan
Katkop
Commissioner's Salt Pan
Rietfontein se Pan
Bitterputs se Pan
Brandvlei
Brospan
Flaminks-vlei
BO-KAROO
Holpan
Ysterdorings-pan
Groenberg Suid
De Kop
Riet se Vloer
Soutputs se Vloer
Blomberg se Vloer
Swartkolkvloer
Krom
Sandkraal
Kamdanie
Loeriesfontein
Sakrivier
Tontelbos
Voëlvlei se Vloer
KNERSVLAKTE
Kanakies
Doring
BOKKEVELDBERG
KAREEBERG
Corbelled House
Droëputs
Klipwerf
Driekop Dam
Hantams
HANTAM
HANTAMSBERG
Brandkop
Kootjieskolk
Hoedjies
Sterling
Bakenklip
Saggiesberg
Nieuwoudtville
Vanrhyns
Oorlogskloof Nature Reserve
Moordenaarspoort
Akkerendam Nature Reserve
Newtown
Calvinia
Swawel
Williston
Uitweg
Downes
Diepdrif
Vanrhynsdorp
Urionskraal
Kobe
Bloukrans
N14
N10
R27
R63
R353
R354
R355
R357
R358
R361
R364
R383
C10
D202
D206
D211
Orange
Molopo
Hartbees
Sout
Tuins
Rugseers
Mottels
Sak
Vis
Riet
Brak
Wolf
Koebee
0 10 20 30 40 50 miles

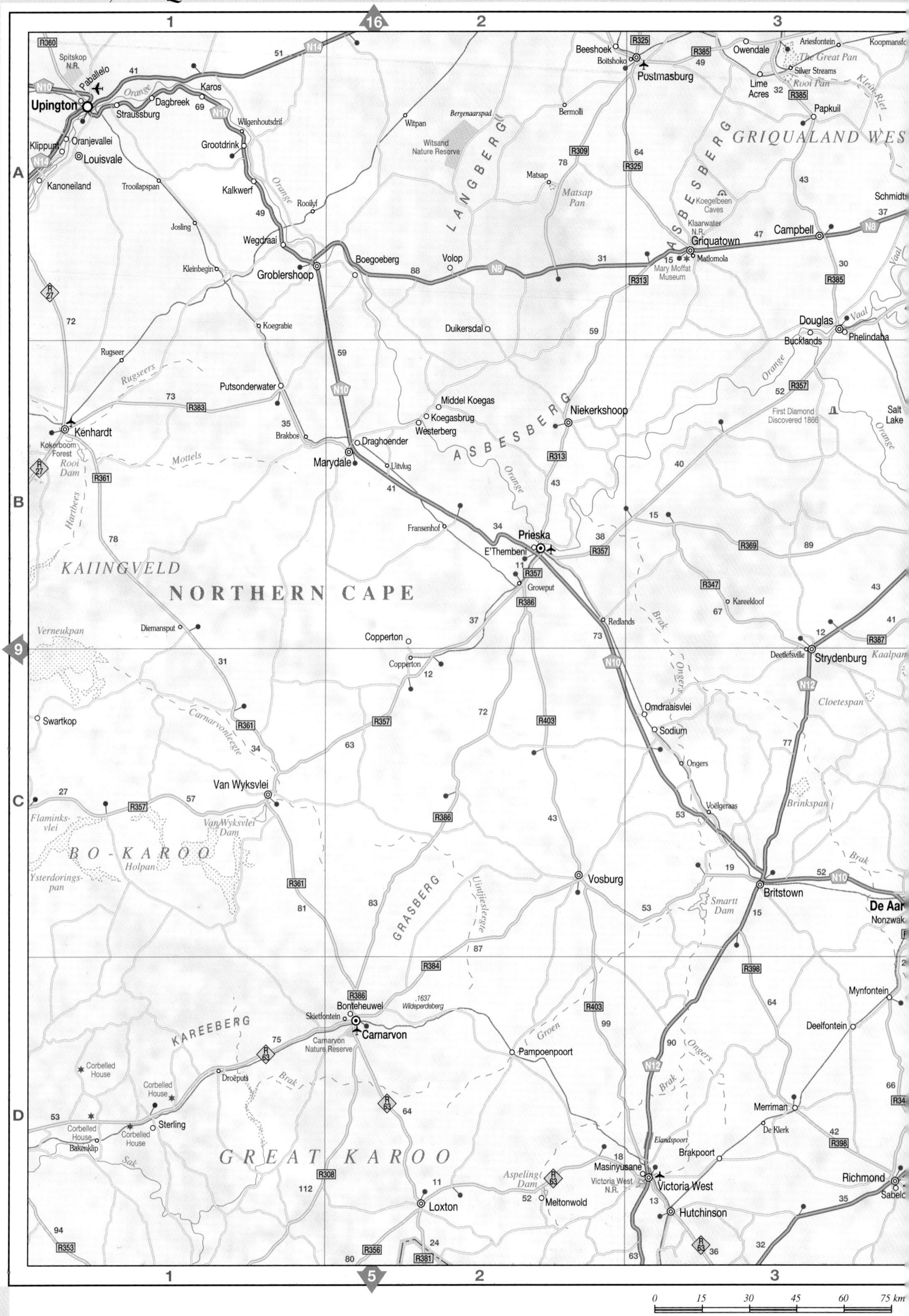
1
16
2
3
R360
Spitskop N.R.
Paballelo
41
Orange
Karos
Dagbreek
69
Upington
Straussburg
N10
Wilgenhoutsdrif
Witpan
Bergenaarspad
Witsand Nature Reserve
LANGBERG
Klippunt
Oranjevallei
Louisvale
Grootdrink
N14
A
Kanoneiland
Trooilapspan
Kalkwerf
Rooilyf
49
Josling
Wegdraai
Kleinbegin
Groblershoop
Boegoeberg
88
Volop
N8
R27
72
Koegrabie
Duikersdal
59
Rugseer
Rugseers
Putsonderwater
73
R383
35
Brakbos
Kenhardt
Kokerboom Forest
Rooi Dam
Mottels
R361
B
Hartbees
78
KAIINGVELD
NORTHERN CAPE
Verneukpan
Diemansput
9
31
Swartkop
Carnarvonleegte
R361
34
Van Wyksvlei
C
27
57
R357
Flaminks-vlei
Van Wyksvlei Dam
BO-KAROO
Holpan
Ysterdorings-pan
R361
81
KAREEBERG
75
R63
Corbelled House
Corbelled House
Droëputs
Brak
53
Corbelled House
Corbelled House
Sterling
D
Bakenklip
Sak
GREAT KAROO
94
R353
112
R308
R356
80
5
1
2
3
Draghoender
Marydale
Uitvlug
41
Middel Koegas
Koegasbrug
Westerberg
ASBESBERG
Niekerkshoop
R313
43
Orange
Fransenhof
34
Prieska
E'Thembeni
11
R357
Groveput
R386
37
Copperton
Copperton
12
R357
63
72
R403
R386
43
Vosburg
GRASBERG
Uintjiesleegte
83
87
R384
R386
Bonteheuwel
Skietfontein
Carnarvon
.1637 Wildeperdeberg
Carnarvon Nature Reserve
Groen
Pampoenpoort
R63
64
11
Loxton
24
R381
Aspeling Dam
R63
52
Meltonwold
Beeshoek
R325
Boitshoko
Postmasburg
R385
49
Owendale
Ariesfontein
Koopmansf
The Great Pan
Silver Streams
Lime Acres
32
Rooi Pan
R385
Klein-Riet
Bermolli
Papkuil
GRIQUALAND WES
R309
64
78
R325
Matsap
Matsap Pan
ASBESBERG
Koegelbeen Caves
Klaarwater N.R.
43
Schmidts
37
Campbell
47
N8
Griquatown
31
15
Matlomola
Mary Moffat Museum
R313
30
R385
Vaal
Douglas
Vaal
Bucklands
Phelindaba
Orange
52
R357
First Diamond Discovered 1866
Salt Lake
Orange
40
15
38
R357
R369
89
R347
Kareekloof
67
43
41
Redlands
Brak
73
12
R387
Deetlefsville
Strydenburg
Kaalpan
N10
Onsgers
N12
Cloetespan
Omdraaisvlei
Sodium
77
Ongers
Brinkspan
Voëlgeraas
53
Brak
19
52
N10
Britstown
De Aar
Nonzwak
Smartt Dam
53
15
R398
Mynfontein
64
Deelfontein
R403
99
90
Ongers
N12
Brak
66
Merriman
De Klerk
42
R398
Elandspoort
Brakpoort
18
Masinyusane
Victoria West N.R.
Victoria West
Richmond
Sabelo
13
Hutchinson
35
R63
36
32
63
0
15
30
45
60
75 km

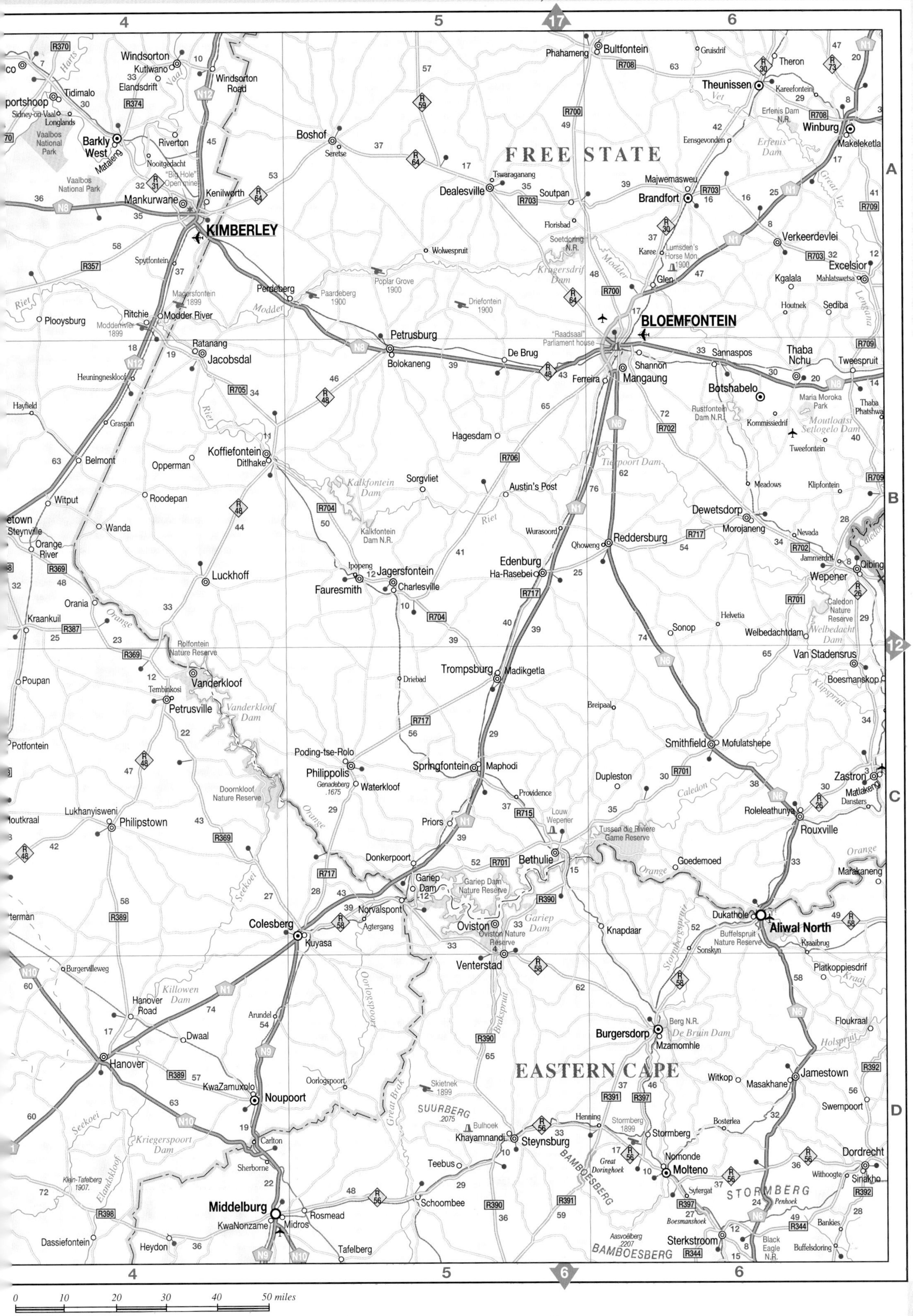
FREE STATE
EASTERN CAPE
KIMBERLEY
BLOEMFONTEIN
Windsorton
Kutlwano
Elandsdrift
Windsorton Road
Tidimalo
Sidney-on-Vaal
Longlands
Vaalbos National Park
Barkly West
Mataleng
Riverton
Nooitgedacht
"Big Hole" Open mine
Mankurwane
Kenilworth
Boshof
Seretse
Dealesville
Tswaraganang
Soutpan
Phahameng
Bultfontein
Gruisdrif
Theron
Theunissen
Kareefontein
Erfenis Dam N.R.
Winburg
Makeleketla
Eensgevonden
Erfenis Dam
Majwemasweu
Brandfort
Florisbad
Soetdoring N.R.
Karee
Lumsden's Horse Mon. 1900
Glen
Verkeerdevlei
Excelsior
Kgalala
Mahlatswetsa
Houtnek
Sediba
Spytfontein
Wolwespruit
Magersfontein 1899
Perdeberg
Paardeberg 1900
Poplar Grove 1900
Driefontein 1900
Ritchie
Modder River
Plooysburg
Moddermer 1899
Petrusburg
Bolokaneng
De Brug
"Raadsaal" Parliament house
Sannaspos
Thaba Nchu
Tweespruit
Shannon
Mangaung
Ferreira
Botshabelo
Rustfontein Dam N.R.
Maria Moroka Park
Thaba Phatshwa
Kommissiedrif
Moutloatsi Setlogelo Dam
Tweefontein
Ratanang
Jacobsdal
Heuningneskloof
Hayfield
Graspan
Hagesdam
Koffiefontein
Ditlhake
Opperman
Belmont
Tierpoort Dam
Sorgvliet
Austin's Post
Meadows
Klipfontein
Kalkfontein Dam
Kalkfontein Dam N.R.
Witput
Roodepan
Wanda
Steynville
Orange River
Wurasoord
Qhoweng
Reddersburg
Dewetsdorp
Morojaneng
Nevada
Jammerdrif
Qibing
Wepener
Caledon Nature Reserve
Luckhoff
Ipopeng
Jagersfontein
Charlesville
Fauresmith
Edenburg
Ha-Rasebei
Orania
Kraankuil
Helvetia
Sonop
Welbedachtdam
Welbedacht Dam
Rolfontein Nature Reserve
Van Stadensrus
Boesmanskop
Poupan
Vanderkloof
Tembinkosi
Petrusville
Vanderkloof Dam
Trompsburg
Madikgetla
Driebad
Breipaal
Potfontein
Poding-tse-Rolo
Philippolis
Genadeberg 1675
Waterkloof
Springfontein
Maphodi
Smithfield
Mofulatshepe
Dupleston
Zastron
Matlakeng
Dansters
Doornkloof Nature Reserve
Providence
Louw Wepener
Roleleathunya
Rouxville
Lukhanyisweni
Philipstown
Priors
Tussen die Riviere Game Reserve
Donkerpoort
Bethulie
Goedemoed
Marakaneng
Gariep Dam
Gariep Dam Nature Reserve
Norvalspont
Agtergang
Colesberg
Kuyasa
Oviston
Oviston Nature Reserve
Knapdaar
Dukathole
Aliwal North
Buffelspruit Nature Reserve
Sonskyn
Kraaibrug
Venterstad
Burgervilleweg
Killowen Dam
Hanover Road
Arundel
Dwaal
Platkoppiesdrif
Berg N.R.
Burgersdorp
De Bruin Dam
Mzamomhle
Floukraal
Hanover
Oorlogspoort
KwaZamuxolo
Noupoort
Skietnek 1899
SUURBERG 2075
Bulhoek
Witkop
Masakhane
Jamestown
Swempoort
Henning
Stormberg 1899
Stormberg
Bosterlea
Krieggerspoort Dam
Carlton
Khayamnandi
Steynsburg
Great Doringhoek
Nomonde
Molteno
Dordrecht
Withoogte
Sinakho
Klein-Tafelberg 1907
Sherborne
Teebus
BAMBOESBERG
STORMBERG
Penhoek
Sytergat
Boesmanshoek
Middelburg
KwaNonzame
Midros
Rosmead
Schoombee
Bankies
Dassiefontein
Heydon
Tafelberg
Aasvoëlberg 2207
Sterkstroom
Black Eagle N.R.
Buffelsdoring
Modder
Riet
Orange
Vaal
Caledon
Seekoei
Oorlogspoort
Great Brak
Brakspruit
Stormbergspruit
Kraai
Holspruit
Klipspruit
Great Vet
Vet
Harts
Elandskloof
0 10 20 30 40 50 miles

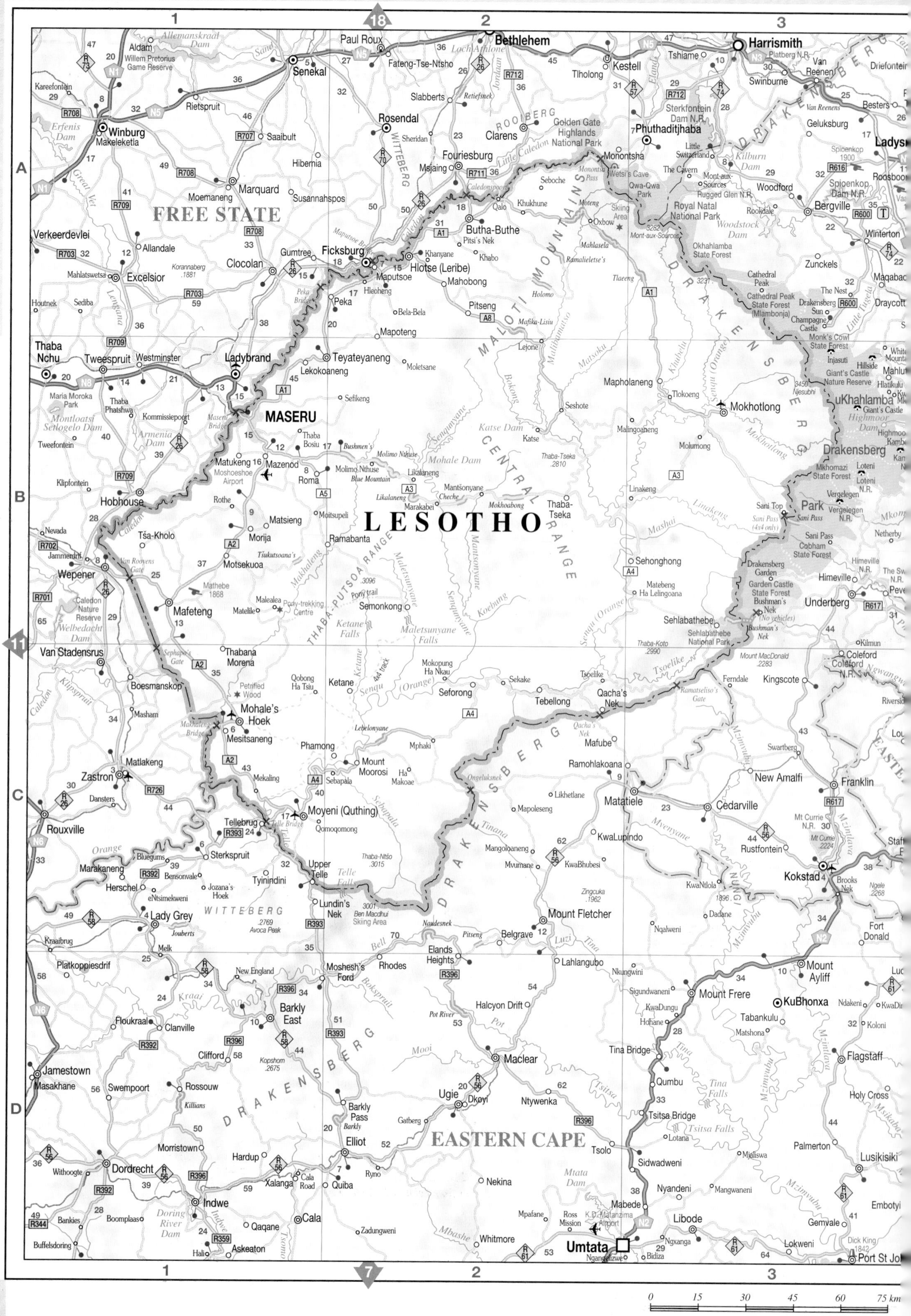
FREE STATE
LESOTHO
EASTERN CAPE
MASERU
Bethlehem
Harrismith
Senekal
Paul Roux
Winburg
Rosendal
Fouriesburg
Clarens
Ficksburg
Clocolan
Marquard
Excelsior
Ladybrand
Thaba Nchu
Tweespruit
Hobhouse
Wepener
Van Stadensrus
Zastron
Rouxville
Sterkspruit
Lady Grey
Barkly East
Jamestown
Dordrecht
Indwe
Elliot
Maclear
Ugie
Umtata
Kokstad
Matatiele
Cedarville
Mount Fletcher
Mount Frere
Mount Ayliff
Flagstaff
Lusikisiki
Libode
Tsolo
Qumbu
Tsitsa Bridge
Bergville
Winterton
Underberg
Himeville
Franklin
Kestell
Phuthaditjhaba
Butha-Buthe
Hlotse (Leribe)
Maputsoe
Teyateyaneng
Roma
Morija
Mafeteng
Mohale's Hoek
Moyeni (Quthing)
Qacha's Nek
Thaba-Tseka
Mokhotlong
Semonkong
Sehonghong
Sani Top
Golden Gate Highlands National Park
Qwa-Qwa Park
Royal Natal National Park
Sehlabathebe National Park
Katse Dam
Mohale Dam
MALOTI MOUNTAINS
CENTRAL RANGE
THABA-PUTSOA RANGE
DRAKENSBERG
WITTEBERG
uKhahlamba Drakensberg Park
0 15 30 45 60 75 km

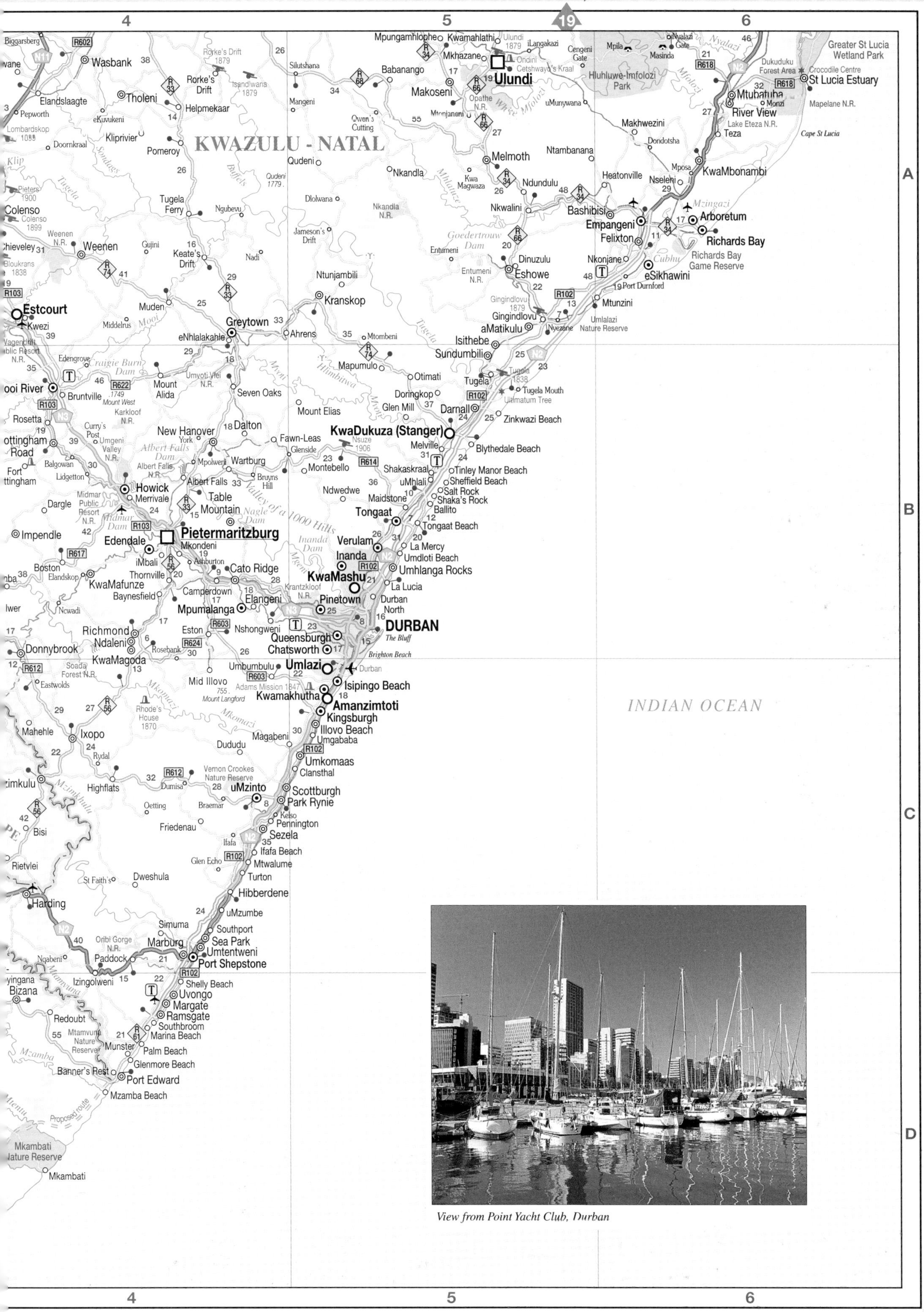

View from Point Yacht Club, Durban

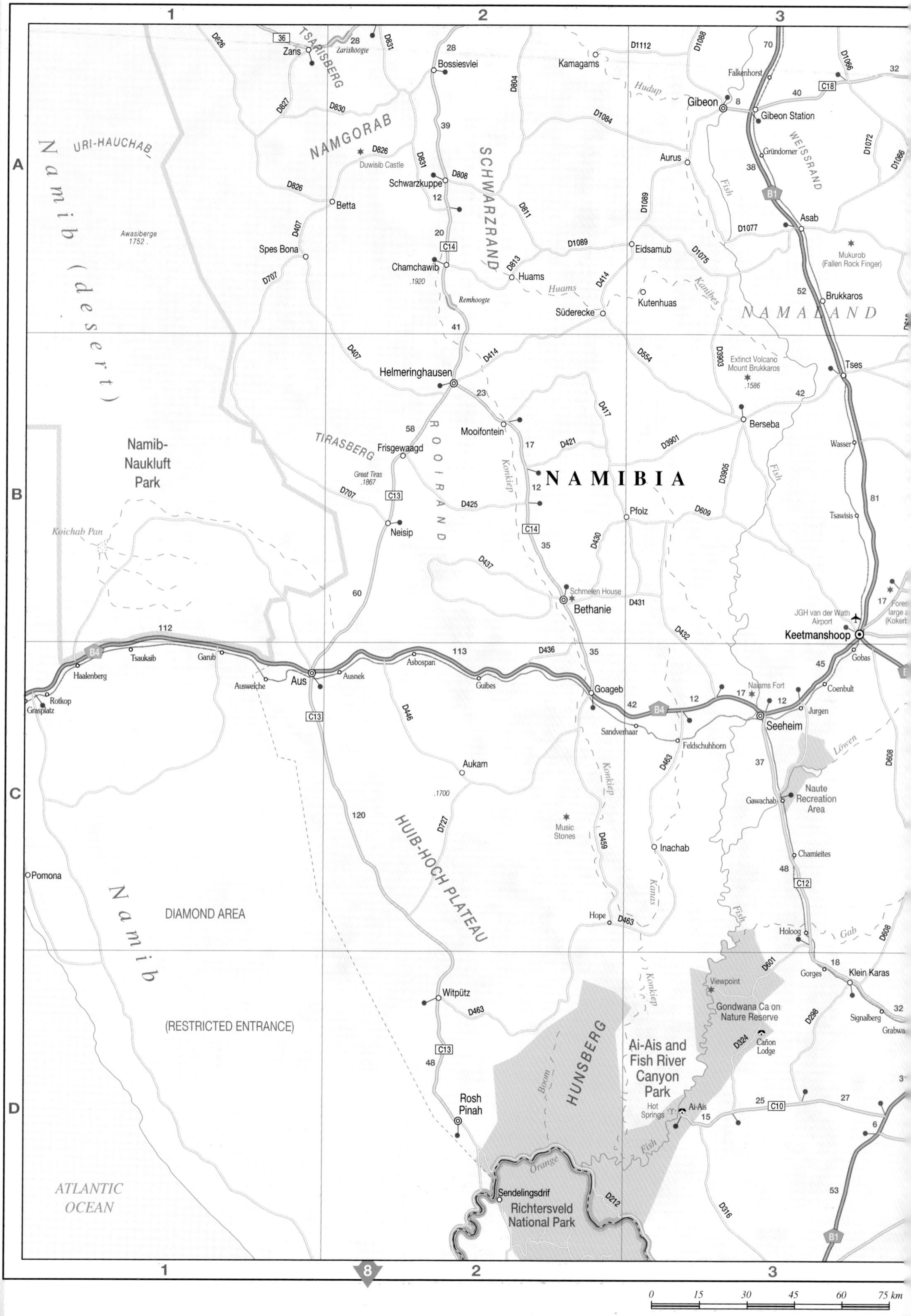
Namib (desert)
URI-HAUCHAB
NAMGORAB
TSARISBERG
SCHWARZRAND
TIRASBERG
ROOIRAND
WEISSRAND
NAMALAND
NAMIBIA
HUIB-HOCH PLATEAU
HUNSBERG
Namib-Naukluft Park
Koichab Pan
Awasiberge 1752
Zaris
Zarishoogte
Bossiesvlei
Kamagams
Hudup
Gibeon
Gibeon Station
Falkenhorst
Gründorner
Duwisib Castle
Schwarzkuppe
Betta
Spes Bona
Aurus
Fish
Asab
Mukurob (Fallen Rock Finger)
Chamchawib
1920
Remhoogte
Huams
Eidsamub
Kutenhuas
Kanibes
Süderecke
Brukkaros
Helmeringhausen
Extinct Volcano Mount Brukkaros 1586
Tses
Mooifontein
Berseba
Frisgewaagd
Great Tiras 1867
Konkiep
Wasser
Neisip
Pfolz
Tsawisis
Schmelen House
Bethanie
JGH van der Wath Airport
Keetmanshoop
Gobas
Coenbult
Haalenberg
Tsaukaib
Garub
Rotkop
Grasplatz
Ausweiche
Aus
Ausnek
Asbospan
Guibes
Goageb
Naiams Fort
Seeheim
Jurgen
Sandverhaar
Feldschuhhorn
Löwen
Aukam
1700
Gawachab
Naute Recreation Area
Music Stones
Inachab
Chamieites
Pomona
DIAMOND AREA
Hope
Kanas
Holoog
Gab
Gorges
Klein Karas
Viewpoint
Gondwana Cañon Nature Reserve
Cañon Lodge
Signalberg
Witpütz
(RESTRICTED ENTRANCE)
Ai-Ais and Fish River Canyon Park
Boom
Hot Springs
Ai-Ais
Rosh Pinah
Orange
Sendelingsdrif
Richtersveld National Park
ATLANTIC OCEAN
B1
B4
C10
C12
C13
C14
C18
D212
D298
D316
D324
D407
D414
D417
D421
D425
D430
D431
D432
D436
D437
D446
D459
D463
D554
D601
D608
D609
D707
D727
D804
D808
D811
D813
D826
D827
D830
D831
D1066
D1072
D1075
D1077
D1084
D1088
D1089
D1112
D3901
D3903
D3905
A
B
C
D
1
2
3
8
0 15 30 45 60 75 km

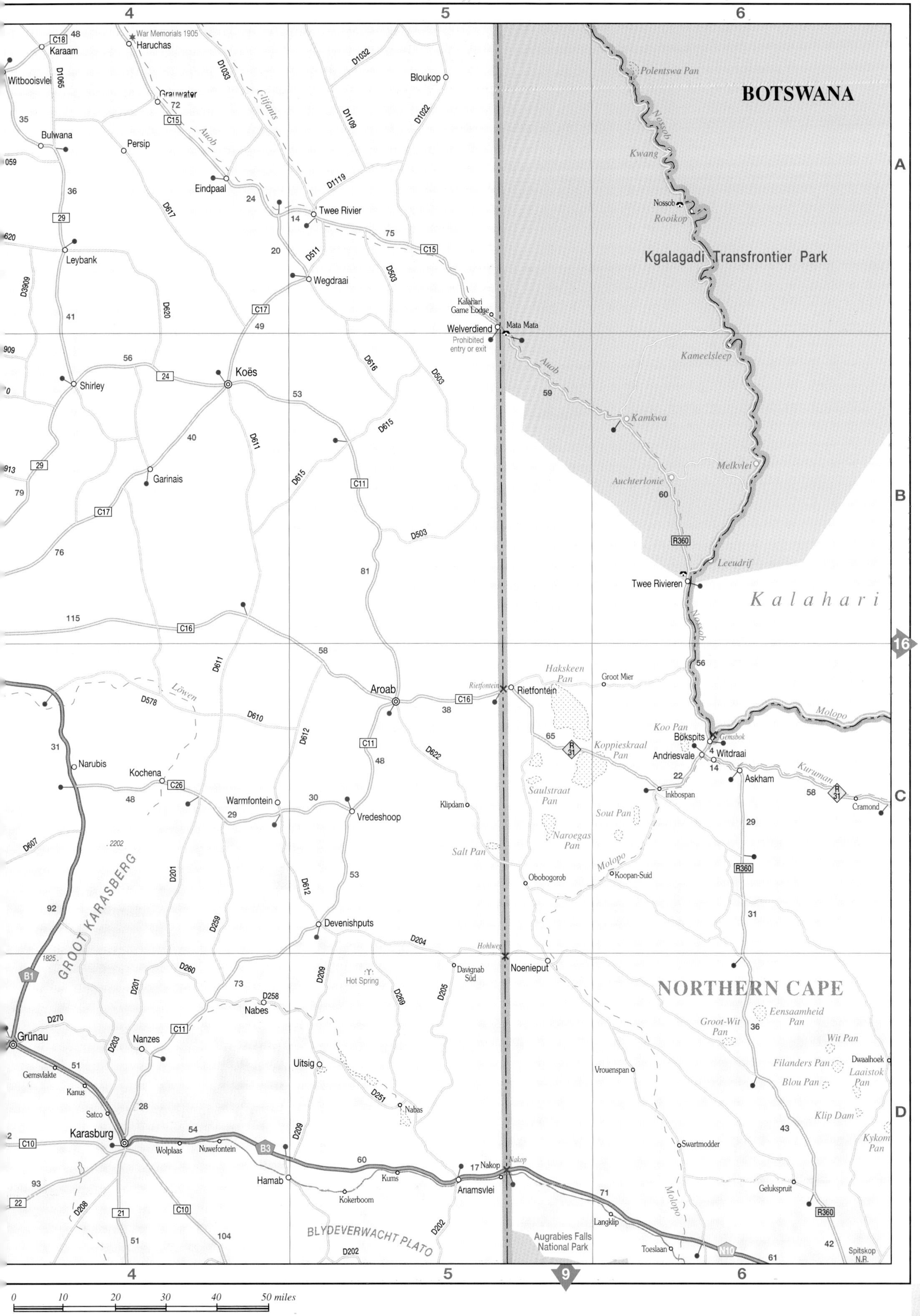
4
5
6
A
B
C
D
16
9
BOTSWANA
Kgalagadi Transfrontier Park
Kalahari
NORTHERN CAPE
War Memorials 1905
Haruchas
Karaam
C18
48
Witbooisvlei
D1065
Grauwater
72
C15
Auob
Clifants
D1033
D1032
Bloukop
D1109
D1022
Polentswa Pan
Nossob
Kwang
Nossob
Rooikop
35
Bulwana
Persip
059
36
Eindpaal
24
D1119
Twee Rivier
14
75
29
D617
620
Leybank
20
D511
D503
D3909
Wegdraai
D620
41
C17
49
Kalahari Game Lodge
Welverdiend
Prohibited entry or exit
Mata Mata
Kameelsleep
909
56
Shirley
24
Koës
D616
D503
Auob
59
Kamkwa
53
40
D611
D615
D615
913
29
Garinais
C11
Melkvlei
Auchterlonie
60
79
C17
D503
R360
76
81
Leeudrif
Twee Rivieren
115
C16
58
D611
Haksheen Pan
Groot Mier
56
Löwen
D578
D610
Aroab
Rietfontein
Rietfontein
C16
38
D612
Molopo
Koo Pan
Bokspits
Gemsbok
31
Narubis
C11
48
D622
65
Koppieskraal Pan
Andriesvale
Witdraai
14
22
Askham
Kuruman
Kochena
C26
48
Warmfontein
30
Vredeshoop
Klipdam
Saulstraat Pan
Inkbospan
58
Cramond
29
Sout Pan
29
D607
2202
GROOT KARASBERG
Naroegas Pan
Salt Pan
Molopo
Koopan-Suid
R360
D201
53
D612
Obobogorob
92
D259
Devenishputs
31
D204
Hohlweg
1825
B1
D260
D201
73
D209
Hot Spring
Davignab Süd
D269
D205
Noenieput
D258
Nabes
Groot-Wit Pan
36
Eensaamheid Pan
D270
Grünau
Nanzes
D203
C11
Wit Pan
Dwaalhoek
Filanders Pan
Gemsvlakte
51
Kanus
Uitsig
Vrouenspan
Laaistok Pan
Blou Pan
28
Satco
D251
Nabas
Klip Dam
D
43
Kykom Pan
2
C10
Karasburg
54
Wolplaas
Nuwefontein
B3
D209
Swartmodder
60
17
Nakop
Nakop
93
Hamab
Kums
Anamsvlei
71
Molopo
Gelukspruit
22
Kokerboom
D208
21
C10
Langklip
R360
104
BLYDEVERWACHT PLATO
D202
Augrabies Falls National Park
42
Toeslaan
N10
Spitskop N.R.
51
D202
61
0
10
20
30
40
50 miles

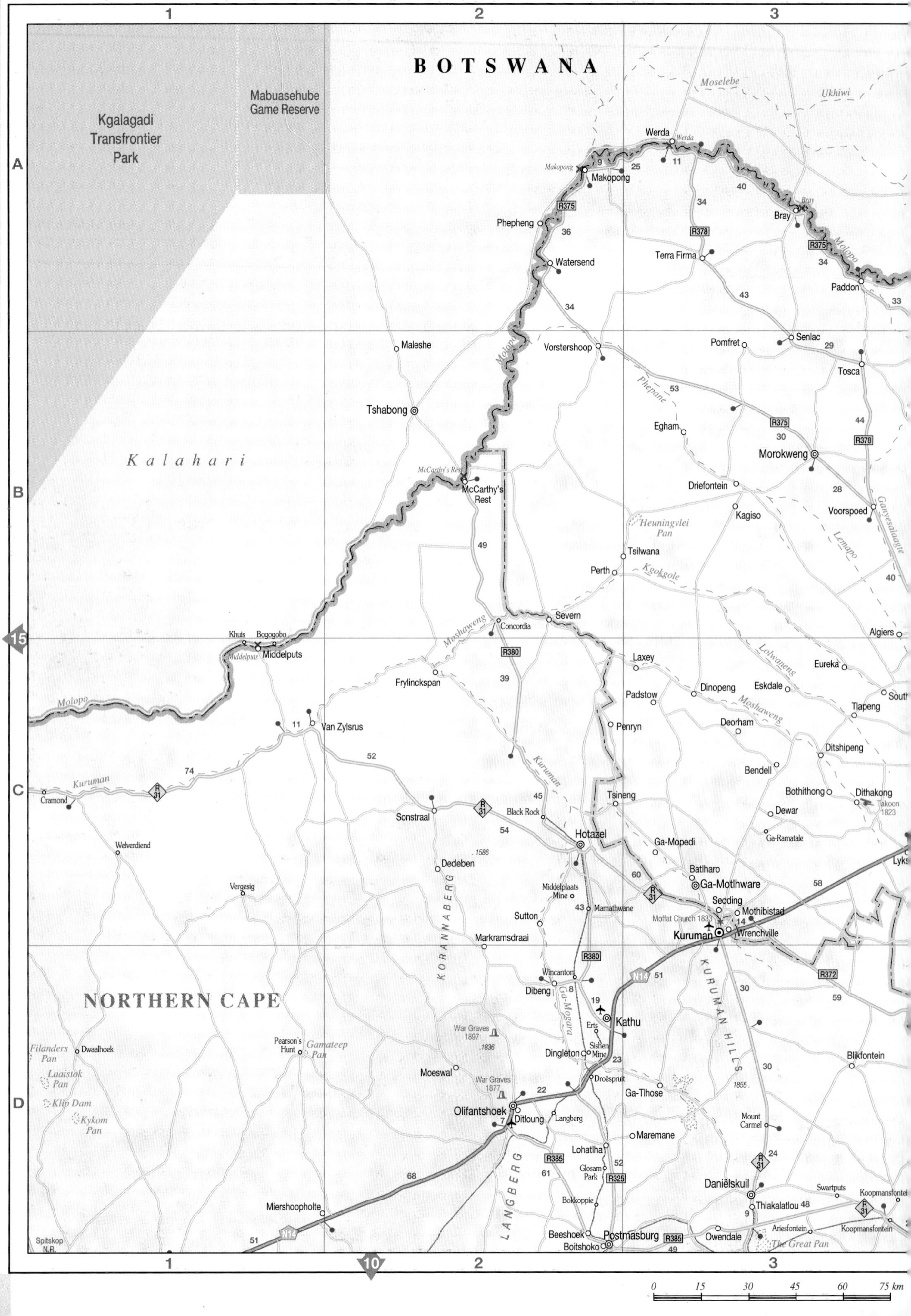
BOTSWANA
NORTHERN CAPE
Kgalagadi Transfrontier Park
Mabuasehube Game Reserve
Kalahari
Moselebe
Ukhiwi
Werda
Makopong
Phepheng
Watersend
Terra Firma
Bray
Paddon
Molopo
Senlac
Pomfret
Tosca
Maleshe
Vorstershoop
Phepane
Tshabong
Egham
Morokweng
McCarthy's Rest
Driefontein
Kagiso
Voorspoed
Ganyesa
Heuningvlei Pan
Lemapo
Tsilwana
Perth
Kgokgole
Concordia
Severn
Moshaweng
Algiers
Khuis
Bogogobo
Middelputs
Laxey
Lotlwaneng
Eureka
Frylinckspan
Padstow
Dinopeng
Eskdale
Tlapeng
Penryn
Deorham
Van Zylsrus
Ditshipeng
Bendell
Kuruman
Cramond
Tsineng
Bothithong
Dithakong
Takoon 1823
Sonstraal
Black Rock
Dewar
Ga-Ramatale
Hotazel
Ga-Mopedi
Welverdiend
Dedeben
Batlharo
Ga-Motlhware
Vergesig
Middelplaats Mine
Seoding
Mothibistad
Sutton
Mamathwane
Moffat Church 1833
Kuruman
Wrenchville
Markramsdraai
KORANNABERG
KURUMAN HILLS
Wincanton
Dibeng
Ga-Mogara
Kathu
Erts
Sishen Mine
War Graves 1897
War Graves 1877
Filanders Pan
Dwaalhoek
Laaistok Pan
Klip Dam
Kykom Pan
Pearson's Hunt
Gamateep Pan
Moeswal
Dingleton
Droëspruit
Ga-Tlhose
Blikfontein
Olifantshoek
Ditloung
Langberg
Maremane
Mount Carmel
Lohatlha
Glosam Park
LANGBERG
Daniëlskuil
Thlakalatlou
Swartputs
Koopmansfontein
Miershoopholte
Bokkoppie
Beeshoek
Postmasburg
Boitshoko
Owendale
Ariesfontein
The Great Pan
Spitskop N.R.
R375
R378
R380
R31
R385
R325
R372
N14
1
2
3
A
B
C
D
15
10
0 15 30 45 60 75 km

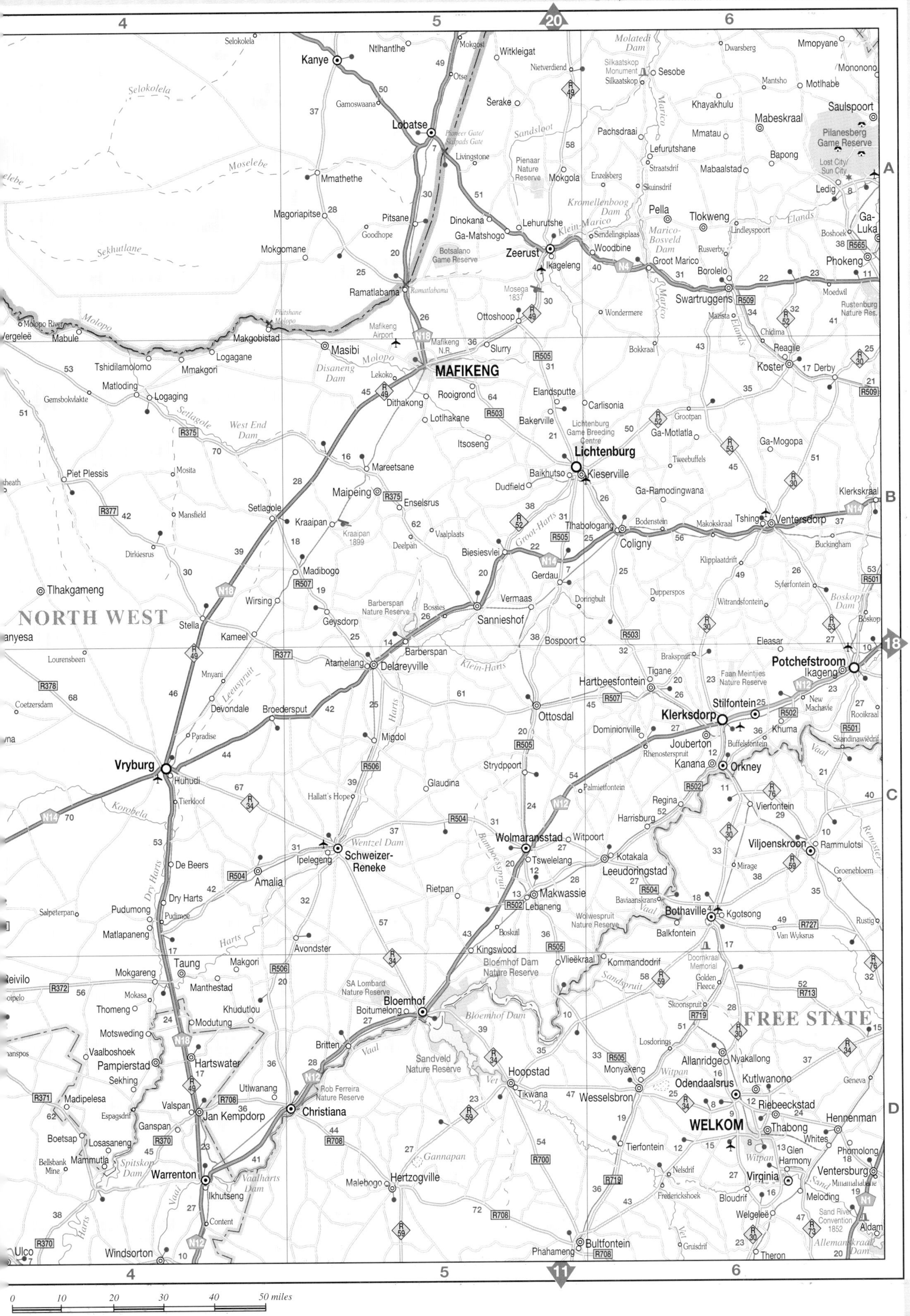
4
5
6
20
11
18
A
B
C
D
Kanye
Lobatse
Ntlhantlhe
Mokgosi
Otse
Witkleigat
Nietverdiend
Molatedi Dam
Silkaatskop Monument
Silkaatskop
Sesobe
Dwarsberg
Mmopyane
Mononono
Mantsho
Motlhabe
Khayakhulu
Saulspoort
Mabeskraal
Pilanesberg Game Reserve
Selokolela
Gamoswaana
Serake
Sandsloot
Pachsdraai
Mmatau
Lefurutshane
Straatsdrif
Bapong
Lost City/ Sun City
Mabaalstad
Pioneer Gate/ Skilpads Gate
Livingstone
Pienaar Nature Reserve
Mokgola
Enzelsberg
Skuinsdrif
Moselebe
Mmathethe
Kromellenboog Dam
Ledig
Pella
Tlokweng
Magoriapitse
Pitsane
Dinokana
Lehurutshe
Klein-Marico
Sendelingsplaas
Marico-Bosveld Dam
Lindleyspoort
Elands
Boshoek
Ga-Luka
Goodhope
Ga-Matshogo
Zeerust
Woodbine
Rusverby
Sekhutlane
Mokgomane
Botsalano Game Reserve
Ikageleng
Groot Marico
Borolelo
Phokeng
Ramatlabama
Mosega 1837
Swartruggens
Moedwil
Rustenburg Nature Res.
Molopo River
Molopo
Pitshane Molopo
Mafikeng Airport
Ottoshoop
Wondermere
Mazista
Chidima
Marico
Vergeleë
Mabule
Makgobistad
Masibi
Mafikeng N.R.
Slurry
Bokkraal
Reagile
Koster
Derby
Logagane
Tshidilamolomo
Mmakgori
Disaneng Dam
Lekoko
MAFIKENG
Matloding
Gemsbokvlakte
Logaging
Dithakong
Rooigrond
Elandsputte
Carlisonia
Grootpan
Lotlhakane
Bakerville
Lichtenburg Game Breeding Centre
Ga-Motlatla
Ga-Mogopa
Setlagole
West End Dam
Itsoseng
Lichtenburg
Tweebuffels
Mosita
Mareetsane
Baikhutso
Kieserville
Piet Plessis
Dudfield
Ga-Ramodingwana
Klerkskraal
Maipeing
Enselsrus
Setlagole
Kraaipan
Kraaipan 1899
Vaalplaats
Groot-Harts
Tlhabologang
Bodenstein
Makokskraal
Tshing
Ventersdorp
Mansfield
Deelpan
Biesiesvlei
Coligny
Buckingham
Dirkiesrus
Klipplaatdrift
Madibogo
Gerdau
Syferfontein
Tlhakgameng
Wirsing
Vermaas
Doringbult
Dupperspos
Boskop Dam
Barberspan Nature Reserve
Bossies
Witrandsfontein
NORTH WEST
Stella
Geysdorp
Sannieshof
Boskop
Kameel
Bospoort
Eleasar
Lourensbeen
Barberspan
Brakspruit
Potchefstroom
Ikageng
Atamelang
Delareyville
Klein-Harts
Tigane
Mnyani
Hartbeesfontein
Faan Meintjies Nature Reserve
Coetzersdam
Leeuspruit
New Machavie
Devondale
Broederspuit
Ottosdal
Stilfontein
Klerksdorp
Rooikraal
Paradise
Migdol
Dominionville
Khuma
Skandinawiëdrif
Jouberton
Buffelsfontein
Rhenosterspruit
Vryburg
Strydpoort
Kanana
Orkney
Huhudi
Glaudina
Palmietfontein
Hallatt's Hope
Regina
Vierfontein
Tierkloof
Harrisburg
Korobela
Wentzel Dam
Wolmaransstad
Witpoort
Viljoenskroon
Rammulotsi
Ipelegeng
Schweizer-Reneke
Tswelelang
Kotakala
Bamboesspruit
Mirage
Renoster
De Beers
Amalia
Leeudoringstad
Groenebloem
Dry Harts
Rietpan
Makwassie
Dry Harts
Lebaneng
Baviaanskrans
Bothaville
Kgotsong
Pudumong
Salpeterpan
Pudimoe
Wolwespruit Nature Reserve
Vaal
Rustig
Matlapaneng
Boskuil
Balkfontein
Van Wyksrus
Avondster
Harts
Kingswood
Taung
Makgori
Bloemhof Dam Nature Reserve
Vlieëkraal
Kommandodrif
Doornkraal Memorial
Mokgareng
Manthestad
SA Lombard Nature Reserve
Sandspruit
Golden Fleece
Reivilo
Mokasa
Thomeng
Khudutlou
Bloemhof
Boitumelong
Skoonspruit
FREE STATE
Modutung
Bloemhof Dam
Motsweding
Britten
Losdorings
Vaalboshoek
Pampierstad
Hartswater
Sandveld Nature Reserve
Hoopstad
Allanridge
Nyakallong
Monyakeng
Witpan
Sekhing
Utlwanang
Tikwana
Odendaalsrus
Kutlwanong
Geneva
Madipelesa
Valspan
Rob Ferreira Nature Reserve
Wesselsbron
Riebeeckstad
Espagsdrif
Jan Kempdorp
Christiana
Hennenman
Ganspan
WELKOM
Thabong
Boetsap
Losasaneng
Whites
Tierfontein
Glen Harmony
Phomolong
Bellsbank Mine
Mammutla
Spitskop Dam
Gannapan
Nelsdrif
Warrenton
Vaalharts Dam
Malebogo
Hertzogville
Virginia
Ventersburg
Ikhutseng
Fredericksheok
Bloudrif
Meloding
Content
Welgeleë
Sand River Convention 1852
Aldam
Ulco
Windsorton
Phahameng
Bultfontein
Gruisdrif
Theron
Allemanskraal Dam
0 10 20 30 40 50 miles

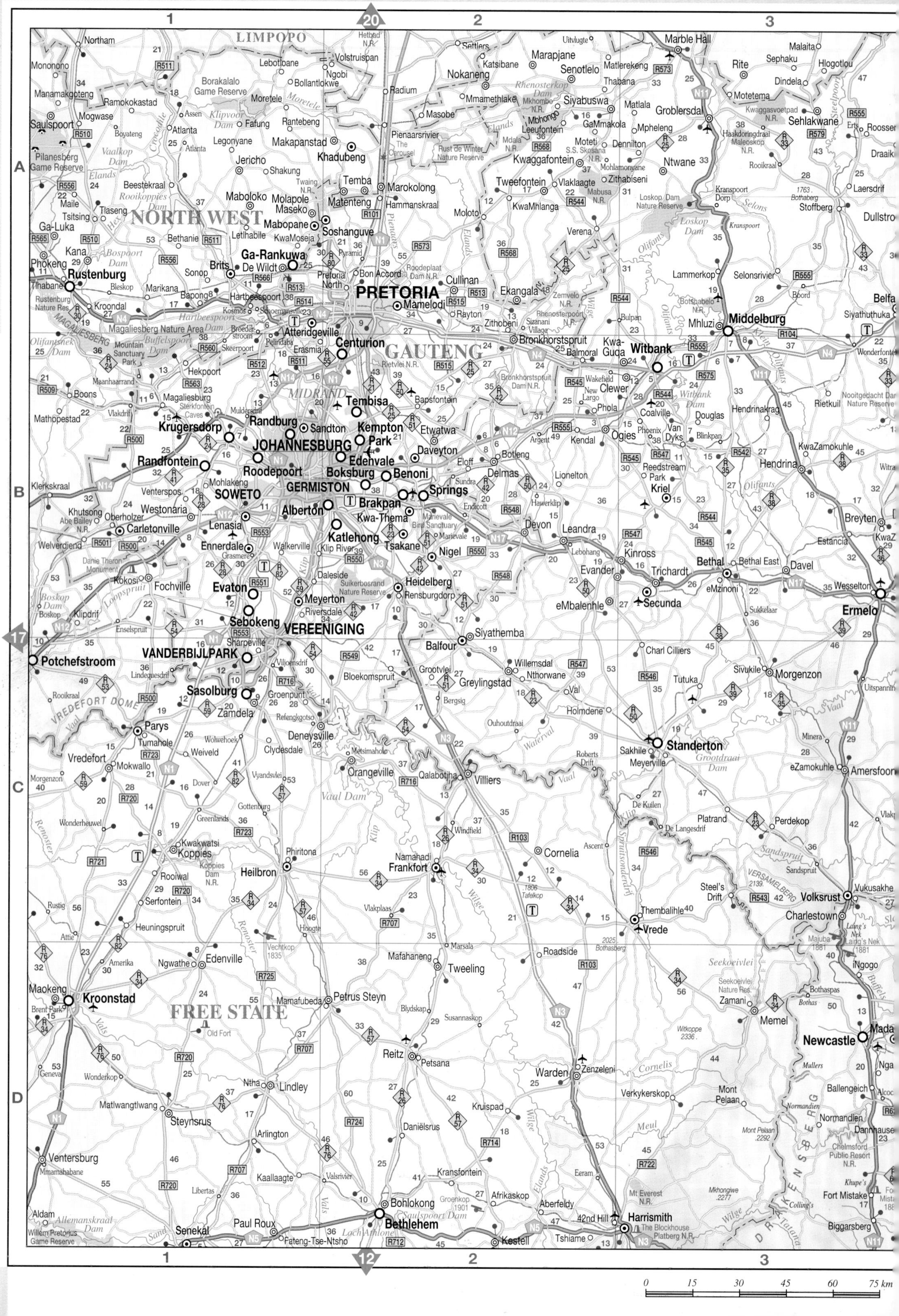

1
2
3
A
B
C
D
20
17
12
LIMPOPO
NORTH WEST
GAUTENG
FREE STATE
MIDRAND
PRETORIA
JOHANNESBURG
GERMISTON
SOWETO
VEREENIGING
VANDERBIJLPARK
Rustenburg
Brits
Ga-Rankuwa
Soshanguve
Mabopane
Centurion
Mamelodi
Cullinan
Tembisa
Kempton Park
Randburg
Sandton
Krugersdorp
Randfontein
Roodepoort
Boksburg
Benoni
Edenvale
Daveyton
Springs
Brakpan
Alberton
Katlehong
Tsakane
Nigel
Heidelberg
Lenasia
Ennerdale
Evaton
Sebokeng
Meyerton
Carletonville
Westonaria
Fochville
Potchefstroom
Sasolburg
Zamdela
Parys
Vredefort
Koppies
Heilbron
Frankfort
Villiers
Deneysville
Orangeville
Balfour
Greylingstad
Delmas
Devon
Leandra
Kinross
Evander
Secunda
Trichardt
Bethal
Davel
Ermelo
Wesselton
Morgenzon
Standerton
Amersfoort
Volksrust
Charlestown
Vrede
Cornelia
Tweeling
Edenville
Kroonstad
Maokeng
Petrus Steyn
Reitz
Lindley
Steynsrus
Ventersburg
Senekal
Paul Roux
Bethlehem
Bohlokong
Kestell
Harrismith
Warden
Memel
Newcastle
Witbank
Middelburg
Ogies
Kriel
Hendrina
Breyten
Groblersdal
Marble Hall
Siyabuswa
Bronkhorstspruit
Ekangala
Vaal Dam
Loskop Dam
Pilanesberg Game Reserve
Magaliesberg Nature Area
Hartbeespoort Dam
Suikerbosrand Nature Reserve
VREDEFORT DOME
Nature Res.
Old Fort
0
15
30
45
60
75 km

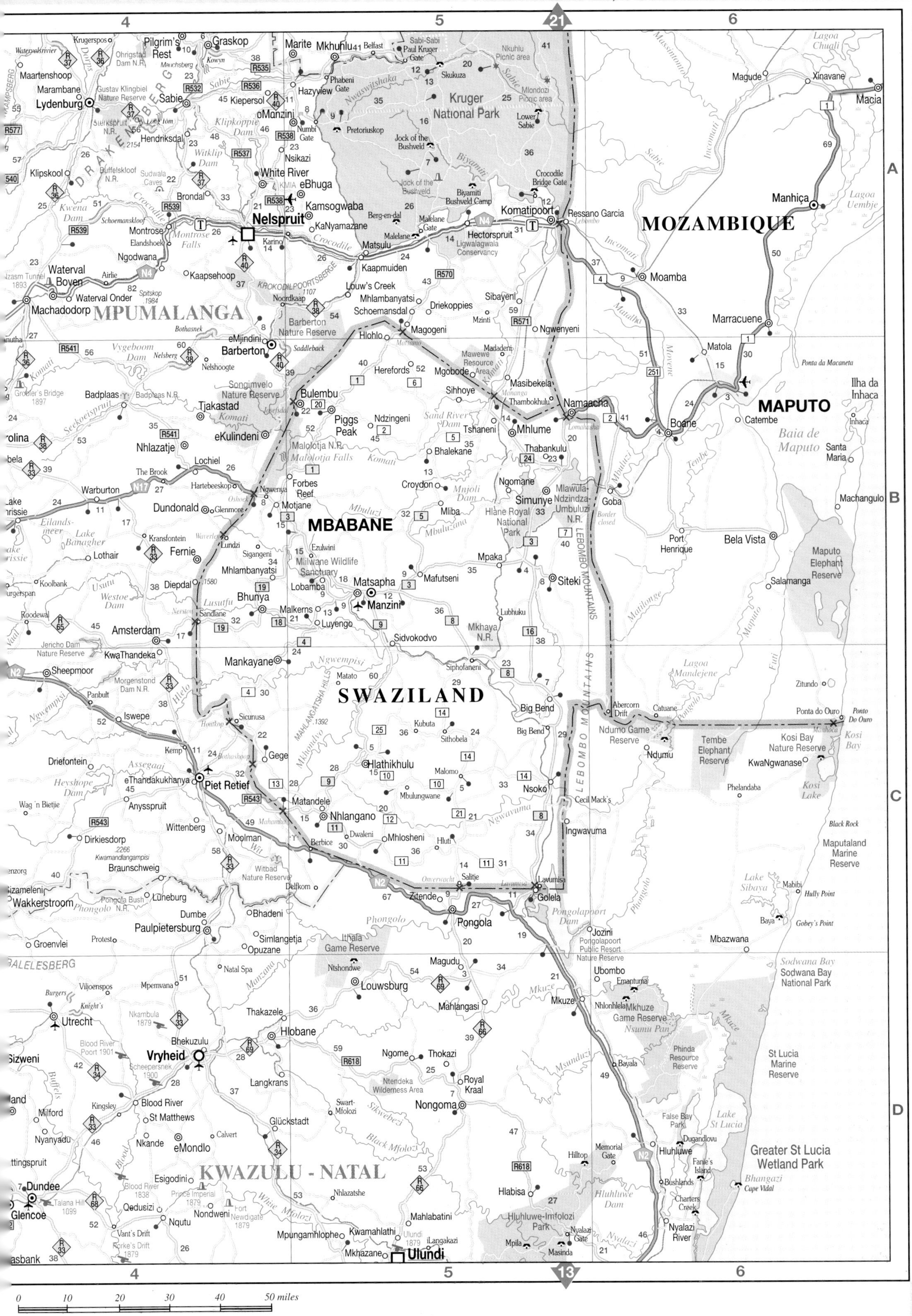
MOZAMBIQUE
MAPUTO
MPUMALANGA
MBABANE
SWAZILAND
KWAZULU - NATAL
Kruger National Park
Nelspruit
Lydenburg
Sabie
Graskop
Pilgrim's Rest
White River
Barberton
Komatipoort
Ressano Garcia
Manhiça
Marracuene
Matola
Boane
Namaacha
Moamba
Macia
Xinavane
Magude
Bela Vista
Maputo Elephant Reserve
Baia de Maputo
Ilha da Inhaca
Manzini
Matsapha
Lobamba
Piggs Peak
Bulembu
Mhlume
Simunye
Siteki
Big Bend
Nhlangano
Hlathikhulu
Mankayane
Pongola
Golela
Piet Retief
Amsterdam
Ermelo
Badplaas
Machadodorp
Waterval Boven
Dundonald
Wakkerstroom
Paulpietersburg
Vryheid
Utrecht
Dundee
Glencoe
Nongoma
Louwsburg
Ulundi
Mkuze
Hluhluwe
Hluhluwe-Imfolozi Park
Greater St Lucia Wetland Park
Sodwana Bay National Park
Kosi Bay Nature Reserve
Tembe Elephant Reserve
Ndumo Game Reserve
LEBOMBO MOUNTAINS
DRAKENSBERG
0 10 20 30 40 50 miles

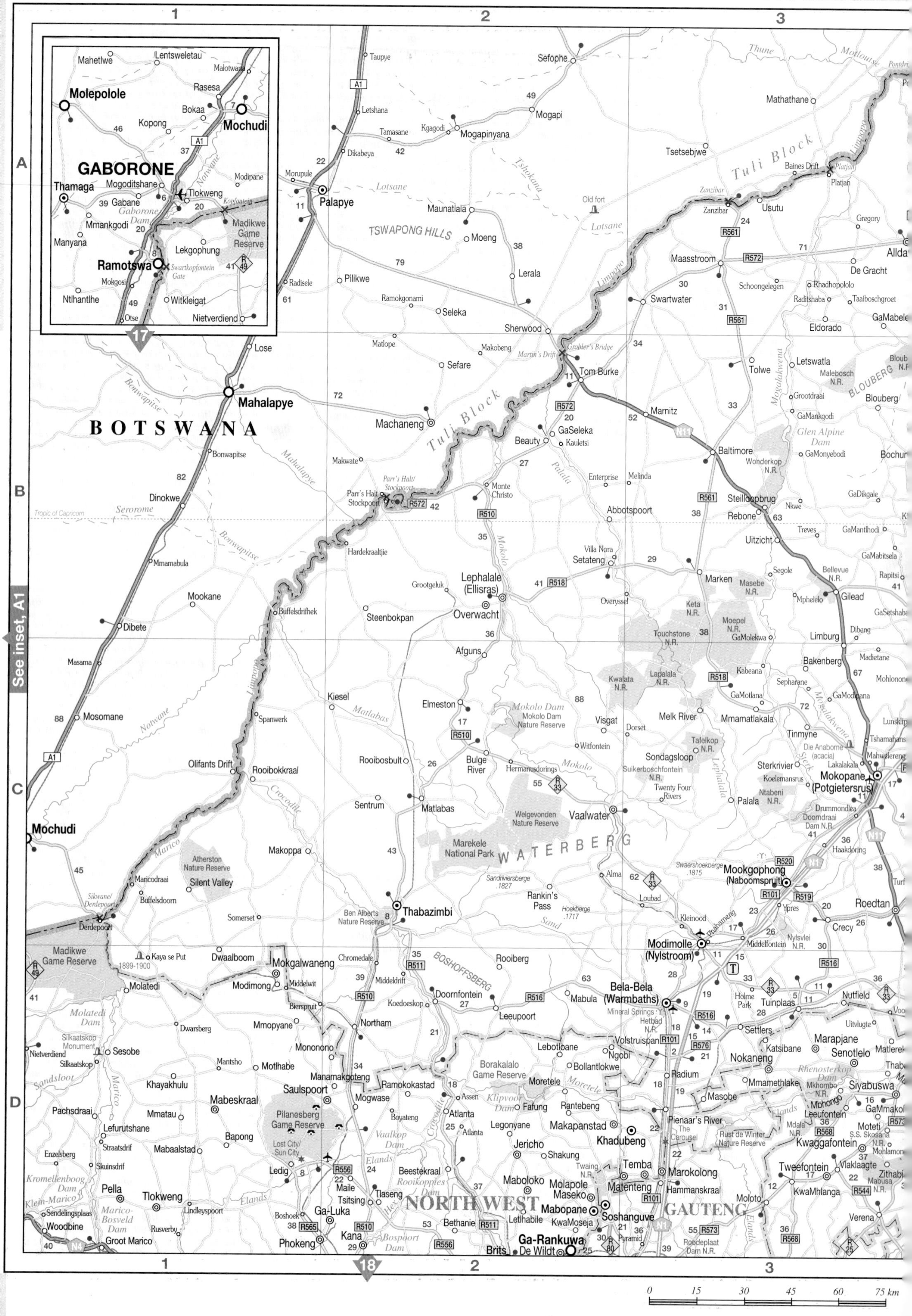
GABORONE
Molepolole
Mochudi
Thamaga
Mogoditshane
Gabane
Tlokweng
Gaborone Dam
Mmankgodi
Manyana
Lekgophung
Madikwe Game Reserve
Ramotswa
Swartkopfontein Gate
Mokgosi
Ntlhantlhe
Witkleigat
Nietverdiend
Otse
Kopong
Bokaa
Rasesa
Malotwana
Lentsweletau
Mahetlwe
Modipane
Kopfontein
17
BOTSWANA
Palapye
Morupule
Taupye
Letshana
Dikabeya
Tamasane
Kgagodi
Mogapinyana
Mogapi
Sefophe
Lotsane
TSWAPONG HILLS
Maunatlala
Moeng
Lerala
Old fort
Pilikwe
Radisele
Ramokgonami
Seleka
Sherwood
Lose
Mahalapye
Matlope
Makobeng
Sefare
Machaneng
Martin's Drift
Grobler's Bridge
Tom Burke
Tuli Block
Mathathane
Tsetsebjwe
Baines Drift
Platjan
Zanzibar
Usutu
Maasstroom
Swartwater
Schoongelegen
Rhadhopololo
Raditshaba
Taaibosgroet
De Gracht
Gregory
Alldays
Eldorado
GaMabele
Tolwe
Letswatla
Malebosch N.R.
BLOUBERG
Blouberg
Grootdraai
GaMankgodi
Glen Alpine Dam
GaMonyebodi
Bochum
Marnitz
Baltimore
Wonderkop N.R.
Beauty
GaSeleka
Kauletsi
Makwate
Bonwapitse
Dinokwe
Serorome
Tropic of Capricorn
Parr's Halt/Stockpoort
Monte Christo
Enterprise
Melinda
Abbotspoort
Steilloopbrug
Rebone
Nkwe
GaDikgale
Treves
GaMantlhodi
Uitzicht
GaMabitsela
Hardekraaltjie
Mmamabula
Mookane
Villa Nora
Setateng
Marken
Segole
Bellevue N.R.
Rapitsi
Grootgeluk
Lephalale (Ellisras)
Overwacht
Steenbokpan
Buffelsdrifhek
Overyssel
Masebe N.R.
Keta N.R.
Moepel N.R.
Mphelelo
Gilead
GaSetshaba
Dibete
Touchstone N.R.
GaMolekwa
Limburg
Dibeng
Afguns
Masama
Bakenberg
Madietane
Mohlonong
Kwalata N.R.
Lapalala N.R.
Kabeana
Sepharane
GaMotlana
GaModipana
Kiesel
Matlabas
Elmeston
Mokolo Dam
Mokolo Dam Nature Reserve
Visgat
Dorset
Melk River
Mmamatlakala
Tinmyne
Lunsklip
Mosomane
Spanwerk
Witfontein
Sondagsloop
Tafelkop N.R.
Die Anaboom (acacia)
Tshamahansi
Bulge River
Rooibosbult
Hermanusdorings
Suikerboschfontein N.R.
Sterkrivier
Lakalakala
Mahwelereng
Olifants Drift
Rooibokkraal
Twenty Four Rivers
Koelemansrus
Mokopane (Potgietersrus)
Ntabeni N.R.
Palala
Sentrum
Matlabas
Welgevonden Nature Reserve
Vaalwater
Drummondlea
Doorndraai Dam N.R.
Mochudi
Marico
Marekele National Park
WATERBERG
Haakdoring
Makoppa
Atherston Nature Reserve
Silent Valley
Alma
Swaershoekberge 1815
Mookgophong (Naboomspruit)
Sandriviersberge 1827
Maricodraai
Buffelsdoorn
Sikwane/Derdepoort
Rankin's Pass
Hoekberge 1717
Loubad
Roedtan
Thabazimbi
Ben Alberts Nature Reserve
Somerset
Kleinood
Ypres
Crecy
Derdepoort
Modimolle (Nylstroom)
Middelfontein
Nylsvlei N.R.
Madikwe Game Reserve
Kaya se Put 1899-1900
Dwaalboom
Mokgalwaneng
Chromedale
BOSHOFFSBERG
Rooiberg
Molatedi
Modimong
Middelwit
Middeldrift
Doornfontein
Bela-Bela (Warmbaths)
Mabula
Holme Park
Tuinplaas
Nutfield
Molatedi Dam
Biersspruit
Koedoeskop
Leeupoort
Mineral Springs
Hetbad N.R.
Silkaatskop Monument
Dwarsberg
Mmopyane
Northam
Settlers
Uitvlugte
Marapjane
Nietverdiend
Sesobe
Silkaatskop
Mononono
Volstruispan
Lebotloane
Ngobi
Katsibane
Senotlelo
Matlerekeng
Mantsho
Motlhabe
Bollantlokwe
Nokaneng
Rhenosterkop Dam
Thabana
Sandsloot
Khayakhulu
Manamakgoteng
Ramokokastad
Borakalalo Game Reserve
Moretele
Radium
Mmamethlake
Mkhombo Dam N.R.
Siyabuswa
Mabeskraal
Saulspoort
Mogwase
Assen
Klipvoor Dam
Fafung
Rantebeng
Masobe
Mbhongo
Leeufontein
GaMmakola
Pachsdraai
Mmatau
Pilanesberg Game Reserve
Boyateng
Atlanta
Pienaar's River
Moteti
S.S. Skosana N.R.
Lefurutshane
Bapong
Vaalkop Dam
Legonyane
Makapanstad
Khadubeng
The Carousel
Rust de Winter Nature Reserve
Mdala N.R.
Kwaggafontein
Mohlamonyane
Straatsdrif
Mabaalstad
Lost City/Sun City
Jericho
Shakung
Enzelsberg
Skuinsdrif
Ledig
Beestekraal
Twaing N.R.
Temba
Marokolong
Tweefontein
Vlaklaagte
Zithabiseni
Kromellenboog Dam
Maile
Rooikopjies Dam
Maboloko
Molapole
Matenteng
Hammanskraal
KwaMhlanga
Mabusa N.R.
Pella
Tlokweng
Klein-Marico
Tsitsing
Tlaseng
Maseko
Moloto
Sendelingsplaas
Marico-Bosveld Dam
Lindleyspoort
Boshoek
Ga-Luka
NORTH WEST
Mabopane
Soshanguve
GAUTENG
Verena
Letlhabile
KwaMoseja
Woodbine
Rusverby
Kana
Bethanie
Pyramid
Roodeplaat Dam N.R.
Groot Marico
Phokeng
Bospoort Dam
Brits
De Wildt
Ga-Rankuwa
See inset, A1
18
0 15 30 45 60 75 km

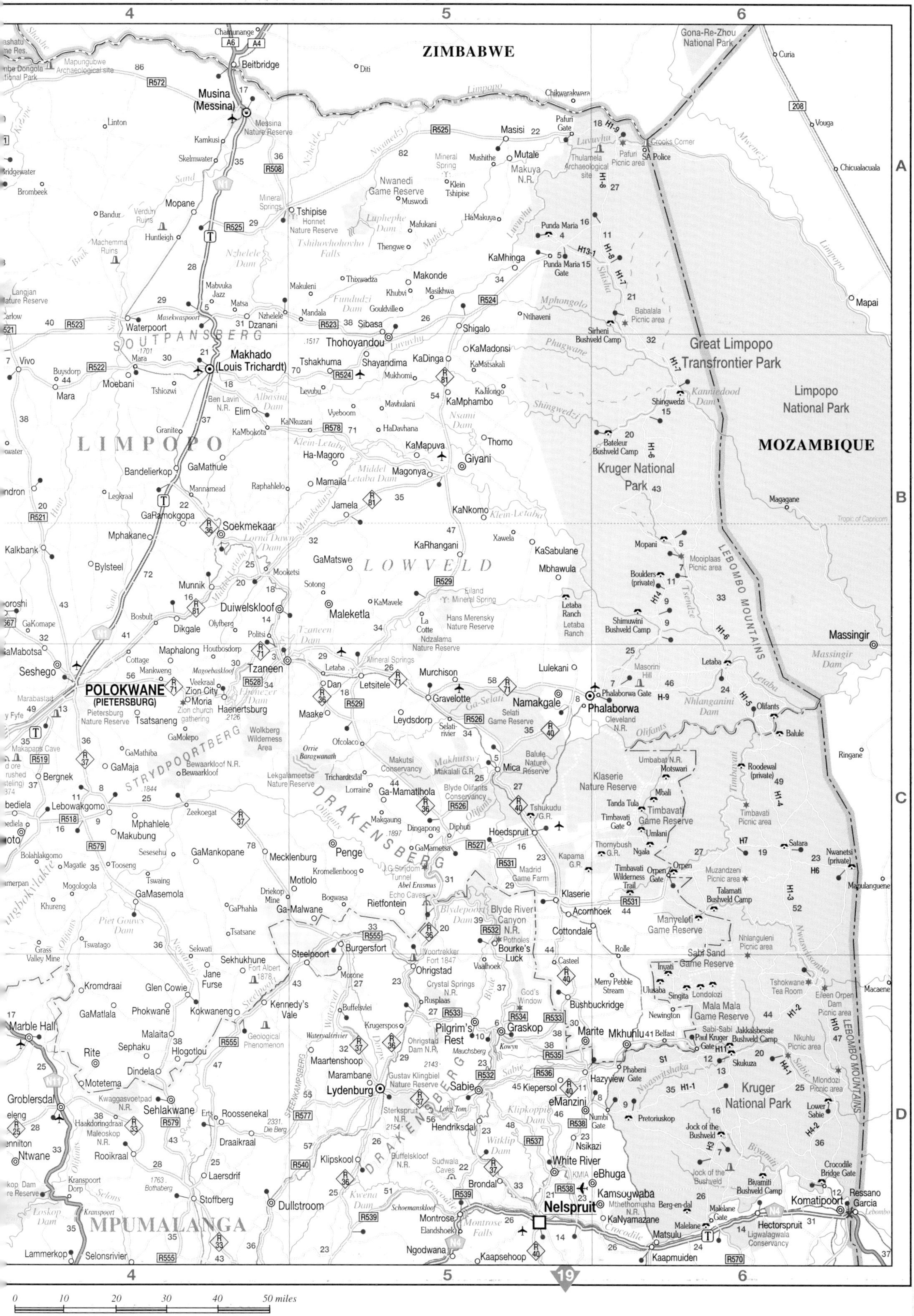
4
5
6
A
B
C
D
ZIMBABWE
MOZAMBIQUE
LIMPOPO
MPUMALANGA
LOWVELD
SOUTPANSBERG
STRYDPOORTBERG
DRAKENSBERG
LEBOMBO MOUNTAINS
Gona-Re-Zhou National Park
Great Limpopo Transfrontier Park
Limpopo National Park
Kruger National Park
Musina (Messina)
Beitbridge
Chamunange
Mapungubwe Archaeological site
Messina Nature Reserve
Linton
Kamkusi
Skelmwater
Bridgewater
Brombeek
Mopane
Bandur
Verdun Ruins
Huntleigh
Machemma Ruins
Nzhelele Dam
Mabvuka Jazz
Matsa
Nzhelele
Waterpoort
Dzanani
Langjan Nature Reserve
Vivo
Buysdorp
Mara
Moebani
Makhado (Louis Trichardt)
Tshiozwi
Ben Lavin N.R.
Elim
Albasini Dam
Granite
KaMbokota
Bandelierkop
GaMathule
Mannamead
Legkraal
GaRamokgopa
Soekmekaar
Mphakane
Kalkbank
Bylsteel
Munnik
Duiwelskloof
Dikgale
Bosbult
Olyfberg
Politsi
Maphalong
Houtbosdorp
Cottage
Mankweng
Tzaneen
Tzaneen Dam
Seshego
POLOKWANE (PIETERSBURG)
Pietersburg Nature Reserve
Tsatsaneng
Zion City
Moria
Haenertsburg
Ebenezer Dam
GaMolepo
Makapans Cave
GaMathiba
GaMaja
Bergneek
Bewaarkloof N.R.
Bewaarkloof
Lebowakgomo
Mphahlele
Makubung
Zeekoegat
Sesesehu
GaMankopane
Mecklenburg
Magatle
Tooseng
Mogologola
Tswaing
GaMasemola
Khureng
GaPhahla
Tsatsane
Piet Gouws Dam
Tswatago
Grass Valley Mine
Sekwati
Sekhukhune
Fort Albert 1878
Jane Furse
Kromdraai
Glen Cowie
Phokwane
Kokwaneng
Kennedy's Vale
GaMatlala
Marble Hall
Malaita
Sephaku
Hlogotlou
Geological Phenomenon
Rite
Dindela
Motetema
Groblersdal
Kwaggasvoetpad N.R.
Sehlakwane
Roossenekal
Haakdoringdraai
Maleoskop N.R.
Rooikraal
Draaikraal
Ntwane
Laersdrif
Kranspoort Dorp
Stoffberg
Loskop Dam
Lammerkop
Selonsrivier
Dullstroom
Tshipise
Honnet Nature Reserve
Mineral Springs
Nwanedi Game Reserve
Muswodi
Klein Tshipise
Luphephe Dam
Mafukani
Tshihovhohovho Falls
Thengwe
HaMakuya
Makuleni
Thixwadza
Makonde
Khubvi
Masikhwa
Fundudzi Dam
Gouldville
Mandala
Sibasa
Shigalo
Thohoyandou
Tshakhuma
Shayandima
KaDinga
KaMadonsi
KaMatsakali
Mukhomi
Levubu
Mavhulani
Kadilongo
KaMphambo
Nsami Dam
Vyeboom
KaNkuzani
HaDavhana
Thomo
KaMapuva
Giyani
Ha-Magoro
Magonya
Middel Letaba Dam
Mamaila
Raphahlelo
Jamela
KaNkomo
Klein-Letaba
KaRhangani
Xawela
KaSabulane
Mbhawula
GaMatswe
Lorna Dawn Dam
Mooketsi
Sotong
Maleketla
KaMavele
Eiland
Mineral Spring
Hans Merensky Nature Reserve
La Cotte
Ndzalama Nature Reserve
Letaba
Dan
Letsitele
Murchison
Gravelotte
Namakgale
Selati Game Reserve
Phalaborwa
Phalaborwa Gate
Cleveland N.R.
Lulekani
Maake
Leydsdorp
Selati-rivier
Ofcolaco
Orrie Baragwanath
Makutsi Conservancy
Makalali G.R.
Balule Nature Reserve
Mica
Lekgalameetse Nature Reserve
Trichardtsdal
Lorraine
Ga-Mamatlhola
Blyde Olifants Conservancy
Makgaung
Dingapong
Diphuti
Hoedspruit
Tshukudu G.R.
GaMametsa
Penge
Kromellenbooq
J.G.Strijdom Tunnel
Abel Erasmus
Echo Caves
Motlolo
Driekop Mine
Bogwasa
Ga-Malwane
Rietfontein
Blydepoort Dam
Blyde River Canyon N.R.
Madrid Game Farm
Kapama G.R.
Klaserie
Acornhoek
Cottondale
Steelpoort
Burgersfort
Voortrekker Fort 1847
Ohrigstad
Morone
Crystal Springs N.R.
Rusplaas
Buffelsvlei
Bourke's Luck Potholes
Vaalhoek
God's Window
Casteel
Rolle
Merry Pebble Stream
Bushbuckridge
Krugerspos
Waterval
Pilgrim's Rest
Graskop
Kowyn
Marite
Mkhuhlu
Belfast
Ohrigstad Dam N.R.
Mauchsberg
Maartenshoop
Marambane
Gustav Klingbiel Nature Reserve
Lydenburg
Sabie
Kiepersol
Hazyview
eManzini
Numbi Gate
Sterkspruit N.R.
Long Tom
Hendriksdal
Klipkoppie Dam
Witklip Dam
Nsikazi
White River
KMIA
eBhuga
Klipskool
Buffelskloof N.R.
Sudwala Caves
Brondal
Kamsogwaba
Kwena Dam
Schoemanskloof
Montrose
Elandshoek
Montrose Falls
Nelspruit
Mthethomusha N.R.
KaNyamazane
Berg-en-dal
Ngodwana
Kaapsehoop
Malelane Gate
Malelane
Matsulu
Kaapmuiden
Hectorspruit
Ligwalagwala Conservancy
Komatipoort
Ressano Garcia
Lebombo
Crocodile
Crocodile Bridge Gate
Biyamiti Bushveld Camp
Jock of the Bushveld
Pretoriuskop
Lower Sabie
Mlondozi Picnic area
Nkuhlu Picnic area
Skukuza
Paul Kruger Gate
Jakkalsbessie
Sabi-Sabi
Phabeni Gate
Mala Mala Game Reserve
Newington
Londolozi
Singita
Ulusaba
Inyati
Sabi Sand Game Reserve
Tshokwane Tea Room
Eileen Orpen Dam Picnic area
Nhlanguleni Picnic area
Manyeleti Game Reserve
Talamati Bushveld Camp
Muzandzeni Picnic area
Orpen Gate
Timbavati Wilderness Trail
Thornybush G.R.
Timbavati Game Reserve
Timbavati Gate
Tanda Tula
Umlani
Mbali
Ngala
Motswari
Umbabat N.R.
Klaserie Nature Reserve
Timbavati Picnic area
Roodewal (private)
Satara
Nwanetsi (private)
Mapulanguene
Macaene
Ringane
Balule
Olifants
Nhlanganini Dam
Letaba
Masorini Hill
Massingir
Massingir Dam
Shimuwini Bushveld Camp
Letaba Ranch
Boulders (private)
Mopani
Mooiplaas Picnic area
Magagane
Tropic of Capricorn
Bateleur Bushveld Camp
Shingwedzi
Kanniedood Dam
Sirheni Bushveld Camp
Babalala Picnic area
Nthaveni
Punda Maria Gate
Punda Maria
KaMhinga
Mphongolo
Thulamela Archaeological site
Pafuri Gate
Pafuri Picnic area
Crooks Corner
SA Police
Masisi
Mushithe
Mutale
Makuya N.R.
Chikwarakwara
Diti
Curia
Vouga
Chicualacuala
Mapai
Limpopo
Mwenezi
Olifants
Sabie
N1
N4
N11
R525
R508
R523
R522
R524
R578
R521
R528
R529
R519
R518
R579
R555
R577
R526
R527
R531
R532
R533
R534
R535
R536
R537
R538
R539
R540
R570
A6
A4
208
19
0 10 20 30 40 50 miles

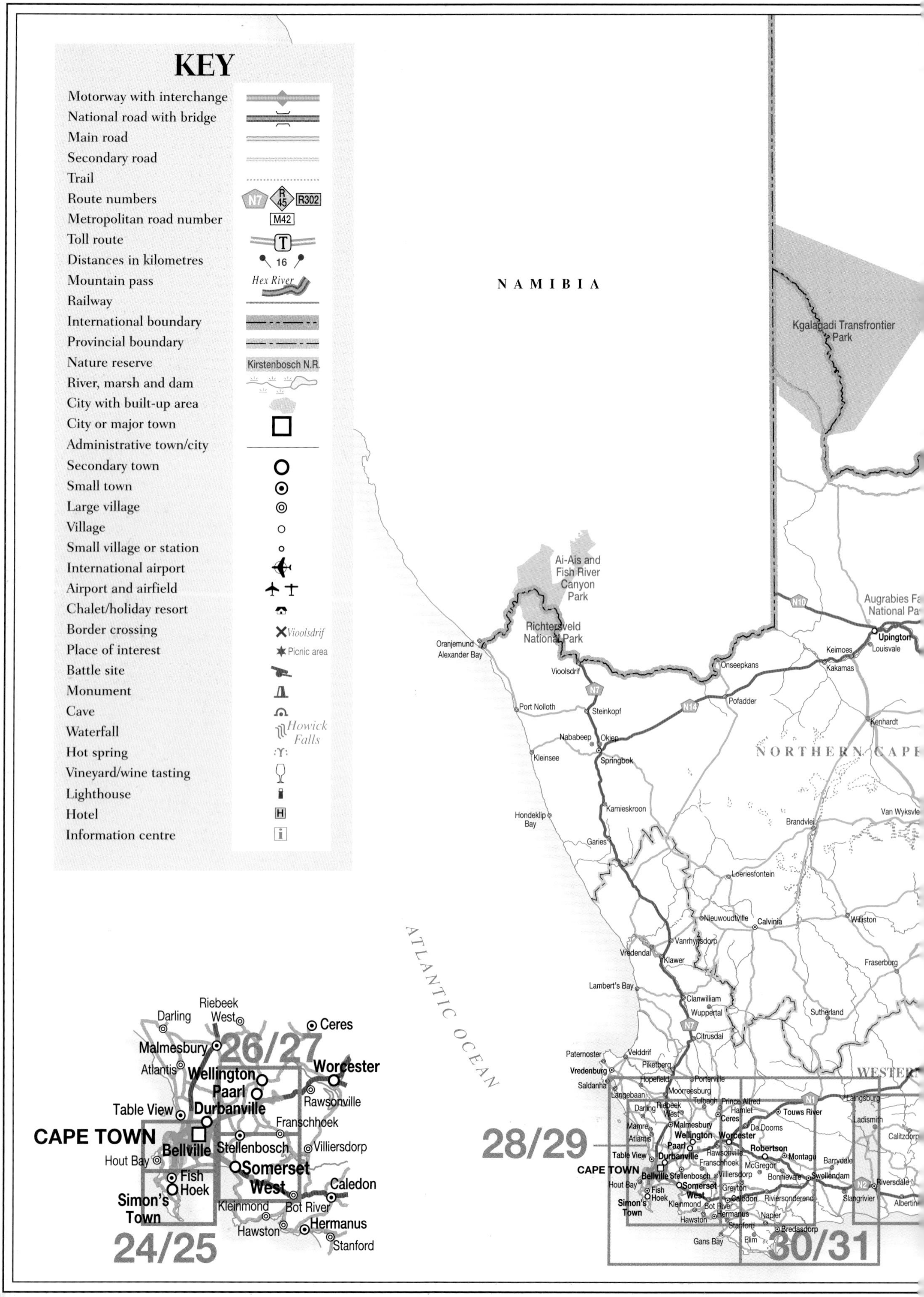
KEY
Motorway with interchange
National road with bridge
Main road
Secondary road
Trail
Route numbers
N7
R 45
R302
Metropolitan road number
M42
Toll route
T
Distances in kilometres
16
Mountain pass
Hex River
Railway
International boundary
Provincial boundary
Nature reserve
Kirstenbosch N.R.
River, marsh and dam
City with built-up area
City or major town
Administrative town/city
Secondary town
Small town
Large village
Village
Small village or station
International airport
Airport and airfield
Chalet/holiday resort
Border crossing
Vioolsdrif
Place of interest
Picnic area
Battle site
Monument
Cave
Waterfall
Howick Falls
Hot spring
Vineyard/wine tasting
Lighthouse
Hotel
H
Information centre
NAMIBIA
Kgalagadi Transfrontier Park
Ai-Ais and Fish River Canyon Park
Richtersveld National Park
Augrabies Falls National Park
Oranjemund
Alexander Bay
Vioolsdrif
Onseepkans
Keimoes
Kakamas
Upington
Louisvale
N10
N7
N14
Port Nolloth
Steinkopf
Pofadder
Kenhardt
Nababeep
Okiep
Kleinsee
Springbok
NORTHERN CAPE
Kamieskroon
Hondeklip Bay
Brandvlei
Van Wyksvlei
Garies
Loeriesfontein
Nieuwoudtville
Calvinia
Williston
Vanrhynsdorp
Vredendal
Klawer
Fraserburg
Lambert's Bay
Clanwilliam
Wuppertal
Sutherland
Citrusdal
ATLANTIC OCEAN
Paternoster
Velddrif
Piketberg
Vredenburg
Saldanha
Hopefield
Porterville
Langebaan
Moorreesburg
WESTERN
Tulbagh
Prince Alfred Hamlet
Ceres
Laingsburg
Darling
Riebeek West
Touws River
Ladismith
Malmesbury
De Doorns
Mamre
Atlantis
Wellington
Worcester
Calitzdorp
Paarl
Robertson
Montagu
Table View
Durbanville
Rawsonville
Barrydale
Franschhoek
McGregor
28/29
CAPE TOWN
Bellville
Stellenbosch
Villiersdorp
Bonnievale
Swellendam
Hout Bay
Somerset West
Riversdale
Fish Hoek
Greyton
N2
Simon's Town
Kleinmond
Bot River
Caledon
Riviersonderend
Slangrivier
Albertinia
Hermanus
Hawston
Napier
Stanford
Bredasdorp
Gans Bay
Elim
30/31
Riebeek West
Darling
Ceres
Malmesbury
26/27
Atlantis
Wellington
Worcester
Paarl
Rawsonville
Table View
Durbanville
Franschhoek
CAPE TOWN
Bellville
Stellenbosch
Villiersdorp
Hout Bay
Somerset West
Fish Hoek
Caledon
Simon's Town
Kleinmond
Bot River
Hermanus
Hawston
Stanford
24/25

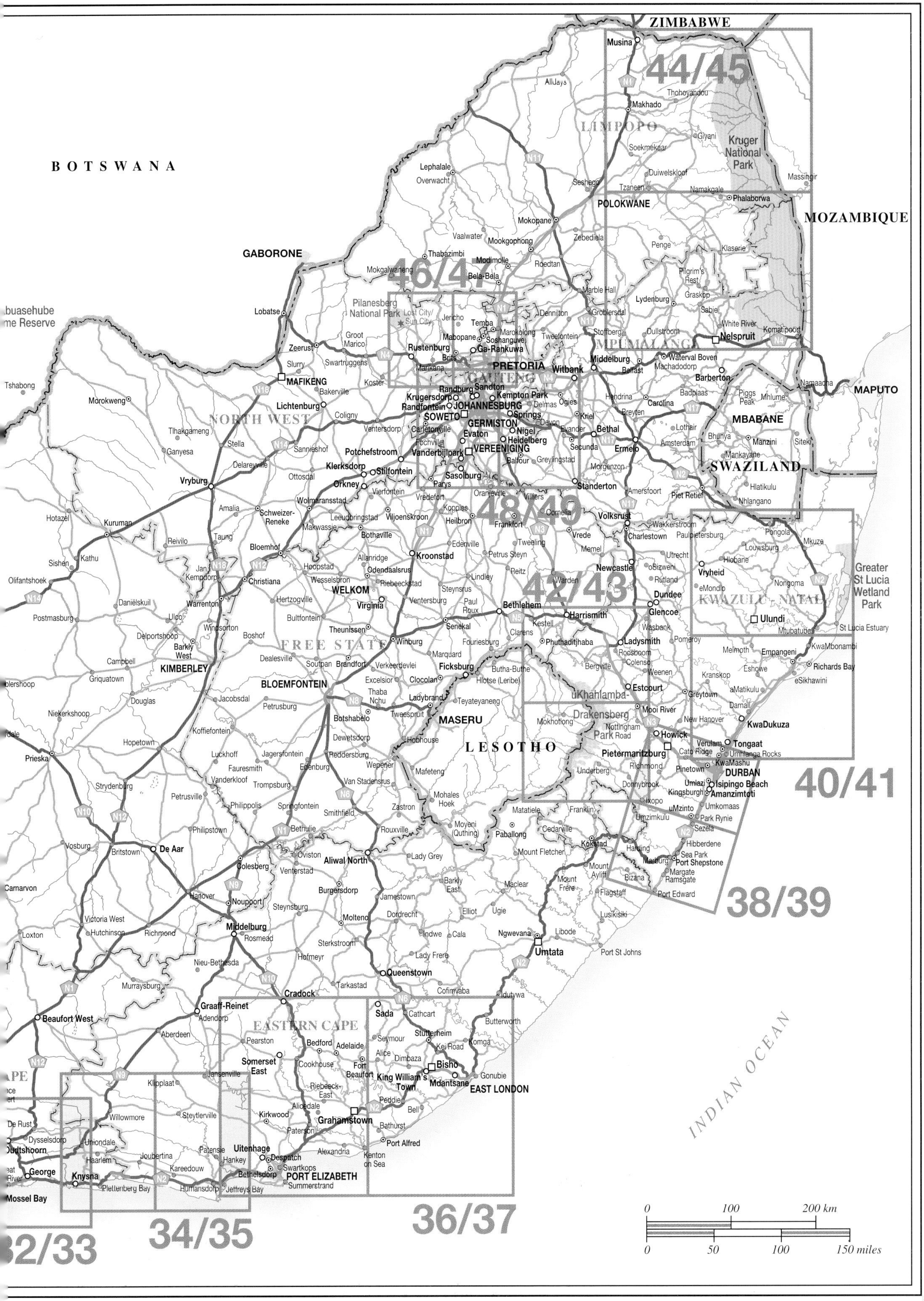
ZIMBABWE
BOTSWANA
MOZAMBIQUE
SWAZILAND
LESOTHO
INDIAN OCEAN
LIMPOPO
NORTH WEST
GAUTENG
MPUMALANGA
FREE STATE
KWAZULU-NATAL
EASTERN CAPE
44/45
46/47
48/49
42/43
40/41
38/39
36/37
34/35
32/33
Kruger National Park
Greater St Lucia Wetland Park
Pilanesberg National Park
GABORONE
MAPUTO
MBABANE
MASERU
PRETORIA
JOHANNESBURG
SOWETO
GERMISTON
VEREENIGING
MAFIKENG
KIMBERLEY
BLOEMFONTEIN
WELKOM
POLOKWANE
DURBAN
EAST LONDON
PORT ELIZABETH
Musina
Makhado
Thohoyandou
Phalaborwa
Mokopane
Nelspruit
Witbank
Middelburg
Rustenburg
Lichtenburg
Potchefstroom
Klerksdorp
Vryburg
Kuruman
Bloemhof
Kroonstad
Bethlehem
Harrismith
Newcastle
Ladysmith
Vryheid
Ulundi
Richards Bay
Pietermaritzburg
Tongaat
KwaDukuza
Port Shepstone
Kokstad
Umtata
Queenstown
Aliwal North
Colesberg
De Aar
Middelburg
Cradock
Graaff-Reinet
Beaufort West
Grahamstown
Uitenhage
Bisho
King William's Town
Mdantsane
Knysna
George
Mossel Bay
Oudtshoorn
Plettenberg Bay
Jeffreys Bay
Port Alfred
Drakensberg
uKhahlamba-
0
100
200 km
0
50
100
150 miles

CAPE TOWN
Table Bay
ATLANTIC OCEAN
TABLE MOUNTAIN
TWELVE APOSTLES
CONSTANTIABERG
Bellville
Parow
Goodwood
Milnerton
Pinelands
Langa
Athlone
Rondebosch
Newlands
Claremont
Kenilworth
Wynberg
Plumstead
Constantia
Hout Bay
Llandudno
Camps Bay
Clifton
Bantry Bay
Sea Point
Green Point
Mouille Point
Woodstock
Observatory
Mowbray
Rosebank
Nyanga
Guguletu
Philippi
Mitchells Plain
Grassy Park
Retreat
Tokai
Bakoven
Oudekraal
Cape Peninsula National Park
Table Mountain Nature Reserve
Kirstenbosch National Botanic Garden
Cape Town International Airport
Duiker Island
Seal Island
Tyger Valley, Paarl
Bellville
Stellenbosch
Somerset West
Kuilsrivier
0 1 2 km
0 (1 cm) 1,2 kilometres

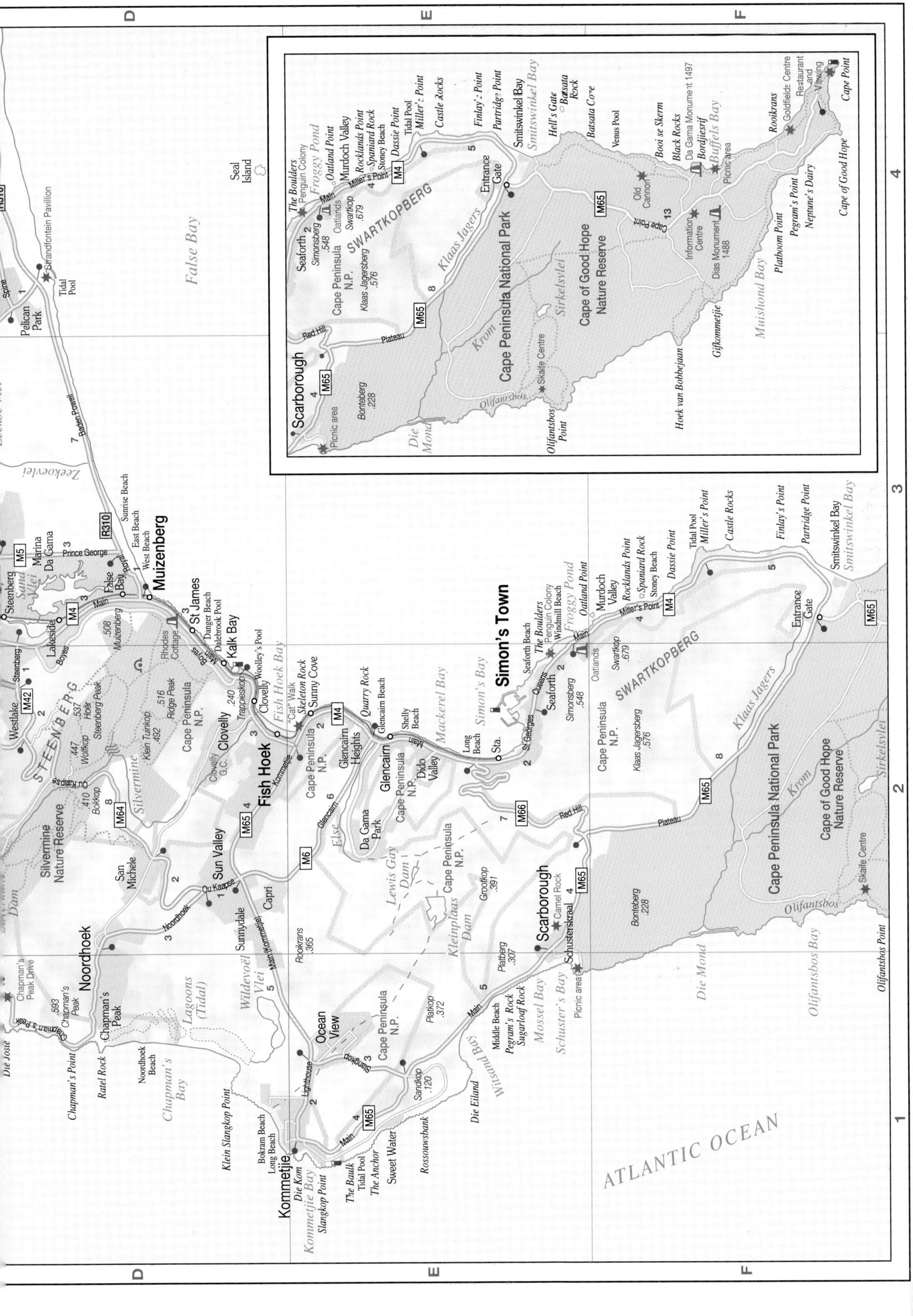
D
E
F
1
2
3
4
False Bay
Seal Island
Muizenberg
St James
Kalk Bay
Fish Hoek
Simon's Town
Scarborough
Kommetjie
Noordhoek
Ocean View
Sun Valley
Capri
Sunnydale
Glencairn
Glencairn Heights
Clovelly
Lakeside
Westlake
Steenberg
Marina Da Gama
Pelican Park
Strandfontein Pavillion
Zeekoevlei
Silvermine Nature Reserve
Cape Peninsula N.P.
Cape Peninsula National Park
Cape of Good Hope Nature Reserve
SWARTKOPBERG
STEENBERG
Fish Hoek Bay
Mackerel Bay
Simon's Bay
Froggy Pond
The Boulders
Penguin Colony
Seaforth
Smitswinkel Bay
Entrance Gate
Chapman's Peak
Chapman's Bay
Noordhoek Beach
Kommetjie Bay
Slangkop Point
Wildevoël Vlei
Lewis Gay Dam
Kleinplaas Dam
Mossel Bay
Schuster's Bay
Witsand Bay
Olifantsbos Bay
Olifantsbos Point
Die Mond
Skaife Centre
Sirkelsvlei
Klaas Jagers
ATLANTIC OCEAN
Cape Point
Cape of Good Hope
Buffels Bay
Dias Monument 1488
Da Gama Monument 1497
Information Centre
Old Cannon
Platboom Point
Pegram's Point
Neptune's Dairy
Rooikrans
Muishond Bay
Hoek van Bobbejaan
Gifkommetjie
M65
M4
M6
M66
M64
M42
M5
R310

STELLENBOSCH, PAARL and FRANSCHHOEK VINEYARDS

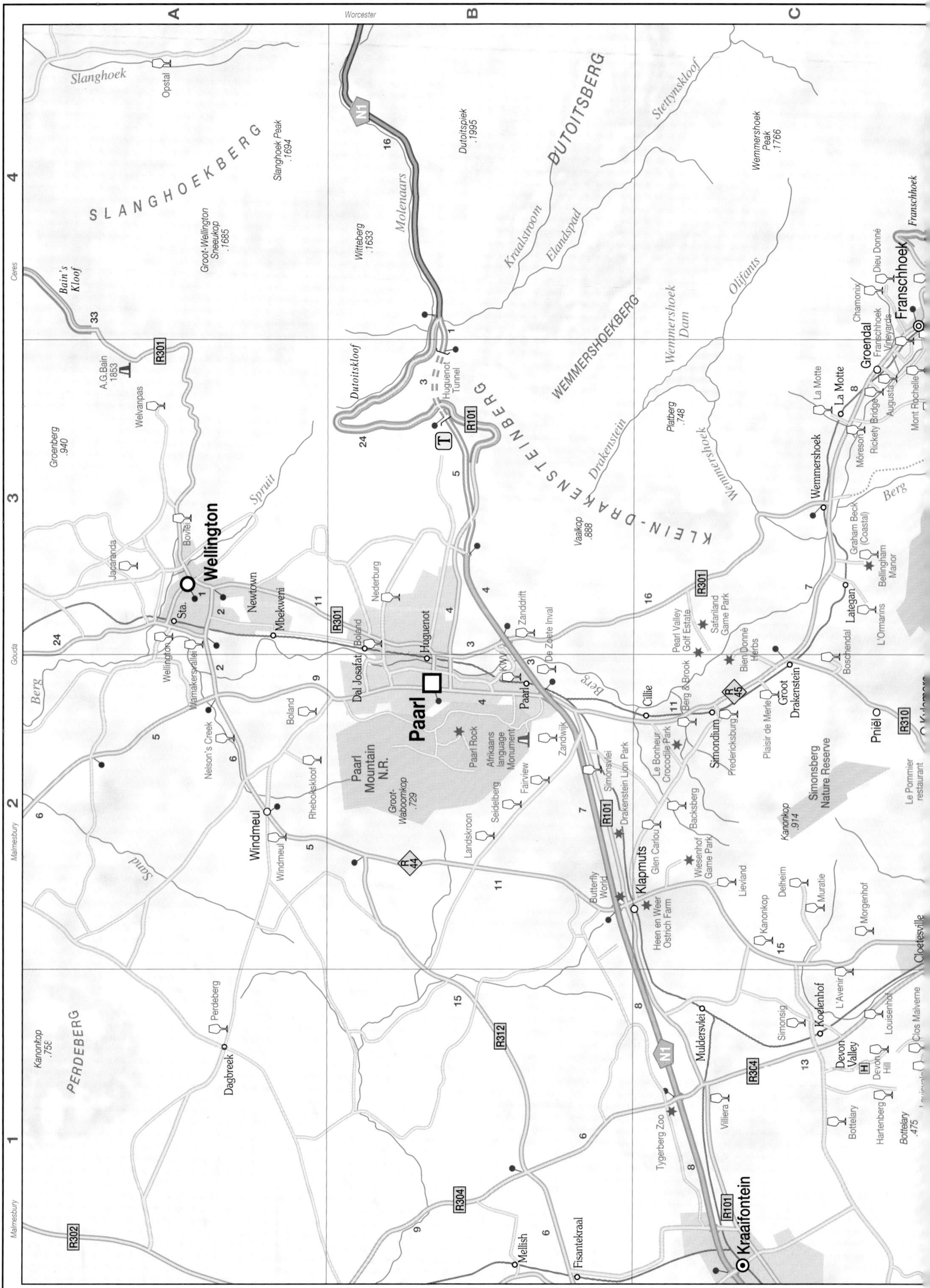

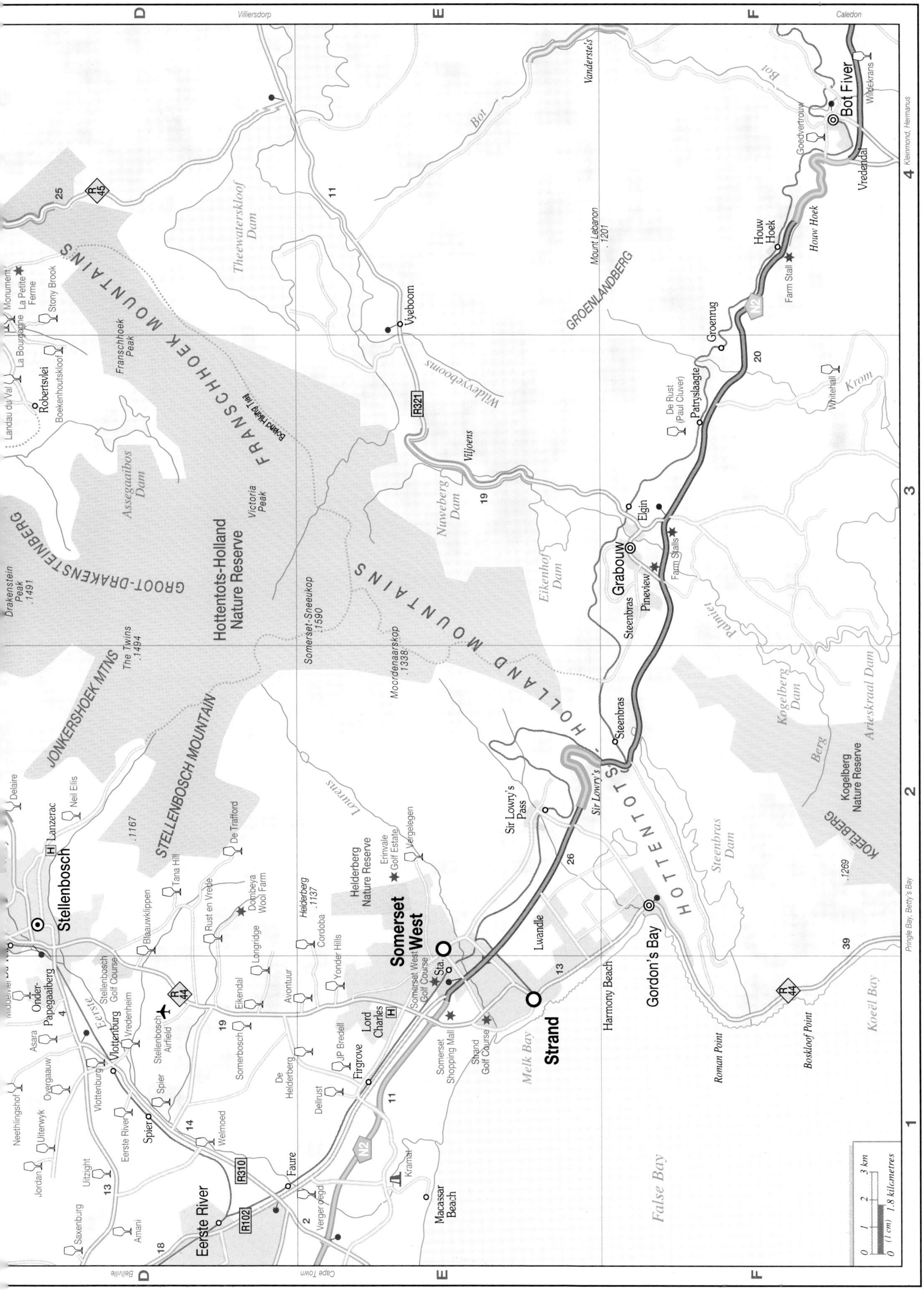
Villiersdorp
Caledon
Bot Fiver
Wildekrans
Goedvertrouw
Vredendal
Kleinmond, Hermanus
Bot
Vandersteis
Theewaterskloof Dam
Mount Lebanon 1201
GROENLANDBERG
Houw Hoek
Farm Stall
N2
Groenrug
Patryslaagte
De Rust (Paul Cluver)
Whitehall
Krom
Vyeboom
R321
Wildevyeboom
Viljoens
Nuweberg Dam
Elgin
Grabouw
Farm Stalls
Pineview
Steenbras
Eikenhof Dam
Palmiet
Kogelberg Dam
Arieskraal Dam
Berg
Kogelberg Nature Reserve
KOGELBERG
.1269
Steenbras Dam
HOTTENTOTS HOLLAND MOUNTAINS
FRANSCHHOEK MOUNTAINS
Sir Lowry's
Sir Lowry's Pass
Boland Hiking Trail
Franschhoek Peak
Victoria Peak
Hottentots-Holland Nature Reserve
Assegaaibos Dam
GROOT-DRAKENSTEINBERG
Drakenstein Peak .1491
Somerset-Sneeukop .1590
Moordenaarskop .1338
The Twins .1494
JONKERSHOEK MTNS
STELLENBOSCH MOUNTAIN
.1167
Robertsvlei
Boekenhoutskloof
Landau du Val
La Bourgogne
Stony Brook
La Petite Ferme
Monument
Delaire
Neil Ellis
Lanzerac
De Trafford
Stellenbosch
Tana Hill
Rust en Vrede
Dombeya Wool Farm
Blaauwklippen
Longridge
Eikendal
Avontuur
Yonder Hills
Cordoba
Helderberg .1137
Helderberg Nature Reserve
Erinvale Golf Estate
Vergelegen
Lourens
Somerset West
Sta.
Somerset West Golf Course
Lord Charles
Stellenbosch Golf Course
Onder-Papegaaiberg
Vredenheim
Stellenbosch Airfield
R44
Asara
Vlottenburg
Somerbosch
De Helderberg
JP Bredell
Firgrove
Somerset Shopping Mall
Strand Golf Course
Strand
Melk Bay
Lwandle
Harmony Beach
Gordon's Bay
26
13
Overgaauw
Neethlingshof
Uiterwyk
Eerste River
Spier
Welmoed
Dellrust
Eerste
R310
Faure
Uitzicht
Jordan
Saxenburg
Amani
Eerste River
R102
Verger gegd
Macassar Beach
Kramat
False Bay
Roman Point
Boskloof Point
Koeël Bay
Pringle Bay, Betty's Bay
Cape Town
Bellville
0 1 2 3 km
(1 cm) 1.8 kilometres
D
E
F
1
2
3
4
11
19
20
25
39
R45
18
14
2

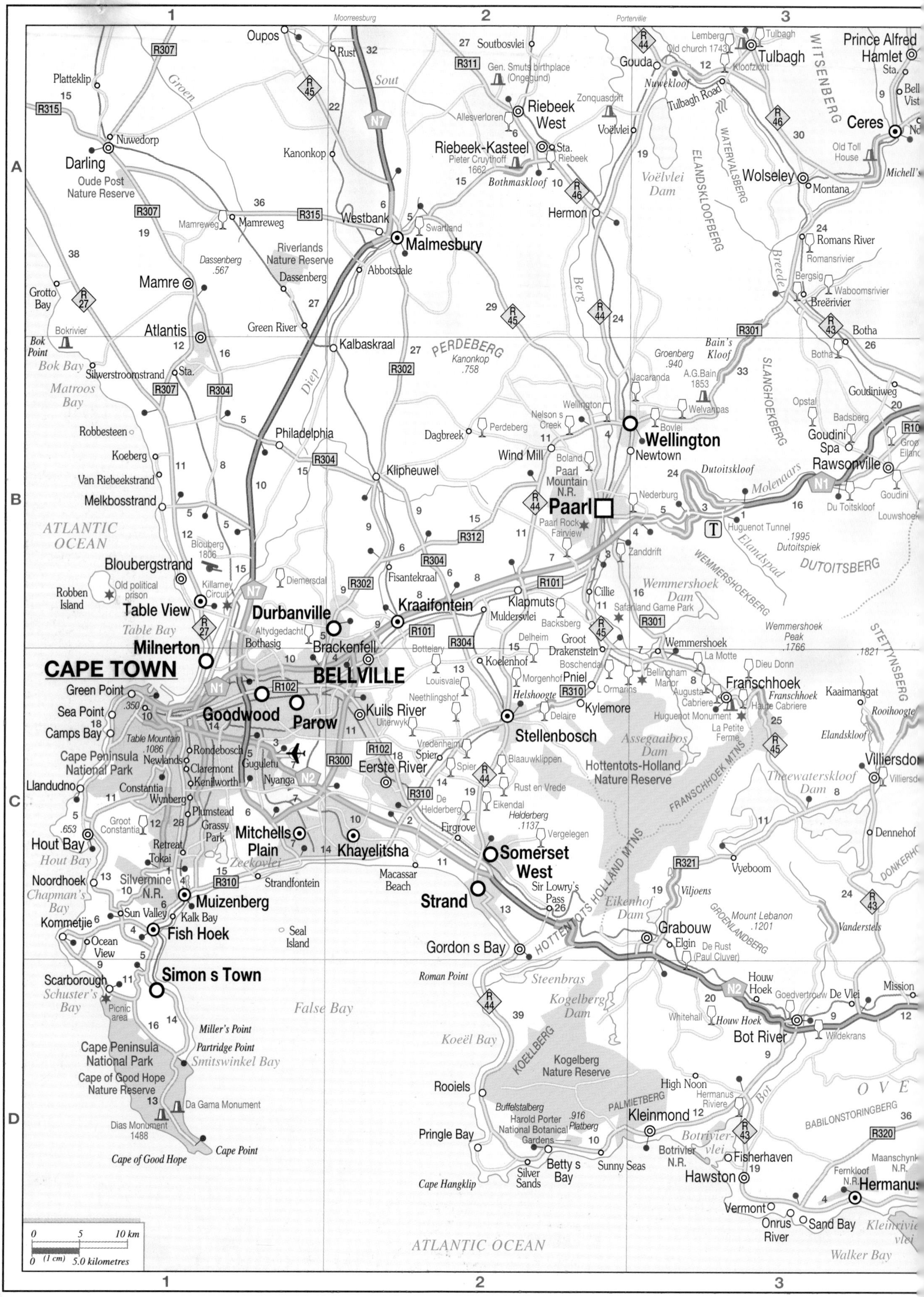
CAPE TOWN
BELLVILLE
Paarl
Wellington
Stellenbosch
Franschhoek
Somerset West
Strand
Malmesbury
Durbanville
Kraaifontein
Tulbagh
Ceres
Wolseley
Riebeek West
Riebeek-Kasteel
Darling
Atlantis
Mamre
Table View
Milnerton
Goodwood
Parow
Kuils River
Eerste River
Mitchells Plain
Khayelitsha
Muizenberg
Fish Hoek
Simon s Town
Hout Bay
Grabouw
Elgin
Bot River
Kleinmond
Hawston
Hermanus
Villiersdorp
Rawsonville
Gordon s Bay
ATLANTIC OCEAN
False Bay
Table Bay
Walker Bay
Cape Point
Cape of Good Hope
Robben Island
Hottentots-Holland Nature Reserve
Kogelberg Nature Reserve
Cape Peninsula National Park
0 5 10 km
0 (1 cm) 5.0 kilometres

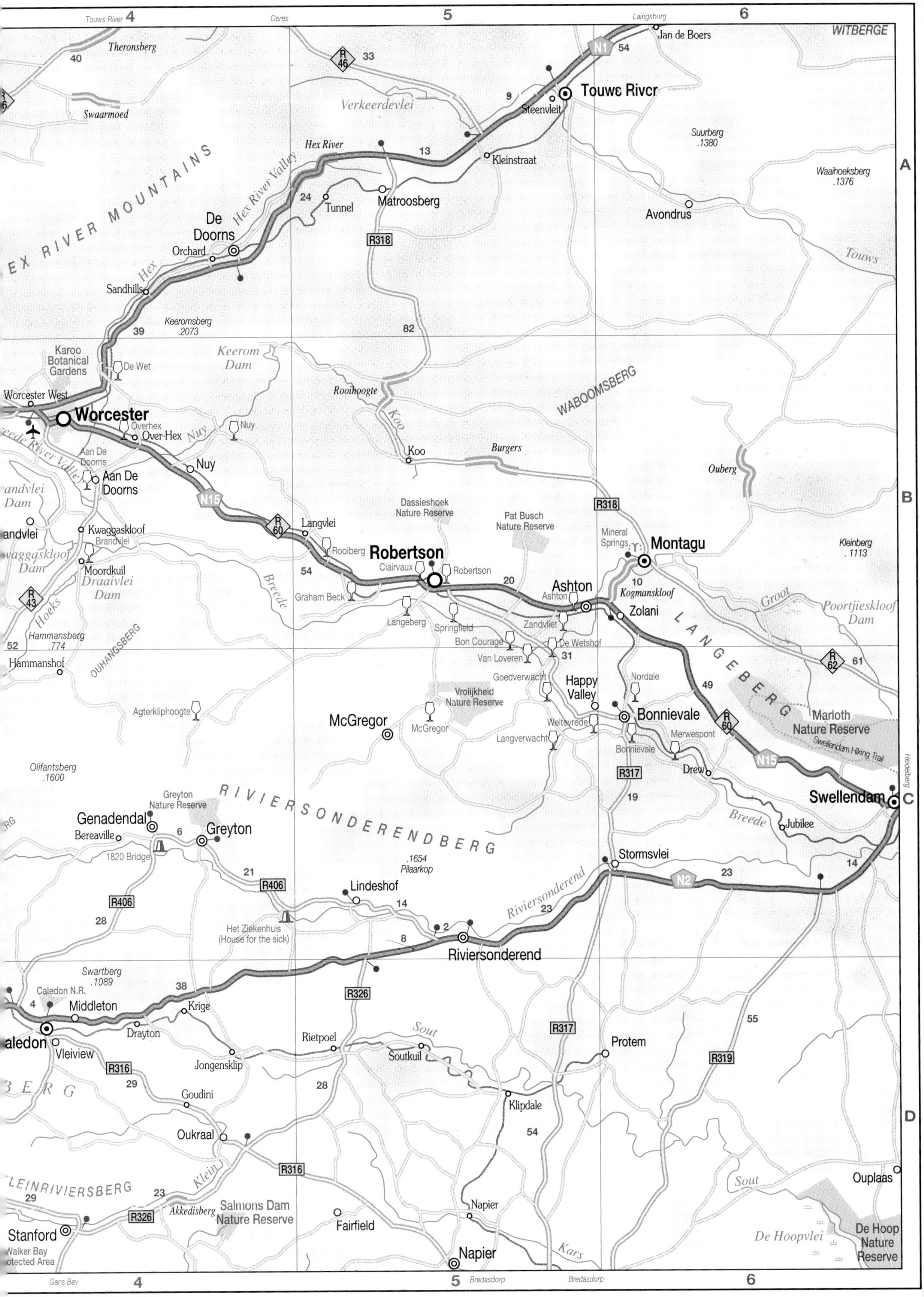

Touws River
Ceres
Laingsburg
Jan de Boers
WITBERGE
Theronsberg
Swaarmoed
Verkeerdevlei
Touws River
Steenvlei
Suurberg
.1380
Hex River
Kleinstraat
Waaihoeksberg
.1376
HEX RIVER MOUNTAINS
Hex River Valley
Tunnel
Matroosberg
Avondrus
De Doorns
Orchard
R318
Touws
Sandhills
Hex
Keeromsberg
.2073
Karoo Botanical Gardens
De Wet
Keerom Dam
Rooihoogte
WABOOMSBERG
Worcester West
Worcester
Overhex
Over-Hex
Nuy
Koo
Burgers
Breede River Valley
Aan De Doorns
Ouberg
Dassieshoek Nature Reserve
Pat Busch Nature Reserve
Mineral Springs
Montagu
Kwaggaskloof
Brandvlei
Langvlei
Rooiberg
Robertson
Clairvaux
Kleinberg
.1113
Moordkuil
Draaivlei Dam
Breede
Graham Beck
Ashton
Kogmanskloof
Zolani
Groot
Poortjieskloof Dam
Hoeks
Langeberg
Springfield
Zandvliet
LANGEBERG
Hammansberg
.774
Hammanshof
OUHANGSBERG
Bon Courage
Van Loveren
De Wetshof
Goedverwacht
Happy Valley
Nordale
Vrolijkheid Nature Reserve
Agterkliphoogte
McGregor
Weltevrede
Bonnievale
Merwespont
Marloth Nature Reserve
Swellendam Hiking Trail
Langverwacht
Olifantsberg
.1600
Drew
Heidelberg
Swellendam
Greyton Nature Reserve
RIVIERSONDERENDBERG
Genadendal
Bereaville
Greyton
1820 Bridge
Breede
Jubilee
Stormsvlei
.1654
Pilaarkop
Lindeshof
N2
Riviersonderend
Het Ziekenhuis
(House for the sick)
Riviersonderend
Swartberg
.1089
Caledon N.R.
Middleton
Krige
Caledon
Drayton
Vleiview
Rietpoel
Sout
Soutkuil
Protem
Jongensklip
Goudini
Klipdale
Oukraal
KLEINRIVIERSBERG
Klein
Salmons Dam Nature Reserve
Akkedisberg
Napier
Fairfield
Ouplaas
Sout
Stanford
Walker Bay
Protected Area
De Hoopvlei
De Hoop Nature Reserve
Kars
Napier
Gans Bay
Bredasdorp

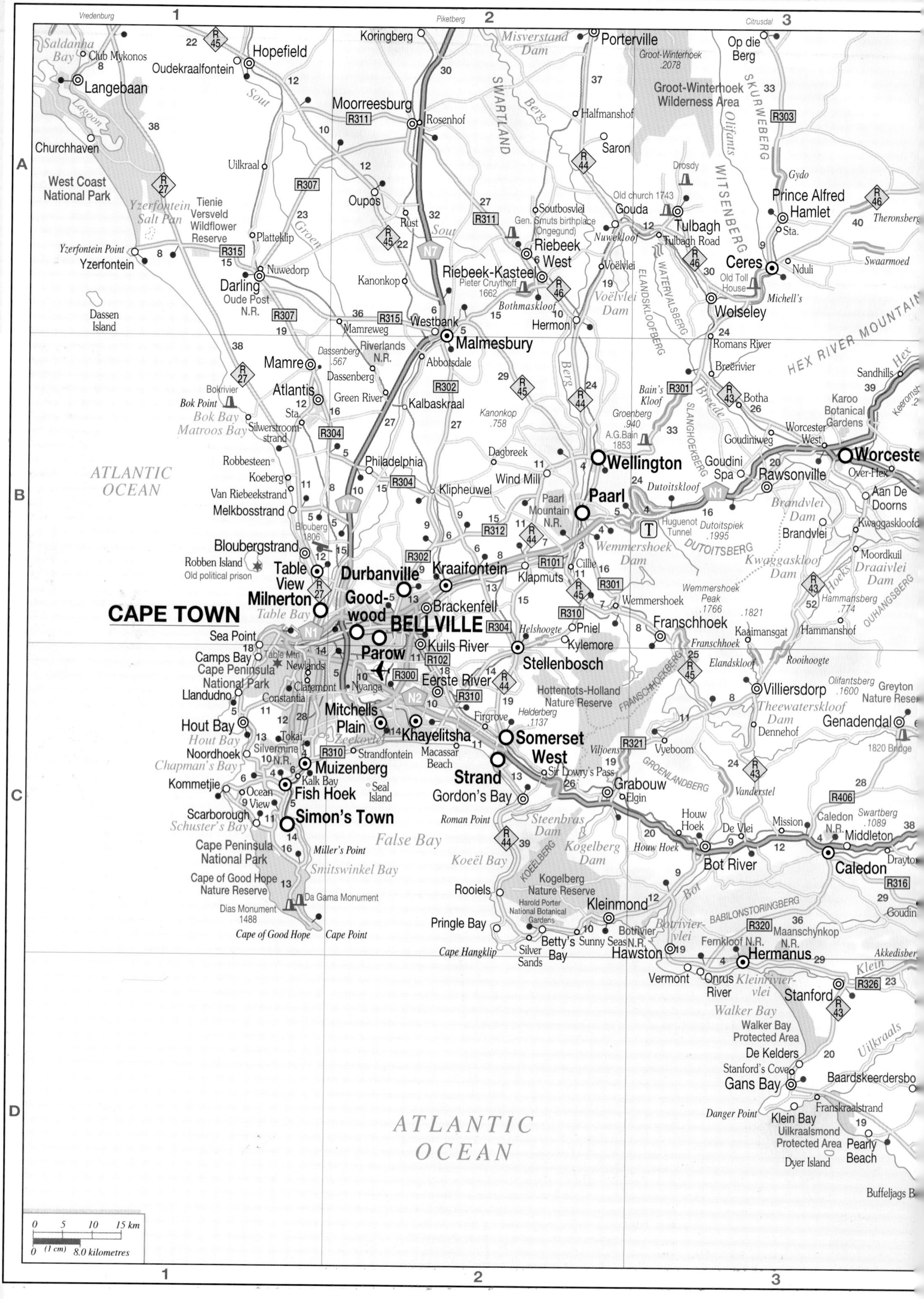
Vredenburg
1
Piketberg
2
Citrusdal
3
Saldanha Bay
Club Mykonos
Langebaan
Langebaan Lagoon
Oudekraalfontein
Hopefield
Koringberg
Misverstand Dam
Porterville
Op die Berg
Groot-Winterhoek .2078
Groot-Winterhoek Wilderness Area
SKURWEBERG
Moorreesburg
R311
Rosenhof
SWARTLAND
Halfmanshof
Churchhaven
Saron
R303
Olifants
A
Uilkraal
West Coast National Park
R27
Oupos
R307
Drosdy
WITSENBERG
Gydo
Prince Alfred Hamlet
Sta.
Theronsberg
Old church 1743
Gouda
Tulbagh
Tulbagh Road
Yzerfontein Salt Pan
Tienie Versveld Wildflower Reserve
Rust
Sout
R311
Soutbosvlei
Gen. Smuts birthplace (Ongegund)
Nuwekloof
Platteklip
Groen
N7
Riebeek West
R315
Yzerfontein Point
Yzerfontein
Darling
Nuwedorp
Oude Post N.R.
Kanonkop
Riebeek-Kasteel
Pieter Cruythoff 1662
Voëlvlei
Voëlvlei Dam
Bothmaskloof
ELANDSKLOOFBERG
WATERVALSBERG
Ceres
Nduli
Swaarmoed
Old Toll House
Michell's
Wolseley
Dassen Island
R307
Mamreweg
R315
Westbank
Malmesbury
Hermon
Romans River
HEX RIVER MOUNTAINS
Mamre
Dassenberg .567
Riverlands N.R.
Dassenberg
Abbotsdale
Breërivier
Sandhills
Hex
Atlantis
Sta.
Green River
R302
Kalbaskraal
Berg
Bain's Kloof
R301
Botha
Karoo Botanical Gardens
Bokrivier
Bok Point
Bok Bay
Matroos Bay
Silwerstroomstrand
R304
Kanonkop .758
Groenberg .940
A.G.Bain 1853
SLANGHOEKBERG
Breede
Worcester West
Goudiniweg
Worcester
Over-Hex
Robbesteen
Philadelphia
Dagbreek
Wellington
Goudini Spa
Rawsonville
ATLANTIC OCEAN
B
Koeberg
Van Riebeekstrand
Melkbosstrand
R304
Klipheuwel
Wind Mill
Paarl Mountain N.R.
Paarl
Dutoitskloof
N1
Aan De Doorns
Brandvlei Dam
Brandvlei
Blouberg .1806
N7
R312
Huguenot Tunnel
Dutoitspiek .1995
Kwaggaskloof
Moordkuil
Bloubergstrand
Robben Island
Old political prison
Table View
R302
Durbanville
Kraaifontein
Klapmuts
R101
Cillié
Wemmershoek Dam
DUTOITSBERG
Kwaggaskloof Dam
Draaivlei Dam
Milnerton
Table Bay
Goodwood
Brackenfell
R301
Wemmershoek
Wemmershoek Peak .1766
.1821
Hammansberg .774
OUHANGSBERG
CAPE TOWN
BELLVILLE
R304
R310
Helshoogte
Pniel
Franschhoek
Kaaimansgat
Hammanshof
Sea Point
N1
Parow
Kuils River
Kylemore
Stellenbosch
Franschhoek
Camps Bay
Table Mtn
Newlands
Cape Peninsula National Park
R102
R300
Eerste River
Elandskloof
Rooihoogte
Claremont
Nyanga
Hottentots-Holland Nature Reserve
FRANSCHHOEKBERG
Villiersdorp
Olifantsberg .1600
Greyton Nature Reserve
Llandudno
Constantia
N2
R310
Helderberg .1137
Theewaterskloof Dam
Mitchells Plain
Khayelitsha
Firgrove
Genadendal
Dennehof
Hout Bay
Tokai
Zeekoevlei
Somerset West
Viljoens
R321
Vyeboom
1820 Bridge
Noordhoek
Silvermine N.R.
R310
Strandfontein
Macassar Beach
Strand
GROENLANDBERG
Chapman's Bay
Muizenberg
Sir Lowry's Pass
Kommetjie
Kalk Bay
Seal Island
Grabouw
Elgin
Vanderstel
C
Ocean View
Fish Hoek
Gordon's Bay
R406
Scarborough
Schuster's Bay
Simon's Town
Roman Point
Steenbras Dam
Houw Hoek
Mission
Caledon N.R.
Swartberg .1089
Middleton
False Bay
De Vlei
Houw Hoek
Cape Peninsula National Park
Miller's Point
KOEËLBERG
Kogelberg Dam
Bot River
Caledon
Drayton
Koeël Bay
Smitswinkel Bay
R316
Cape of Good Hope Nature Reserve
Rooiels
Kogelberg Nature Reserve
Bot
BABILONSTORINGBERG
Da Gama Monument
Harold Porter National Botanical Gardens
Kleinmond
Goudini
Dias Monument 1488
Pringle Bay
Botrivier
Botriviervlei
R320
Maanschynkop N.R.
Cape of Good Hope
Cape Point
Betty's Bay
Sunny Seas N.R.
Fernkloof N.R.
Cape Hangklip
Silver Sands
Hawston
Hermanus
Akkedisberg
Vermont
Onrus River
Kleinriviervlei
Klein
R326
Stanford
R43
Walker Bay
Walker Bay Protected Area
De Kelders
Uilkraals
Stanford's Cove
Gans Bay
Baardskeerdersbos
D
Danger Point
Franskraalstrand
Klein Bay
Uilkraalsmond Protected Area
Pearly Beach
ATLANTIC OCEAN
Dyer Island
Buffeljags Bay
0 5 10 15 km
0 (1 cm) 8.0 kilometres

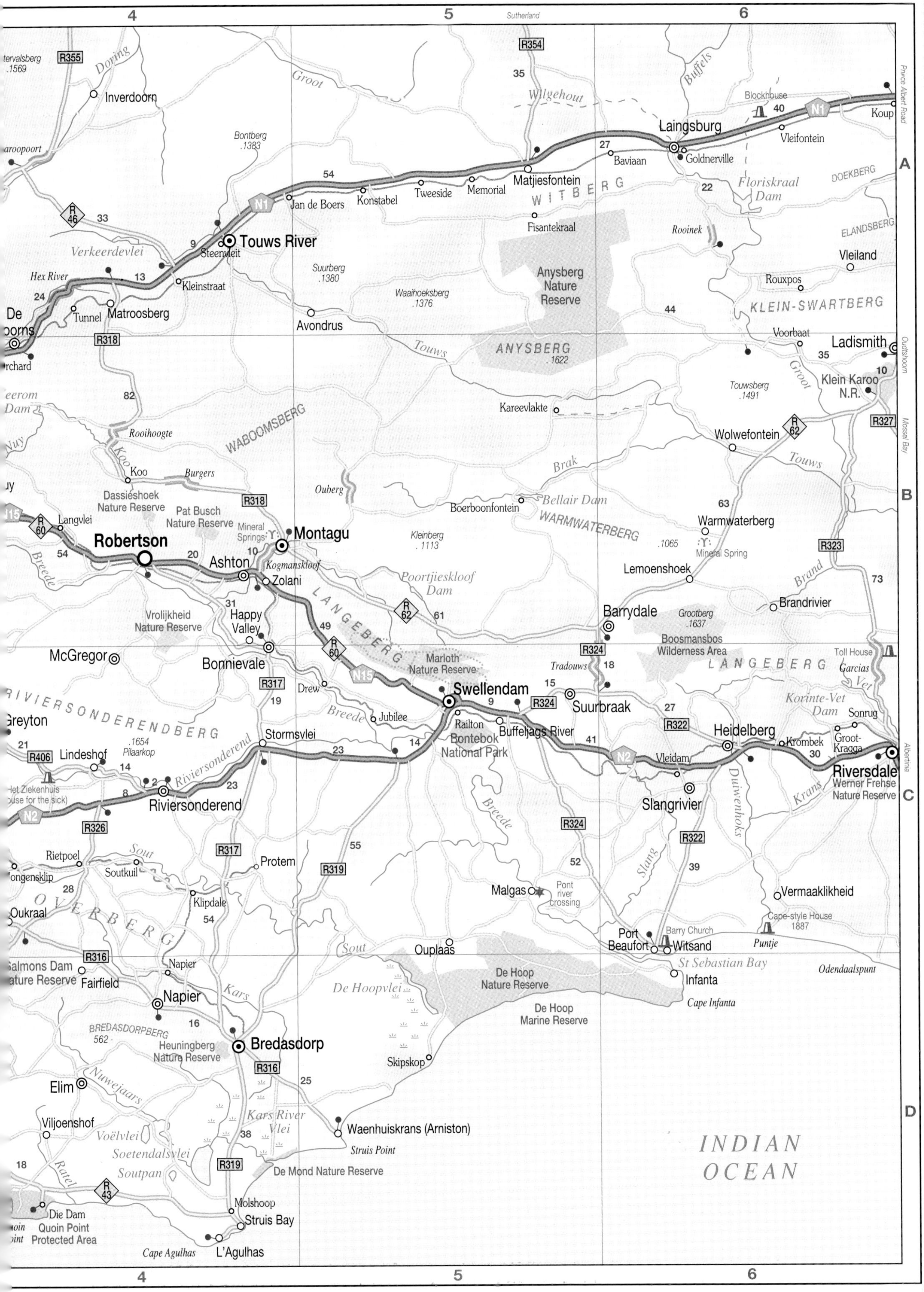
4
5
6
A
B
C
D
Sutherland
R354
R355
Doring
Inverdoorn
Groot
Wilgehout
Buffels
Blockhouse
40
N1
Koup
Prince Albert Road
Laingsburg
Vleifontein
Bontberg
.1383
27
Baviaan
Goldnerville
54
Matjiesfontein
Memorial
Tweeside
Konstabel
Jan de Boers
WITBERG
22
Floriskraal
Dam
DOEKBERG
R
46
33
Fisantekraal
Rooinek
ELANDSBERG
9
Touws River
Steenvleit
Verkeerdevlei
Hex River
13
Kleinstraat
Suurberg
.1380
Anysberg
Nature
Reserve
Vleiland
Rouxpos
24
De
Tunnel
Matroosberg
Waaihoeksberg
.1376
Avondrus
44
KLEIN-SWARTBERG
R318
Touws
ANYSBERG
.1622
Voorbaat
Ladismith
35
Oudtshoorn
10
Klein Karoo
N.R.
82
Touwsberg
.1491
Groot
Kareevlakte
R327
Wolwefontein
R
62
Mossel Bay
Rooihoogte
WABOOMSBERG
Nuy
Brak
Touws
Koo
Koo
Burgers
Ouberg
Bellair Dam
Boerboonfontein
WARMWATERBERG
Dassieshoek
Nature Reserve
Pat Busch
Nature Reserve
R318
63
Warmwaterberg
R
60
Langvlei
Robertson
Mineral
Springs
Montagu
Kleinberg
.1113
.1065
Mineral Spring
R323
54
Breede
20
Ashton
10
Kogmanskloof
Zolani
Poortjieskloof
Dam
Lemoenshoek
Brand
73
Vrolijkheid
Nature Reserve
31
Happy
Valley
LANGEBERG
R
62
61
Barrydale
Grootberg
.1637
Brandrivier
49
Boosmansbos
Wilderness Area
Toll House
McGregor
Bonnievale
R
60
Marloth
Nature Reserve
R324
Tradouws
18
LANGEBERG
Garcias
RIVIERSONDERENDBERG
R317
19
Drew
N15
Swellendam
15
Suurbraak
Korinte-Vet
Dam
Sonrug
Vet
Greyton
Breede
Jubilee
9
R324
27
Railton
Buffeljags River
R322
Heidelberg
Groot-
Kragga
.1654
Pilaarkop
Stormsvlei
14
Bontebok
National Park
41
Krombek
21
R406
Lindeshof
Riviersonderend
23
N2
Vleidam
30
Riversdale
14
Albertinia
Het Ziekenhuis
2
8
23
Riviersonderend
Slangrivier
Werner Frehse
Nature Reserve
Krans
N2
Duiwenhoks
R326
Breede
R324
R322
Rietpoel
Sout
R317
55
Protem
R319
52
Slang
39
Soutkuil
Jongensklip
28
OVERBERG
Klipdale
Malgas
Pont
river
crossing
Vermaaklikheid
Oukraal
54
Cape-style House
1887
Port
Beaufort
Barry Church
Witsand
Sout
Ouplaas
Puntje
R316
Salmons Dam
Nature Reserve
Fairfield
Napier
De Hoop
Nature Reserve
St Sebastian Bay
Infanta
Odendaalspunt
Kars
De Hoopvlei
Napier
De Hoop
Marine Reserve
Cape Infanta
BREDASDORPBERG
562
16
Heuningberg
Nature Reserve
Bredasdorp
Skipskop
R316
Elim
Nuwejaars
25
Kars River
Vlei
Viljoenshof
Voëlvlei
38
Waenhuiskrans (Arniston)
Soetendalsvlei
Struis Point
INDIAN
OCEAN
18
Ratel
Soutpan
R319
De Mond Nature Reserve
R
43
Molshoop
Die Dam
Struis Bay
Quoin Point
Protected Area
Cape Agulhas
L'Agulhas

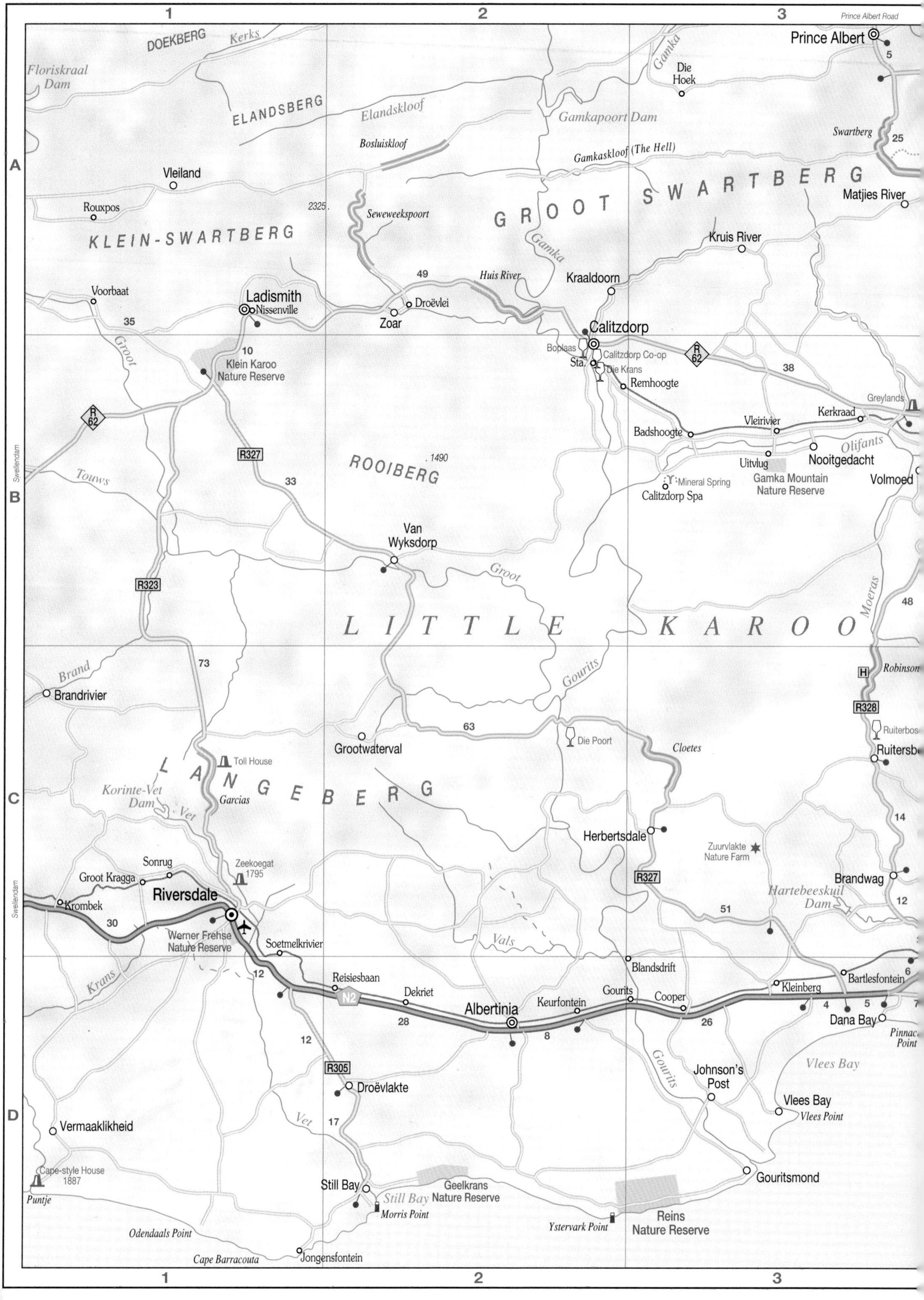

1
2
3
A
B
C
D
Prince Albert Road
Prince Albert
DOEKBERG
Kerks
Floriskraal Dam
ELANDSBERG
Elandskloof
Gamka
Die Hoek
Gamkapoort Dam
Bosluiskloof
Swartberg
25
Gamkaskloof (The Hell)
Vleiland
GROOT SWARTBERG
Matjies River
Rouxpos
2325
Seweweekspoort
KLEIN-SWARTBERG
Kruis River
49
Huis River
Kraaldoorn
Voorbaat
Ladismith
Nissenville
Droëvlei
Zoar
35
Calitzdorp
Groot
10
Klein Karoo Nature Reserve
Boplaas
Sta.
Calitzdorp Co-op
Die Krans
R62
38
Remhoogte
Greylands
Kerkraad
Vleirivier
Badshoogte
Olifants
R327
1490
Uitvlug
Nooitgedacht
ROOIBERG
Touws
Swellendam
33
Mineral Spring
Calitzdorp Spa
Gamka Mountain Nature Reserve
Volmoed
Van Wyksdorp
Groot
R323
Moeras
48
LITTLE KAROO
73
Robinson
Brand
Gourits
Brandrivier
R328
63
Ruiterbos
Die Poort
Grootwaterval
Cloetes
Ruitersb
Toll House
LANGEBERG
Korinte-Vet Dam
Vet
Garcias
14
Herbertsdale
Zuurvlakte Nature Farm
Sonrug
Zeekoegat 1795
Groot Kragga
R327
Brandwag
Hartebeeskuil Dam
12
Krombek
Riversdale
51
30
Werner Frehse Nature Reserve
Vals
Soetmelkrivier
Blandsdrift
Krans
12
Bartlesfontein
6
Reisiesbaan
Kleinberg
Gourits
Dekriet
Cooper
N2
Keurfontein
4
5
7
Albertinia
Dana Bay
28
8
26
Pinnacle Point
12
Vlees Bay
Gourits
R305
Johnson's Post
Droëvlakte
Vlees Bay
Vlees Point
Vet
17
Vermaaklikheid
Cape-style House 1887
Gouritsmond
Still Bay
Geelkrans Nature Reserve
Puntje
Still Bay
Morris Point
Reins Nature Reserve
Ysterva rk Point
Odendaals Point
Cape Barracouta
Jongensfontein

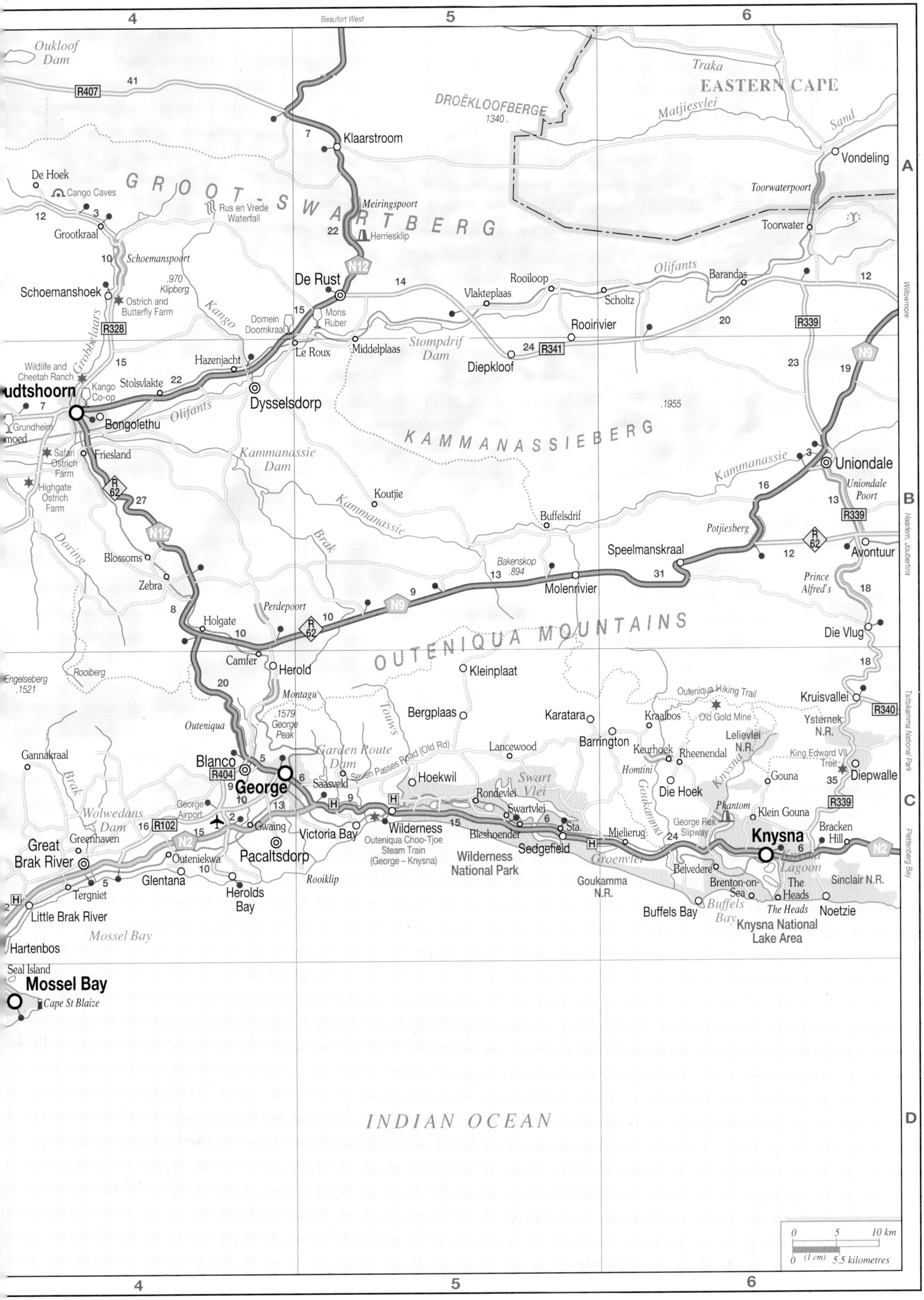
4
5
6
A
B
C
D
Beaufort West
Oukloof Dam
R407
41
Traka
EASTERN CAPE
DROËKLOOFBERGE
1340
Matjiesvlei
Sand
7
Klaarstroom
Vondeling
De Hoek
Cango Caves
GROOT-SWARTBERG
Rus en Vrede Waterfall
Meiringspoort
Toorwaterpoort
12
Grootkraal
3
22
Herriesklip
Toorwater
10
Schoemanspoort
N12
Olifants
Barandas
12
Willowmore
.970 Klipberg
De Rust
14
Rooiloop
Schoemanshoek
Ostrich and Butterfly Farm
Vlakteplaas
Scholtz
Grobbelaars
Kango
15
Domein Doornkraal
Mons Ruber
Rooirivier
20
R339
R328
Le Roux
Middelplaas
Stompdrif Dam
24
R341
Wildlife and Cheetah Ranch
15
Hazenjacht
Diepkloof
23
N9
19
udtshoorn
Kango Co-op
Stolsvlakte
22
7
Dysselsdorp
.1955
Grundheim
moed
Bongolethu
Olifants
KAMMANASSIEBERG
Safari Ostrich Farm
Friesland
Kammanassie Dam
Kammanassie
3
Uniondale
Uniondale Poort
Highgate Ostrich Farm
R62
27
Koutjie
16
13
Kammanassie
Buffelsdrif
R339
Potjiesberg
Haarlem, Joubertina
N12
Doring
Brak
Speelmanskraal
R62
12
Avontuur
Blossoms
Bakenskop .894
13
Molenrivier
31
Prince Alfred's
18
Zebra
9
8
Perdepoort
10
N9
Holgate
R62
10
OUTENIQUA MOUNTAINS
Die Vlug
Camfer
Herold
Kleinplaat
18
Engelseberg .1521
Rooiberg
20
Montagu
Outeniqua Hiking Trail
Kruisvallei
Outeniqua
.1579 George Peak
Towws
Bergplaas
Karatara
Kraaibos
Old Gold Mine
R340
Ystèrnek N.R.
Tsitsikamma National Park
Barrington
Lelievlei N.R.
Gannakraal
Lancewood
Garden Route Dam
Seven Passes Road (Old Rd)
Keurhoek
Rheenendal
King Edward VII Tree
Blanco
5
Homtini
Knysna
Diepwalle
R404
George
6
Hoekwil
Swart Vlei
Gouna
35
Brak
9
Saasveld
Die Hoek
Goukamma
George Airport
10
13
Rondevlei
Wolwedans Dam
H
9
H
Swartvlei
Phantom
Klein Gouna
R339
16
R102
2
Gwaing
6
Sta.
Bracken Hill
15
Wilderness
15
George Rex Slipway
Great Brak River
Greenhaven
N2
Victoria Bay
Outeniqua Choo-Tjoe Steam Train (George – Knysna)
Bleshoender
Sedgefield
H
Mielierug
24
Knysna
6
N2
Outeniekwa
Pacaltsdorp
Groenvlei
Knysna Lagoon
Plettenberg Bay
10
Wilderness National Park
Belvedere
5
Glentana
Rooiklip
Goukamma N.R.
Brenton-on-Sea
The Heads
Sinclair N.R.
Tergniet
Herolds Bay
H
Buffels Bay
Buffels Bay
The Heads
Noetzie
Little Brak River
Knysna National Lake Area
Mossel Bay
Hartenbos
Seal Island
Mossel Bay
Cape St Blaize
INDIAN OCEAN
0 5 10 km
0 (1 cm) 5.5 kilometres

TSITSIKAMMA NATIONAL PARK

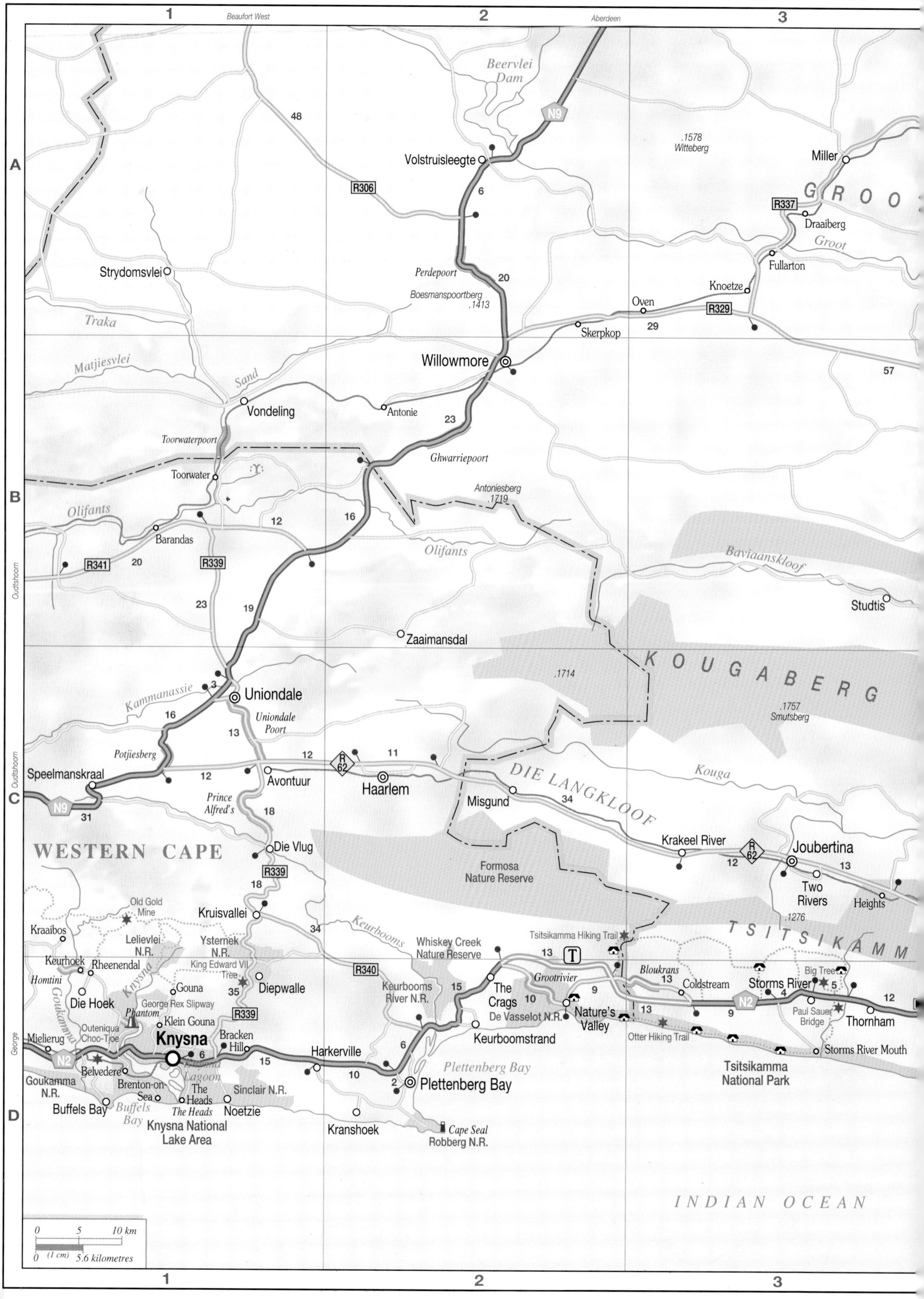

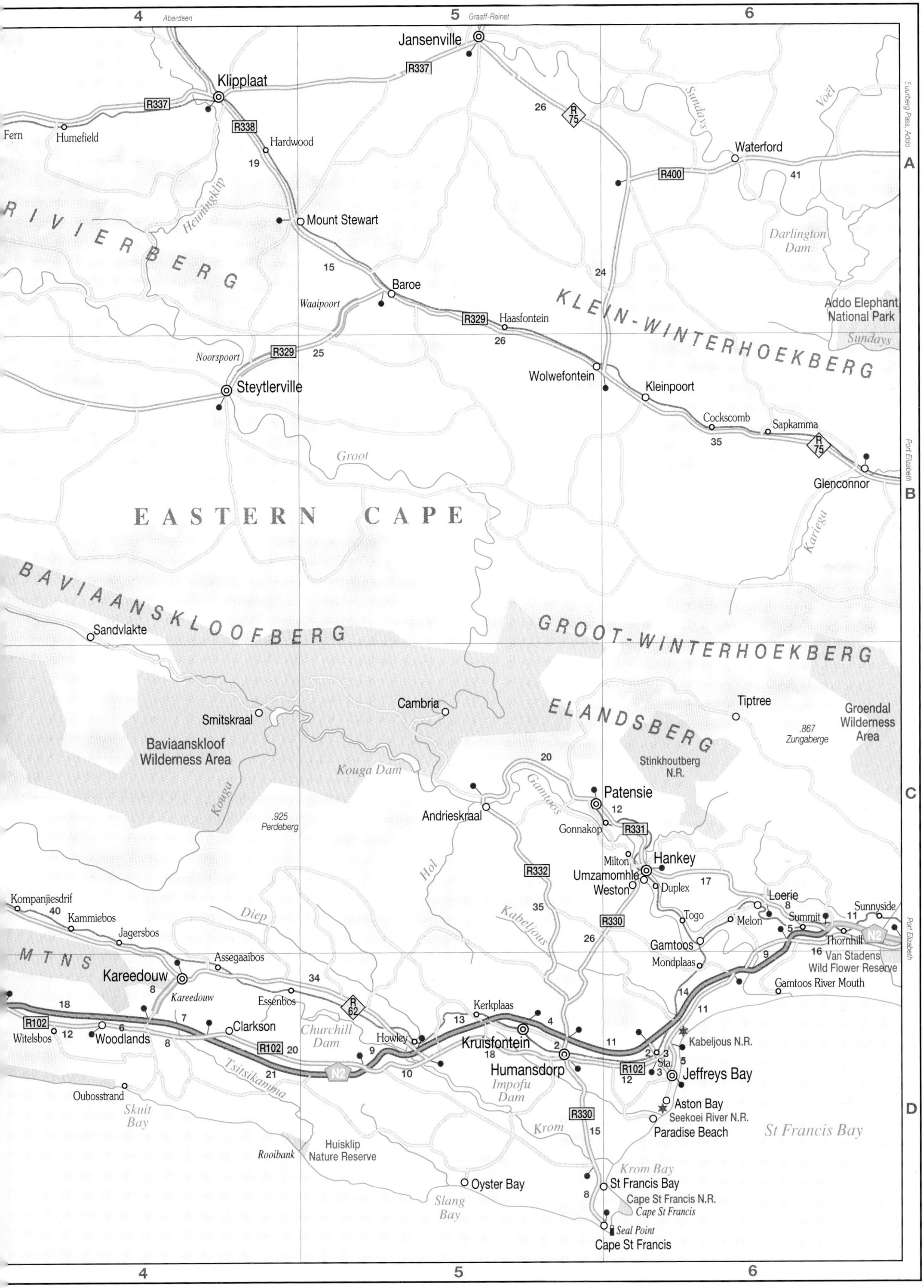

4
Aberdeen
5
Graaff-Reinet
6
Jansenville
R337
Klipplaat
R338
Fern
Humefield
Hardwood
19
26
R 75
Sundays
Voël
Waterford
R400
41
A
Heuningklip
RIVIERBERG
Mount Stewart
Darlington Dam
15
24
Baroe
Waaipoort
R329
Haasfontein
26
KLEIN-WINTERHOEKBERG
Addo Elephant National Park
Sundays
Noorspoort
R329
25
Steytlerville
Wolwefontein
Kleinpoort
Cockscomb
Sapkamma
35
Glenconnor
Port Elizabeth
B
Groot
EASTERN CAPE
Kariega
BAVIAANSKLOOFBERG
Sandvlakte
GROOT-WINTERHOEKBERG
ELANDSBERG
Tiptree
Groendal Wilderness Area
.867 Zungaberge
Cambria
Smitskraal
Baviaanskloof Wilderness Area
Kouga Dam
Kouga
20
Stinkhoutberg N.R.
Gamtoos
Patensie
12
C
Andrieskraal
.925 Perdeberg
Gonnakop
R331
Milton
Hankey
R332
Umzamomhle
Weston
Duplex
17
Hol
Kabeljous
35
Loerie
8
Sunnyside
Kompanjiesdrif
40
Kammiebos
Diep
Togo
Melon
Summit
11
Jagersbos
R330
5
Thornhill
N2
Port Elizabeth
26
Gamtoos
16
Van Stadens Wild Flower Reserve
MTNS
Assegaaibos
Mondplaas
9
Kareedouw
8
Kareedouw
34
Gamtoos River Mouth
Essenbos
R 62
14
18
7
Kerkplaas
4
11
R102
6
Clarkson
13
Churchill Dam
Howley
Kruisfontein
2
11
Kabeljous N.R.
Witelsbos
12
Woodlands
8
R102
20
9
18
2
3
Sta.
5
3
Tsitsikamma
21
N2
10
Humansdorp
R102
12
Jeffreys Bay
Impofu Dam
Aston Bay
Oubosstrand
Skuit Bay
Seekoei River N.R.
D
R330
Krom
15
Paradise Beach
St Francis Bay
Huisklip Nature Reserve
Rooibank
Krom Bay
Oyster Bay
St Francis Bay
8
Cape St Francis N.R.
Slang Bay
Cape St Francis
Seal Point
Cape St Francis
4
5
6

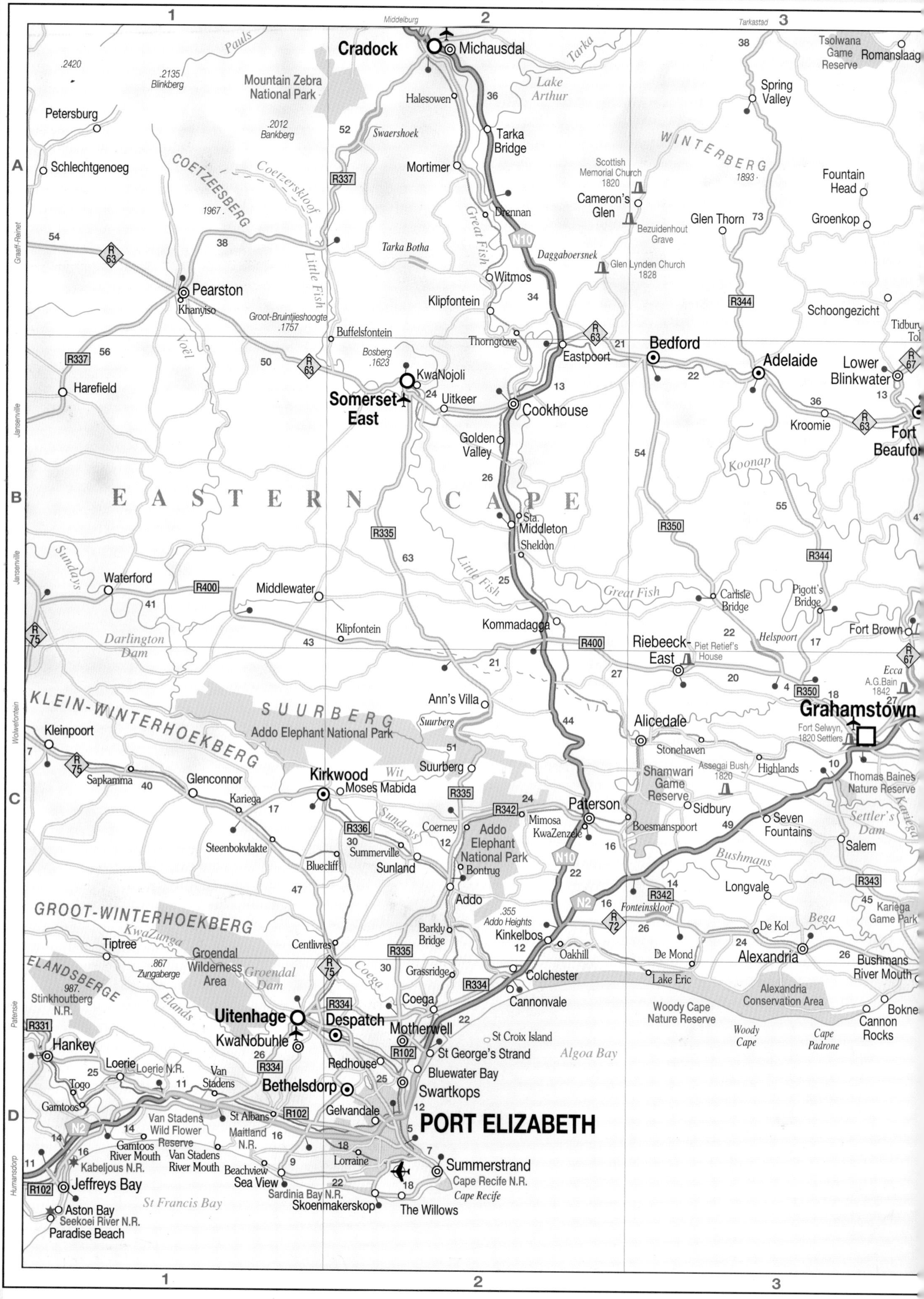
Cradock
Michausdal
Middelburg
Tarkastad
Mountain Zebra National Park
Halesowen
Tarka Bridge
Lake Arthur
Spring Valley
Tsolwana Game Reserve
Romanslaagte
Petersburg
Schlechtgenoeg
COETZEESBERG
Coetzerskloof
Swaershoek
Mortimer
WINTERBERG
Scottish Memorial Church 1820
Cameron's Glen
Fountain Head
Groenkop
Glen Thorn
Drennan
Bezuidenhout Grave
Tarka Botha
Daggaboersnek
Glen Lynden Church 1828
Pearston
Khanyiso
Witmos
Klipfontein
Schoongezicht
Groot-Bruintjieshoogte .1757
Buffelsfontein
Thorngrove
Eastpoort
Bedford
Adelaide
Lower Blinkwater
Harefield
Bosberg .1623
KwaNojoli
Somerset East
Uitkeer
Cookhouse
Kroomie
Fort Beaufort
Golden Valley
Koonap
EASTERN CAPE
Sta. Middleton
Sheldon
Little Fish
Great Fish
Sundays
Waterford
Middlewater
Carlisle Bridge
Pigott's Bridge
Kommadagga
Darlington Dam
Klipfontein
Riebeeck-East
Piet Retief's House
Helspoort
Fort Brown
Ecca
A.G.Bain 1842
Grahamstown
KLEIN-WINTERHOEKBERG
SUURBERG
Addo Elephant National Park
Ann's Villa
Suurberg
Alicedale
Stonehaven
Fort Selwyn, 1820 Settlers
Kleinpoort
Sapkamma
Glenconnor
Kariega
Kirkwood
Moses Mabida
Wit
Assegai Bush 1820
Highlands
Shamwari Game Reserve
Thomas Baines Nature Reserve
Paterson
Sidbury
Steenbokvlakte
Summerville
Sunland
Bluecliff
Coerney
Addo Elephant National Park
Mimosa
KwaZenzele
Boesmanspoort
Seven Fountains
Settler's Dam
Salem
Bontrug
Addo
Bushmans
Longvale
GROOT-WINTERHOEKBERG
KwaZunga
Fonteinskloof
Kariega Game Park
.355 Addo Heights
Barkly Bridge
Kinkelbos
Oakhill
De Mond
De Kol
Bega
Alexandria
Tiptree
Centlivres
Groendal Wilderness Area
Groendal Dam
Coega
Grassridge
Colchester
Lake Eric
Bushmans River Mouth
ELANDSBERGE
.867 Zungaberge
987. Stinkhoutberg N.R.
Elands
Cannonvale
Alexandria Conservation Area
Woody Cape Nature Reserve
Bokne
Cannon Rocks
Uitenhage
Despatch
Coega
Motherwell
KwaNobuhle
Hankey
St Croix Island
Algoa Bay
Woody Cape
Cape Padrone
Loerie
Loerie N.R.
Van Stadens
Redhouse
St George's Strand
Bluewater Bay
Togo
Bethelsdorp
Swartkops
Gamtoos
Van Stadens Wild Flower Reserve
St Albans
Gelvandale
PORT ELIZABETH
Maitland N.R.
Gamtoos River Mouth
Van Stadens River Mouth
Kabeljous N.R.
Lorraine
Summerstrand
Beachview
Sea View
Cape Recife N.R.
Cape Recife
Jeffreys Bay
Sardinia Bay N.R.
Skoenmakerskop
The Willows
St Francis Bay
Aston Bay
Seekoei River N.R.
Paradise Beach
Graaff-Reinet
Jansenville
Wolwefontein
Patensie
Humansdorp
N10
N2
R63
R67
R72
R75
R102
R331
R334
R335
R336
R337
R342
R343
R344
R350
R400

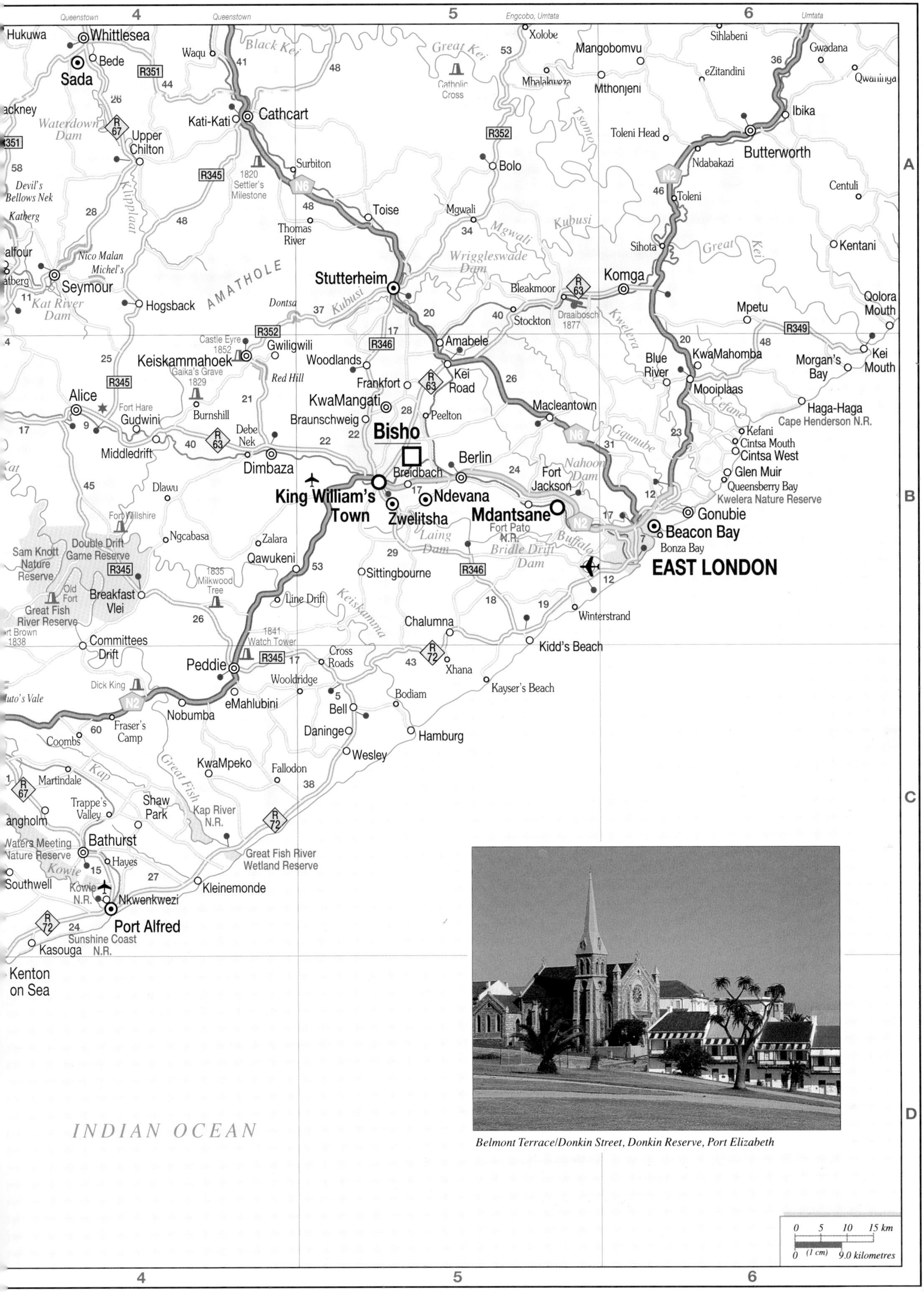

Belmont Terrace/Donkin Street, Donkin Reserve, Port Elizabeth

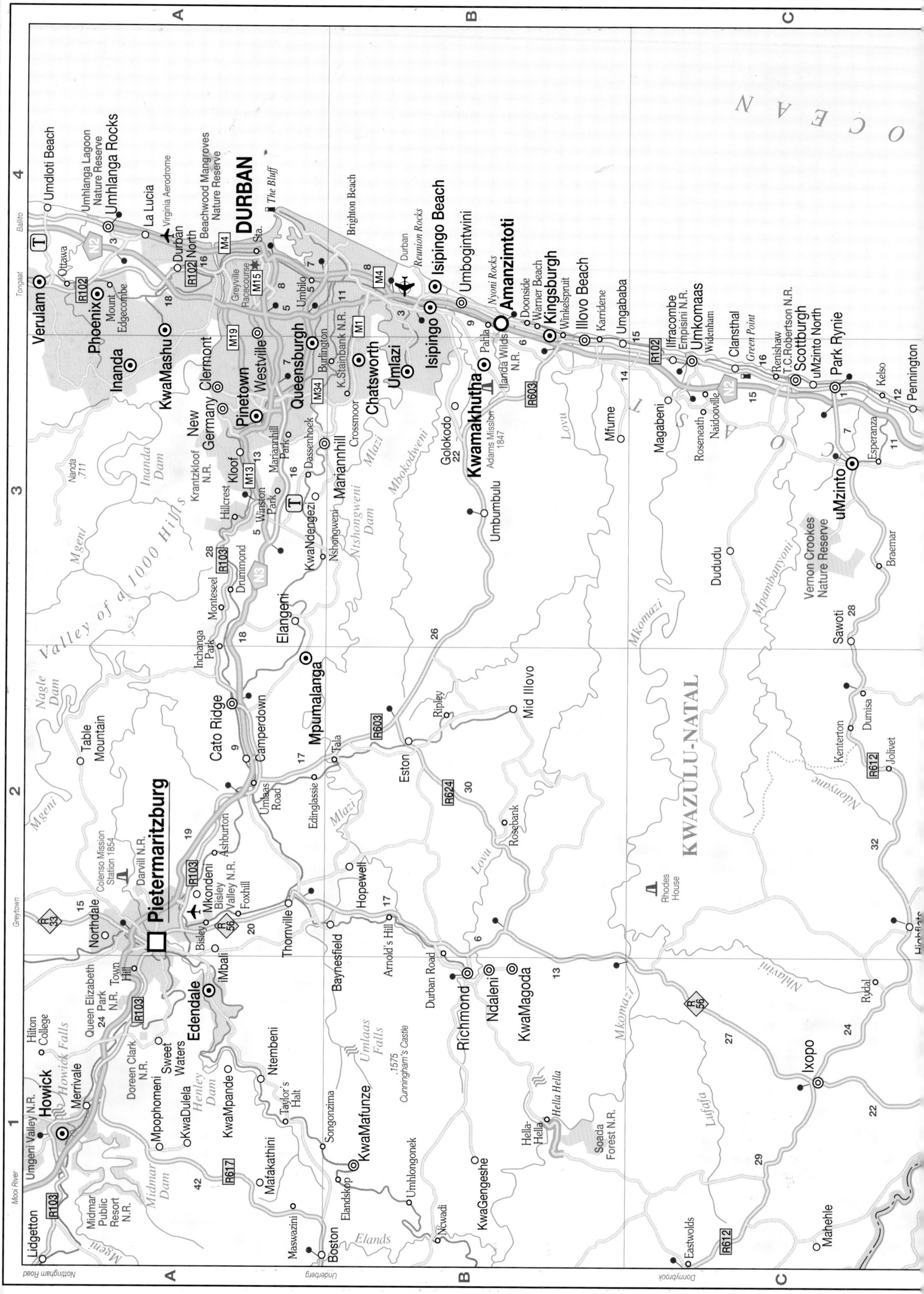

INDIAN OCEAN
KWAZULU-NATAL
DURBAN
Pietermaritzburg
Umdloti Beach
Umhlanga Lagoon Nature Reserve
Umhlanga Rocks
La Lucia
Virginia Aerodrome
Beachwood Mangroves Nature Reserve
Durban North
The Bluff
Brighton Beach
Greyville Racecourse
Sta.
Umbilo
Durban
Reunion Rocks
Isipingo Beach
Umbogintwini
Nyoni Rocks
Amanzimtoti
Doonside
Warner Beach
Winkelspruit
Kingsburgh
Illovo Beach
Karridene
Umgababa
Ilfracombe
Empisini N.R.
Umkomaas
Widenham
Clansthal
Green Point
Renishaw
T.C.Robertson N.R.
Scottburgh
uMzinto North
Park Rynie
Kelso
Pennington
Esperanza
uMzinto
Verulam
Ottawa
Phoenix
Mount Edgecombe
Tongaat
Ballito
Inanda
KwaMashu
Clermont
New Germany
Pinetown
Westville
Queensburgh
Burlington
K.Stainbank N.R.
Chatsworth
Umlazi
Isipingo
Pahla
Ilanda Wilds N.R.
Kwamakhutha
Adams Mission 1847
Golokodo
Mfume
Magabeni
Roseneath
Naidooville
Dududu
Vernon Crookes Nature Reserve
Braemar
Sawoti
Dumisa
Kenterton
Jolivet
Nanda 711
Inanda Dam
Krantzkloof N.R.
Kloof
Hillcrest
Winston Park
Marianhill Park
Dassenhoek
Mariannhill
Crossmoor
KwaNdengezi
Nshongweni
Nshongweni Dam
Umbumbulu
Mbokodweni
Mlazi
Valley of a 1000 Hills
Mgeni
Drummond
Monteseel
Inchanga Park
Elangeni
Mpumalanga
Cato Ridge
Camperdown
Nagle Dam
Table Mountain
Tala
Ripley
Mid Illovo
Eston
Edinglassie
Umlaas Road
Rosebank
Lovu
Mkomazi
Mpambanyoni
Ndonyane
Colenso Mission Station 1854
Darvill N.R.
Ashburton
Mkondeni
Bisley Valley N.R.
Foxhill
Bisley
Northdale
Greytown
Hopewell
Thornville
Baynesfield
Arnold's Hill
Durban Road
Richmond
Ndaleni
KwaMagoda
Rhodes House
Highflats
Nhlavini
Rydal
Ixopo
Lufafa
Mahehle
Eastwolds
Donnybrook
Umgeni Valley N.R.
Howick
Howick Falls
Merrivale
Hilton College
Queen Elizabeth Park N.R.
Town Hill
Edendale
iMbali
Sweet Waters
Doreen Clark N.R.
Mpophomeni
KwaDulela
Henley Dam
KwaMpande
Ntembeni
Taylor's Halt
Umlaas Falls
1575 Cunningham's Castle
Songonzima
KwaMafunze
Umhlongonek
Elandskop
Elands
Ncwadi
Hella-Hella
Hella Hella
Soada Forest N.R.
KwaGengeshe
Matakathini
Maswazini
Boston
Underberg
Midmar Dam
Midmar Public Resort N.R.
Lidgetton
Mooi River
Nottingham Road
N2
N3
R33
R56
R102
R103
R603
R612
R617
R624
M1
M4
M13
M15
M19
M34

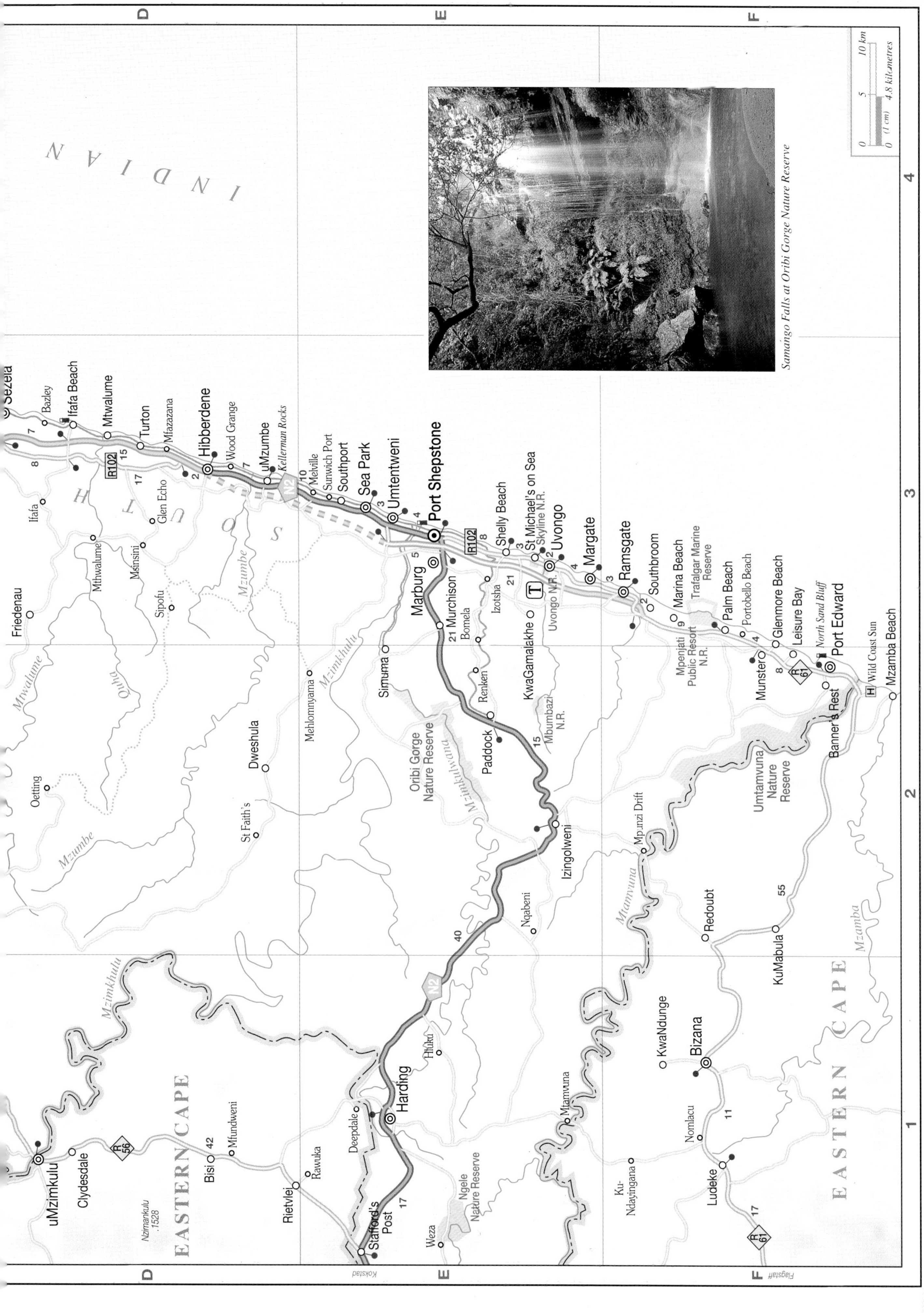

Samango Falls at Oribi Gorge Nature Reserve

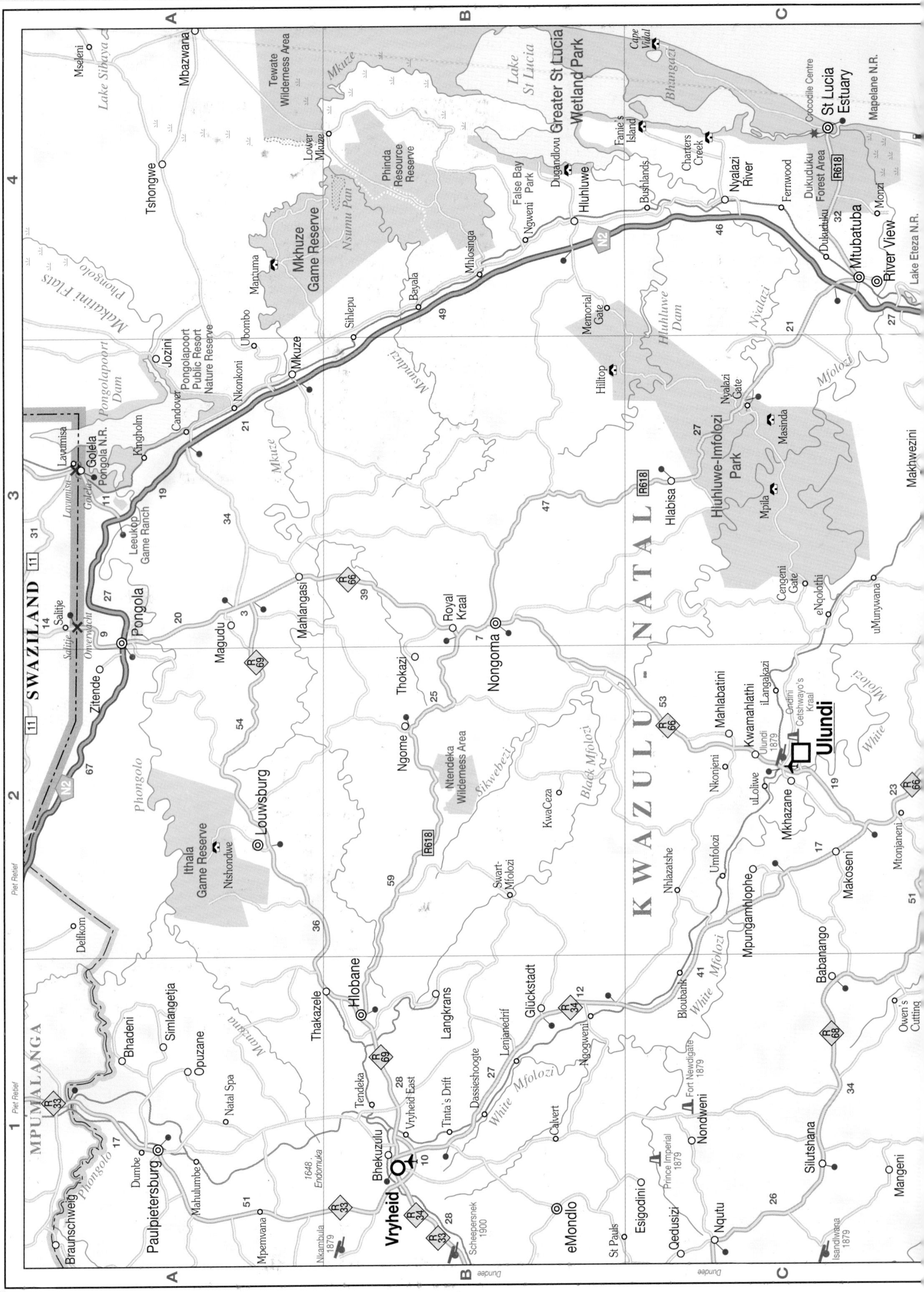
SWAZILAND
MPUMALANGA
KWAZULU - NATAL
Greater St Lucia Wetland Park
Lake St Lucia
Cape Vidal
St Lucia Estuary
Crocodile Centre
Mapelane N.R.
Fanie's Island
Charters Creek
Dugandlovu
False Bay Park
Hluhluwe
Bushlands
Nyalazi River
Fernwood
Dukuduku Forest Area
Dukuduku
Mtubatuba
River View
Monzi
Lake Eteza N.R.
Phinda Resource Reserve
Nsumu Pan
Mkhuze Game Reserve
Mantuma
Lower Mkuze
Tewate Wilderness Area
Mkuze
Lake Sibaya
Mseleni
Mbazwana
Tshongwe
Makatini Flats
Phongolo
Jozini
Pongolapoort Dam
Pongolapoort Public Resort Nature Reserve
Ubombo
Nkonkoni
Candover
Kingholm
Golela
Lavumisa
Pongola N.R.
Leeukop Game Ranch
Sihlepu
Bayala
Mhlosinga
Ngweni
Memorial Gate
Hluhluwe Dam
Hilltop
Nyalazi Gate
Masinda
Hluhluwe-Imfolozi Park
Mpila
Cengeni Gate
eNqolothi
Hlabisa
Makhwezini
uMunywana
Msunduzi
Mfolozi
Nyalazi
Pongola
Salitje
Onverwacht
Zitende
Magudu
Mahlangasi
Royal Kraal
Nongoma
Thokazi
Ngome
Ntendeka Wilderness Area
Sikwebezi
Black Mfolozi
KwaCeza
Mahlabatini
iLangakazi
Ondini Cetshwayo's Kraal
Ulundi
Kwamahlathi
Nkonjeni
uLoliwe
Mkhazane
Mtonjaneni
Makoseni
Mpungamhlophe
Umfolozi
Nhlazatshe
Swart-Mfolozi
Louwsburg
Ithala Game Reserve
Ntshondwe
Delfkom
Piet Retief
Simlangetja
Bhadeni
Opuzane
Natal Spa
Mamba
Thakazele
Hlobane
Langkrans
Glückstadt
Lenjanedrif
Ngogweni
Dassieshoogte
Tinta's Drift
Vryheid East
Tendeka
Bhekuzulu
Vryheid
Calvert
White Mfolozi
Bloubank
Fort Newdigate 1879
Nondweni
Prince Imperial 1879
Esigodini
Qedusizi
Nqutu
St Pauls
eMondlo
Scheepersnek 1900
Nkambula 1879
1648 Endomuka
Mpemvana
Mahlumbe
Dumbe
Paulpietersburg
Braunschweig
Babanango
Owen's Cutting
Silutshana
Mangeni
Isandlwana 1879
Dundee
N2
R618
R66
R69
R33
R34
R68
A
B
C
1
2
3
4

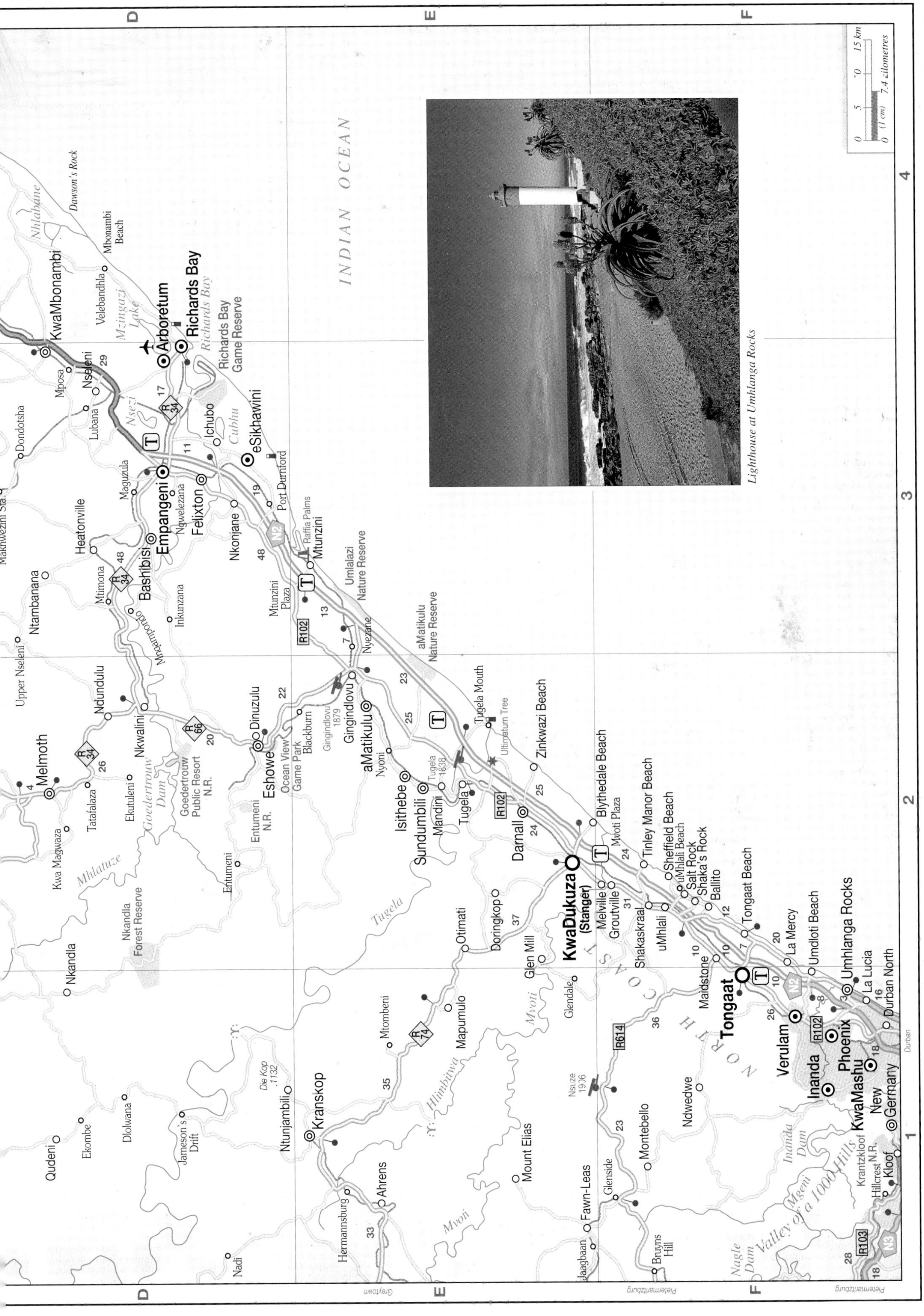

Lighthouse at Umhlanga Rocks

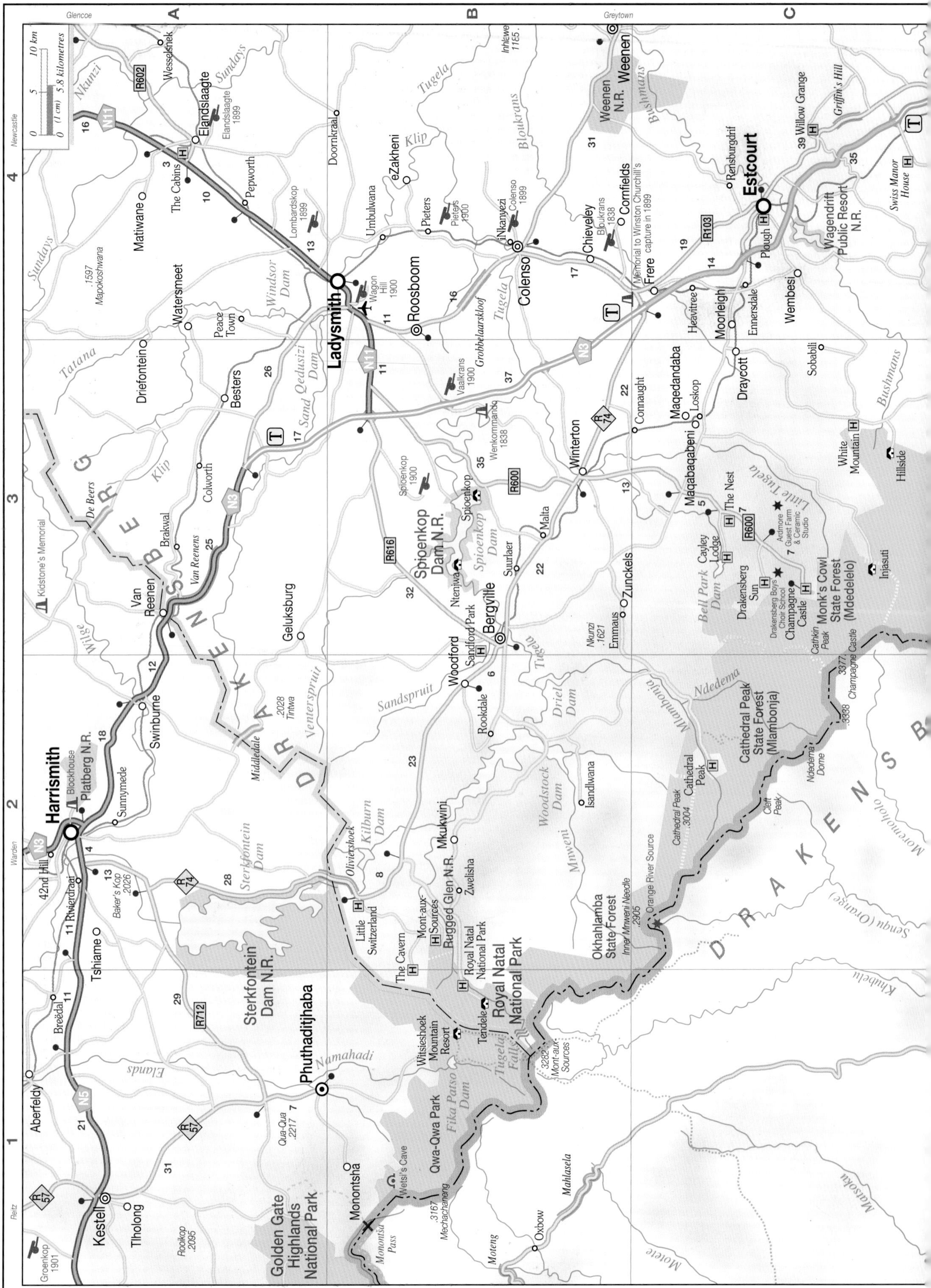
Ladysmith
Estcourt
Harrismith
Phuthaditjhaba
Bergville
Winterton
Colenso
Weenen
Kestell
Van Reenen
Spioenkop Dam N.R.
Royal Natal National Park
Sterkfontein Dam N.R.
Golden Gate Highlands National Park
Qwa-Qwa Park
Cathedral Peak State Forest (Mlambonja)
Monk's Cowl State Forest (Mdedelo)
Okhahlamba State Forest
Weenen N.R.
Wagendrift Public Resort N.R.
Platberg N.R.
D R A K E N S B E R G
0 5 10 km
(1 cm) 5.8 kilometres
Glencoe
Greytown
Newcastle
Warden
Reitz
Bethlehem
Butha-Buthe

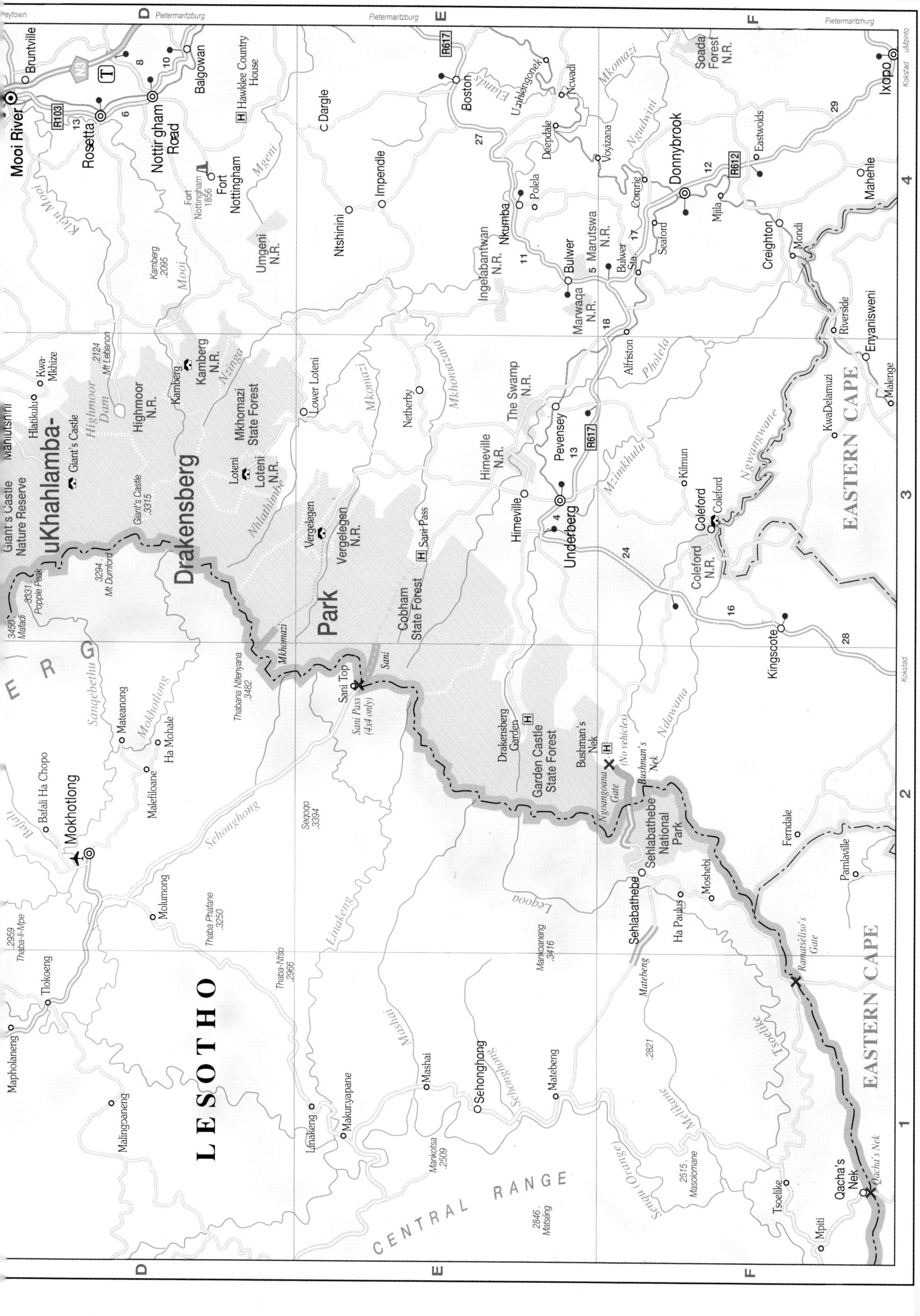
Pietermaritzburg
Kokstad
uMzinto
Mooi River
Bruntville
Rosetta
Nottingham Road
Balgowan
Hawklee Country House
Fort Nottingham
Dargle
Boston
Elands
Umkhongonek
Ncwadi
Mkomazi
Soada Forest N.R.
Ixopo
Donnybrook
Eastwolds
Deepdale
Vozizana
Ngudwini
Impendle
Nkumba
Polela
Comrie
Mjila
Mahehle
Ntshinini
Umgeni N.R.
Mgeni
Kamberg 2095
Mooi
Klein Mooi
Ingelabantwan N.R.
Bulwer
Marutswa N.R.
Bulwer Sta.
Seaford
Creighton
Mondi
Marwaqa N.R.
Alfriston
Riverside
Enyanisweni
Malenge
Pholela
Kwa-Mkhize
Hlatikulu
Mt Lebanon 2124
Highmoor Dam
Highmoor N.R.
Kamberg N.R.
Kamberg
Nzinga
Mkhomazi State Forest
Lower Loteni
Netherby
Mkhomazana
The Swamp N.R.
Pevensey
KwaDelamuzi
EASTERN CAPE
Giant's Castle Nature Reserve
Giant's Castle
uKhahlamba-Drakensberg Park
Giant's Castle 3315
Loteni
Loteni N.R.
Nhlathimbe
Himeville N.R.
Mzimkhulu
Kilmun
Ngwangwane
Coleford
Vergelegen
Vergelegen N.R.
Sani Pass
Himeville
Underberg
Coleford N.R.
3450 Mafadi
3331 Popple Peak
3294 Mt Durnford
Cobham State Forest
Mkhomazi
Kingscote
Sani Top
Sani Pass (4x4 only)
Sani
Thabana Ntlenyana 3482
Sangebethu
Mateanong
Mokhotlong
Ha Mohale
Drakensberg Garden
Garden Castle State Forest
Bushman's Nek
(No vehicles)
Ndawana
Bafali Ha Chopo
Malefiloane
Mokhotlong
Sehonghong
Seqoqo 3394
Ngoangoana Gate
Bushman's Nek
Sehlabathebe National Park
Ferndale
Pamlaville
Molumong
Thaba Phafane 3250
Linakeng
Legooa
Sehlabathebe
Moshebi
Ha Paulus
2959 Thaba-li-Mpe
Tlokoeng
Thaba-Ntšo 2966
Mankoaneng 3416
Matebeng
Ramatšeliso's Gate
LESOTHO
Mapholaneng
Mashai
2821
Tsoelike
Malingoaneng
Makunyapane
Sehonghong
Matebeng
Mankotsa 2509
Senqu (Orange)
Melikane
2515 Masolomane
CENTRAL RANGE
2846 Matsëng
Tsoelike
Qacha's Nek
Mpiti

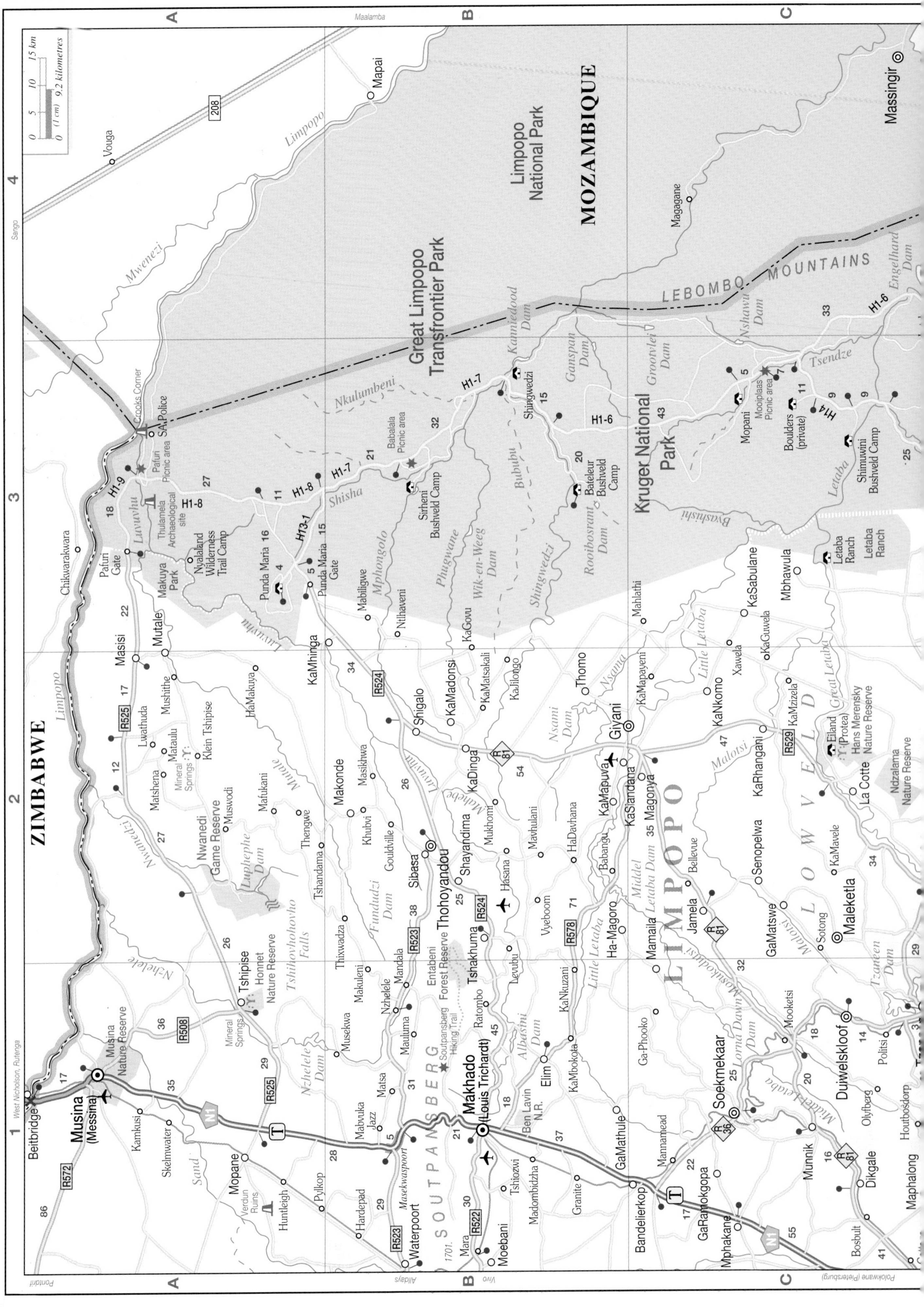
ZIMBABWE
MOZAMBIQUE
Limpopo National Park
Great Limpopo Transfrontier Park
Kruger National Park
LEBOMBO MOUNTAINS
LIMPOPO
LOWVELD
SOUTPANSBERG
Limpopo
Musina (Messina)
Beitbridge
Makhado (Louis Trichardt)
Thohoyandou
Giyani
Soekmekaar
Duiwelskloof
Maleketla
Punda Maria
Punda Maria Gate
Pafuri Gate
Pafuri Picnic area
Crooks Corner
Shingwedzi
Mopani
Boulders (private)
Shimuwini Bushveld Camp
Bateleur Bushveld Camp
Sirheni Bushveld Camp
Babalala Picnic area
Mooiplaas Picnic area
Letaba Ranch
Hans Merensky Nature Reserve
Ndzalama Nature Reserve
Nwanedi Game Reserve
Honnet Nature Reserve
Musina Nature Reserve
Massingir
Mapai
Vouga
Magagane
0 5 10 15 km
0 (1 cm) 9.2 kilometres

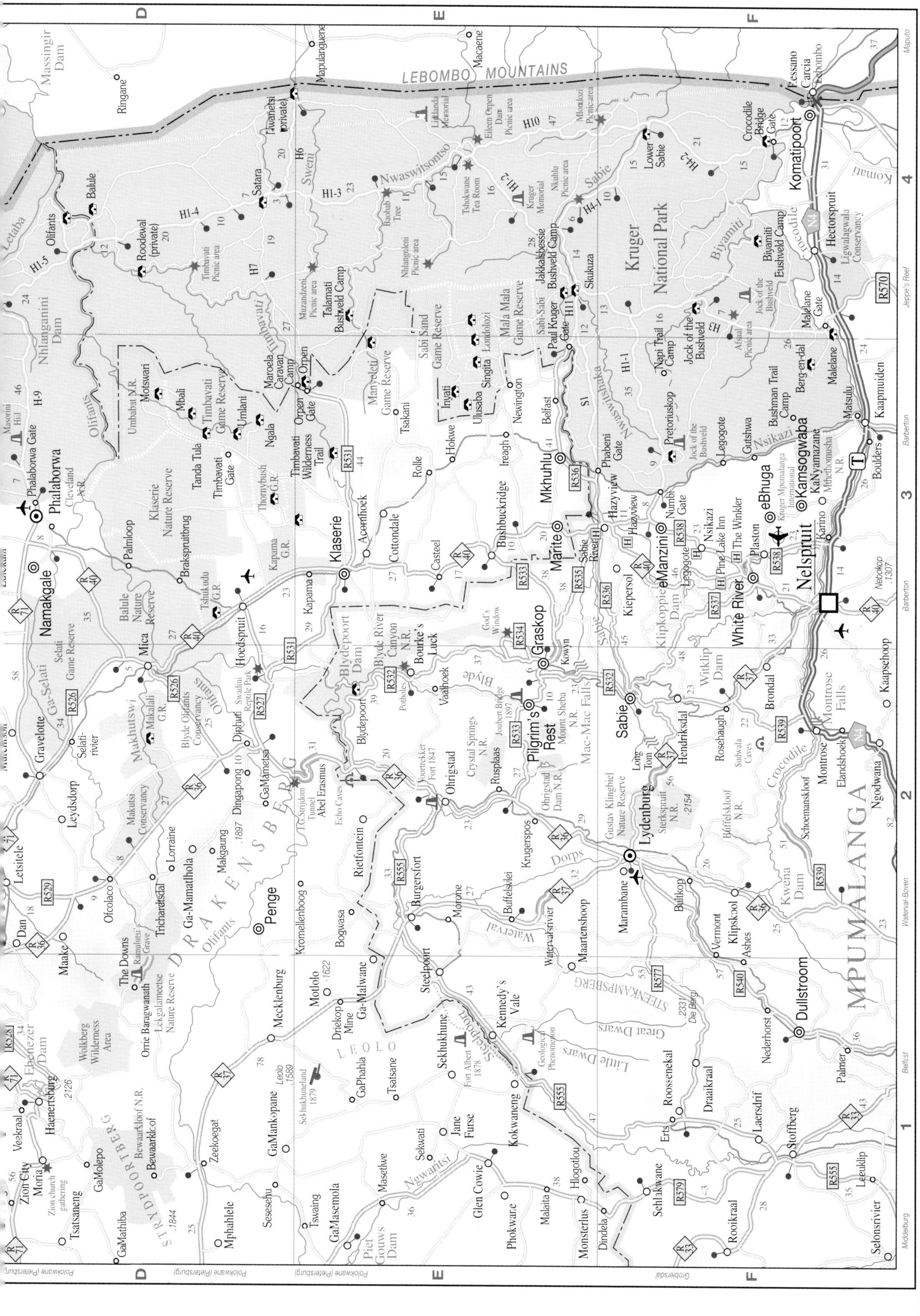

LEBOMBO MOUNTAINS
Kruger National Park
MPUMALANGA
DRAKENSBERG
STRYDPOORTBERG
STEENKAMPSBERG
LEOLO
Phalaborwa
Phalaborwa Gate
Namakgale
Gravelotte
Mica
Hoedspruit
Klaserie
Acornhoek
Graskop
Pilgrim's Rest
Sabie
Lydenburg
Mkhuhlu
Marite
Hazyview
White River
Nelspruit
Kamsogwaba
KaNyamazane
Malelane
Kaapmuiden
Komatipoort
Hectorspruit
Barberton
Dullstroom
Machadodorp
Burgersfort
Steelpoort
Penge
Haenertsburg
Tzaneen
Letsitele
Leydsdorp
Ofcolaco
Trichardtsdal
Mecklenburg
Ohrigstad
Bourke's Luck
God's Window
Blydepoort Dam
Blyde River Canyon N.R.
Klaserie Nature Reserve
Timbavati Game Reserve
Balule Nature Reserve
Sabi Sand Game Reserve
Manyeleti Game Reserve
Mala Mala Game Reserve
Selati Game Reserve
Wolkberg Wilderness Area
Satara
Olifants
Balule
Orpen
Orpen Gate
Skukuza
Lower Sabie
Crocodile Bridge
Berg-en-dal
Pretoriuskop
Numbi Gate
Phabeni Gate
Paul Kruger Gate
Malelane Gate
Tshokwane Tea Room
Talamati Bushveld Camp
Biyamiti Bushveld Camp
Jock of the Bushveld
Roodewal (private)
Mapulanguene
Macaene
Ressano Garcia
Massingir Dam
Ringane
Nhlanganini Dam
Olifants
Sabie
Crocodile
Komati
Timbavati
Nwaswitsontso
Sweni
Letaba
Biyamiti
Nsikazi
Kwena Dam
Witklip Dam
Klipkopjie Dam
Sudwala Caves
Mac-Mac Falls
Montrose Falls
Long Tom
Kaapsehoop
Ngodwana
Elandshoek
Schoemanskloof
Waterval-Boven
Belfast
Middelburg
Polokwane (Pietersburg)
Groblersdal
Maputo

PILANESBERG and MAGALIESBERG REGION

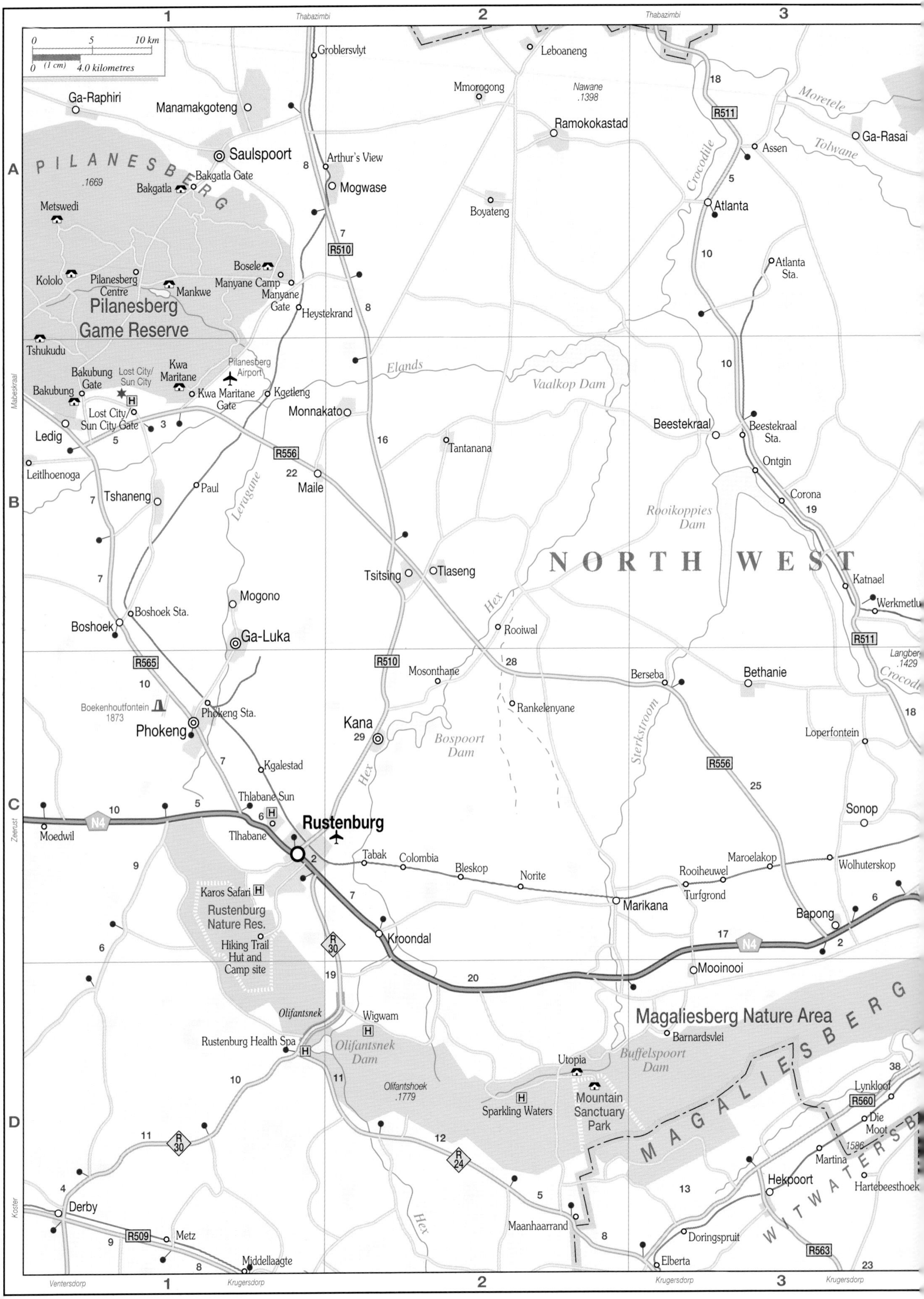

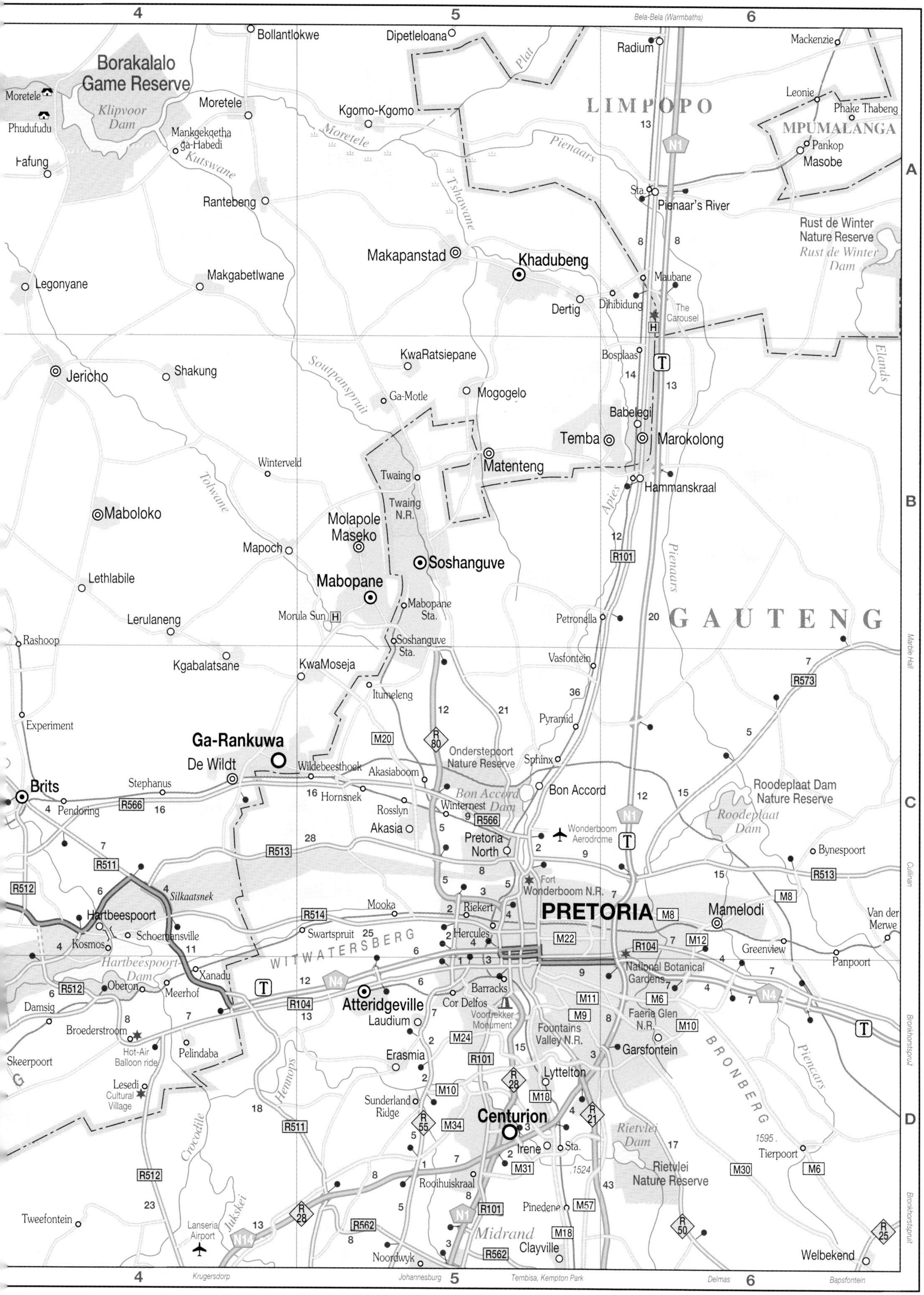

4
5
6
Bela-Bela (Warmbaths)
Bollantlokwe
Dipetleloana
Radium
Mackenzie
Borakalalo
Game Reserve
Moretele
Klipvoor
Dam
Phudufudu
Moretele
Mankgekgetha
ga-Habedi
Kgomo-Kgomo
Moretele
Plat
LIMPOPO
Leonie
Phake Thabeng
MPUMALANGA
Pankop
Masobe
Hafung
Kutswane
Pienaars
Tshawane
N1
Rantebeng
Sta.
Pienaar's River
A
Rust de Winter
Nature Reserve
Rust de Winter
Dam
Makapanstad
Khadubeng
Legonyane
Makgabetlwane
Maubane
Dertig
Dihibidung
The
Carousel
Bosplaas
Jericho
Shakung
KwaRatsiepane
Soutpanspruit
Ga-Motle
Mogogelo
Elands
Babelegi
Temba
Marokolong
Matenteng
Winterveld
Twaing
Twaing
N.R.
Hammanskraal
Tolwane
Apies
B
Maboloko
Molapole
Maseko
Mapoch
Soshanguve
Pienaars
R101
Lethlabile
Mabopane
Mabopane
Sta.
Morula Sun
Lerulaneng
Petronella
GAUTENG
Rashoop
Soshanguve
Sta.
Vasfontein
Marble Hall
Kgabalatsane
KwaMoseja
R573
Itumeleng
Experiment
M20
R80
Pyramid
Ga-Rankuwa
Onderstepoort
Nature Reserve
Sphinx
De Wildt
Wildebeesthoek
Akasiaboom
Brits
Stephanus
Hornsnek
Bon Accord
Bon Accord
Dam
Roodeplaat Dam
Nature Reserve
Pendoring
R566
Rosslyn
Winternest
R566
C
Roodeplaat
Dam
Akasia
Pretoria
North
Wonderboom
Aerodrome
Bynespoort
R511
R513
R513
Cullinan
R512
Silkaatsnek
Fort
Wonderboom N.R.
M8
Hartbeespoort
Riekert
PRETORIA
M8
Mamelodi
Van der
Merwe
Mooka
R514
Kosmos
Schoemansville
Swartspruit
Hercules
M22
R104
M12
Greenview
WITWATERSBERG
Panpoort
Hartbeespoort
Dam
Xanadu
National Botanical
Gardens
Oberon
N4
Barracks
M11
M6
N4
R512
Meerhof
R104
Atteridgeville
Cor Delfos
Voortrekker
Monument
M9
Faerie Glen
N.R.
M10
Damsig
Laudium
Fountains
Valley N.R.
BRONBERG
Broederstroom
M24
Garsfontein
Bronkhorstspruit
Pelindaba
Hot-Air
Balloon ride
Erasmia
R101
Skeerpoort
Hennops
R28
Lyttelton
Pienaars
Lesedi
Cultural
Village
M10
M18
Sunderland
Ridge
R21
Centurion
D
R511
R55
M34
Rietvlei
Dam
Crocodile
1595
Irene
Sta.
Rietvlei
Nature Reserve
Tierpoort
M31
.1524
R512
M30
M6
Rooihuiskraal
Bronkhorstspruit
Tweefontein
R28
Pinedene
M57
N1
R101
Lanseria
Airport
Jukskei
N14
R562
Midrand
M18
R50
R25
Noordwyk
R562
Clayville
Welbekend
Krugersdorp
Johannesburg
Tembisa, Kempton Park
Delmas
Bapsfontein

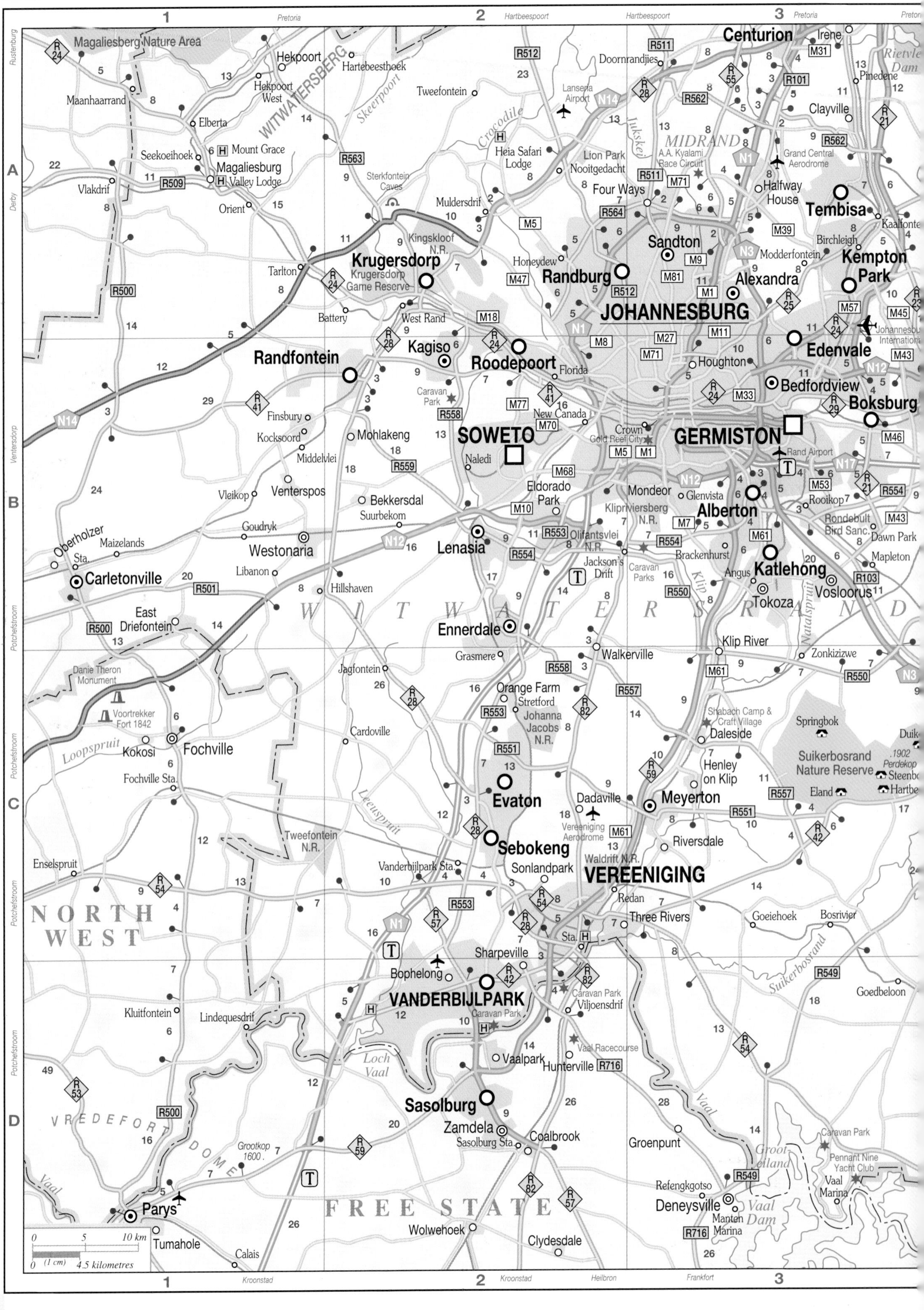
Magaliesberg Nature Area
Hekpoort
Hartebeesthoek
Hekpoort West
WITWATERSBERG
Skeerpoort
Maanhaarrand
Elberta
Seekoeihoek
Mount Grace
Magaliesberg
Valley Lodge
Vlakdrif
Orient
Tweefontein
Crocodile
Lanseria Airport
Heia Safari Lodge
Lion Park
Nooitgedacht
Sterkfontein Caves
Muldersdrif
Kingskloof N.R.
Doornrandjies
Centurion
Irene
Rietvlei Dam
Pinedene
Clayville
MIDRAND
A.A. Kyalami Race Circuit
Grand Central Aerodrome
Halfway House
Tembisa
Kaalfontein
Four Ways
Sandton
Birchleigh
Modderfontein
Kempton Park
Alexandra
Honeydew
Randburg
JOHANNESBURG
Tarlton
Krugersdorp
Krugersdorp Game Reserve
Battery
West Rand
Kagiso
Roodepoort
Florida
Randfontein
Houghton
Edenvale
Johannesburg International
Bedfordview
Boksburg
Caravan Park
New Canada
Finsbury
Kocksoord
Mohlakeng
Middelvlei
SOWETO
Naledi
Crown
Gold Reef City
GERMISTON
Rand Airport
Vleikop
Venterspos
Bekkersdal
Suurbekom
Eldorado Park
Mondeor
Glenvista
Alberton
Rooikop
Klipriviersberg N.R.
Rondebult Bird Sanc.
Dawn Park
Oberholzer Sta.
Maizelands
Goudryk
Westonaria
Lenasia
Olifantsvlei N.R.
Brackenhurst
Katlehong
Mapleton
Carletonville
Libanon
Jackson's Drift
Caravan Parks
Angus
Vosloorus
Tokoza
Hillshaven
East Driefontein
W I T W A T E R S R A N D
Klip
Natalspruit
Ennerdale
Klip River
Zonkizizwe
Danie Theron Monument
Grasmere
Walkerville
Jagfontein
Orange Farm
Stretford
Johanna Jacobs N.R.
Voortrekker Fort 1842
Shabach Camp & Craft Village
Springbok
Daleside
Loopspruit
Kokosi
Fochville
Cardoville
Henley on Klip
Suikerbosrand Nature Reserve
1902 Perdekop
Eland
Fochville Sta.
Leeuspruit
Evaton
Dadaville
Meyerton
Vereeniging Aerodrome
Tweefontein N.R.
Sebokeng
Riversdale
Enselspruit
Vanderbijlpark Sta.
Waldrift N.R.
Sonlandpark
VEREENIGING
Redan
N O R T H W E S T
Three Rivers
Goeiehoek
Bosrivier
Sharpeville
Suikerbosrand
Bophelong
VANDERBIJLPARK
Caravan Park
Viljoensdrif
Goedbeloon
Kluitfontein
Lindequesdrif
Vaal Racecourse
Loch Vaal
Vaalpark
Hunterville
Vaal
Sasolburg
Zamdela
Sasolburg Sta.
Coalbrook
Groenpunt
Caravan Park
Pennant Nine Yacht Club
Vaal Marina
Groot-eiland
V R E D E F O R T D O M E
Grootkop 1600
Refengkgotso
Deneysville
Vaal Dam
Manten Marina
Parys
F R E E S T A T E
Wolwehoek
Clydesdale
Tumahole
Calais
0 5 10 km
0 (1 cm) 4.5 kilometres
Pretoria
Hartbeespoort
Kroonstad
Heilbron
Frankfort
Rustenburg
Derby
Ventersdorp
Potchefstroom

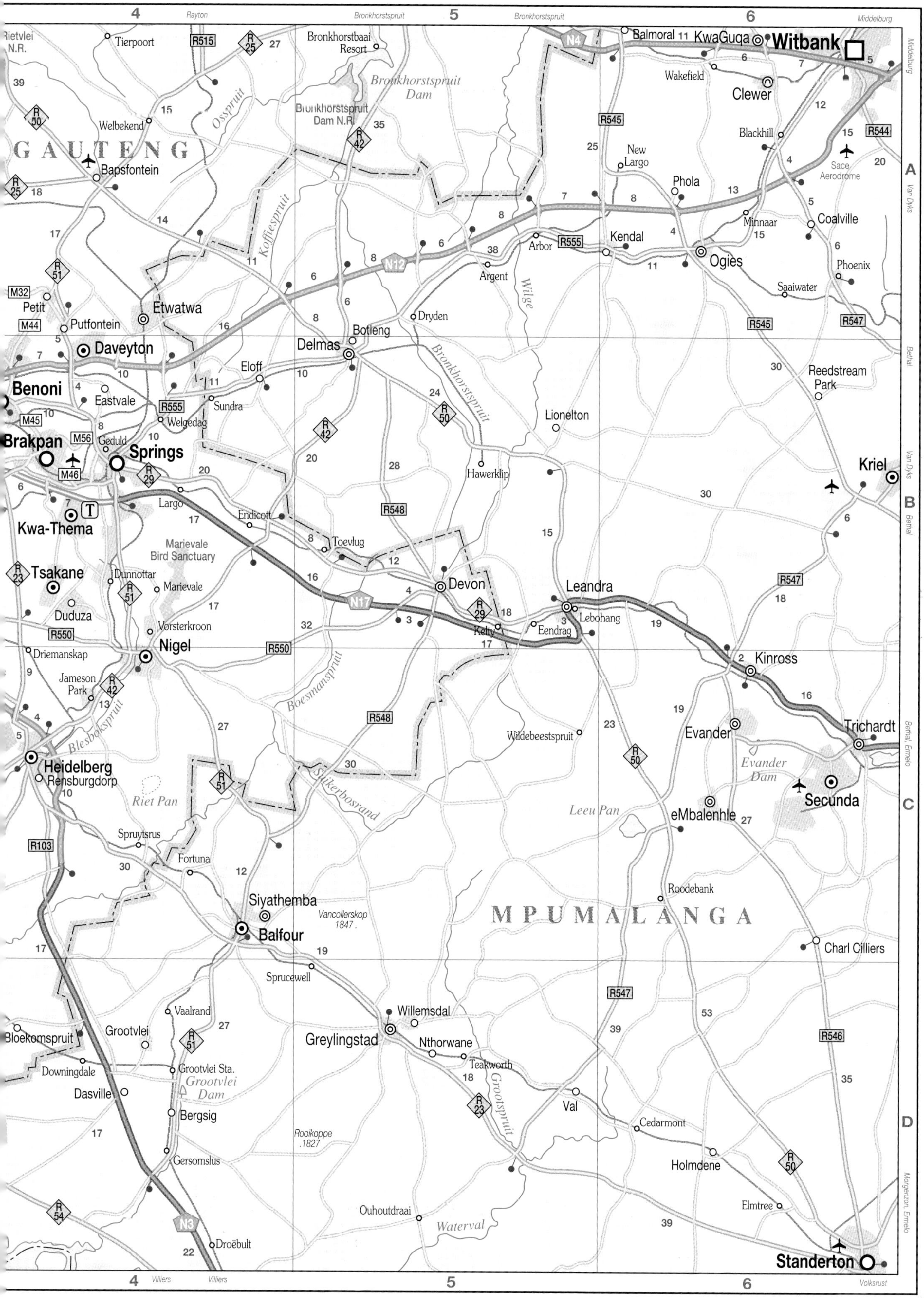

Rayton
Bronkhorstspruit
Bronkhorstspruit
Middelburg
Rietvlei N.R.
Tierpoort
R515
R25
Bronkhorstbaai Resort
Bronkhorstspruit Dam
Bronkhorstspruit Dam N.R.
N4
Balmoral
KwaGuqa
Witbank
Wakefield
Clewer
R545
Blackhill
R544
Sace Aerodrome
R50
Welbekend
Osspruit
R42
GAUTENG
Bapsfontein
New Largo
Phola
Minnaar
Coalville
Kendal
Arbor
R555
Ogies
Phoenix
Saaiwater
Argent
Wilge
Koffiespruit
R51
N12
M32
Petit
M44
Putfontein
Etwatwa
Dryden
Botleng
R545
R547
Daveyton
Delmas
Bronkhorstspruit
Eloff
Benoni
Eastvale
R555
Sundra
M45
Welgedag
Reedstream Park
Lionelton
Brakpan
M56
Geduld
Springs
M46
R29
Hawerklip
Kriel
Largo
Kwa-Thema
Endicott
R548
Marievale Bird Sanctuary
Toevlug
Leandra
Tsakane
Dunnottar
Marievale
Devon
R547
Duduza
N17
Lebohang
Vorsterkroon
Eendrag
Kelty
R550
Driemanskap
Nigel
R550
Kinross
Jameson Park
Boesmanspruit
Blesbokspruit
R548
Wildebeestspruit
Evander
Trichardt
Heidelberg
Rensburgdorp
Riet Pan
Suikerbosrand
Evander Dam
Secunda
Leeu Pan
eMbalenhle
R103
Spruytsrus
Fortuna
Roodebank
Siyathemba
Vancollerskop 1847
MPUMALANGA
Balfour
Charl Cilliers
Sprucewell
R547
Vaalrand
Willemsdal
Bloekomspruit
Grootvlei
Greylingstad
Nthorwane
R546
Downingdale
Grootvlei Sta.
Teakworth
Grootvlei Dam
Grootspruit
Dasville
Val
Bergsig
R23
Rooikoppe 1827
Cedarmont
Gersomslus
Holmdene
R54
Elmtree
Ouhoutdraai
Waterval
N3
Droëbult
Standerton
Villiers
Villiers
Volksrust
Van Dyks
Bethal
Van Dyks
Bethal
Bethal, Ermelo
Morgenzon, Ermelo

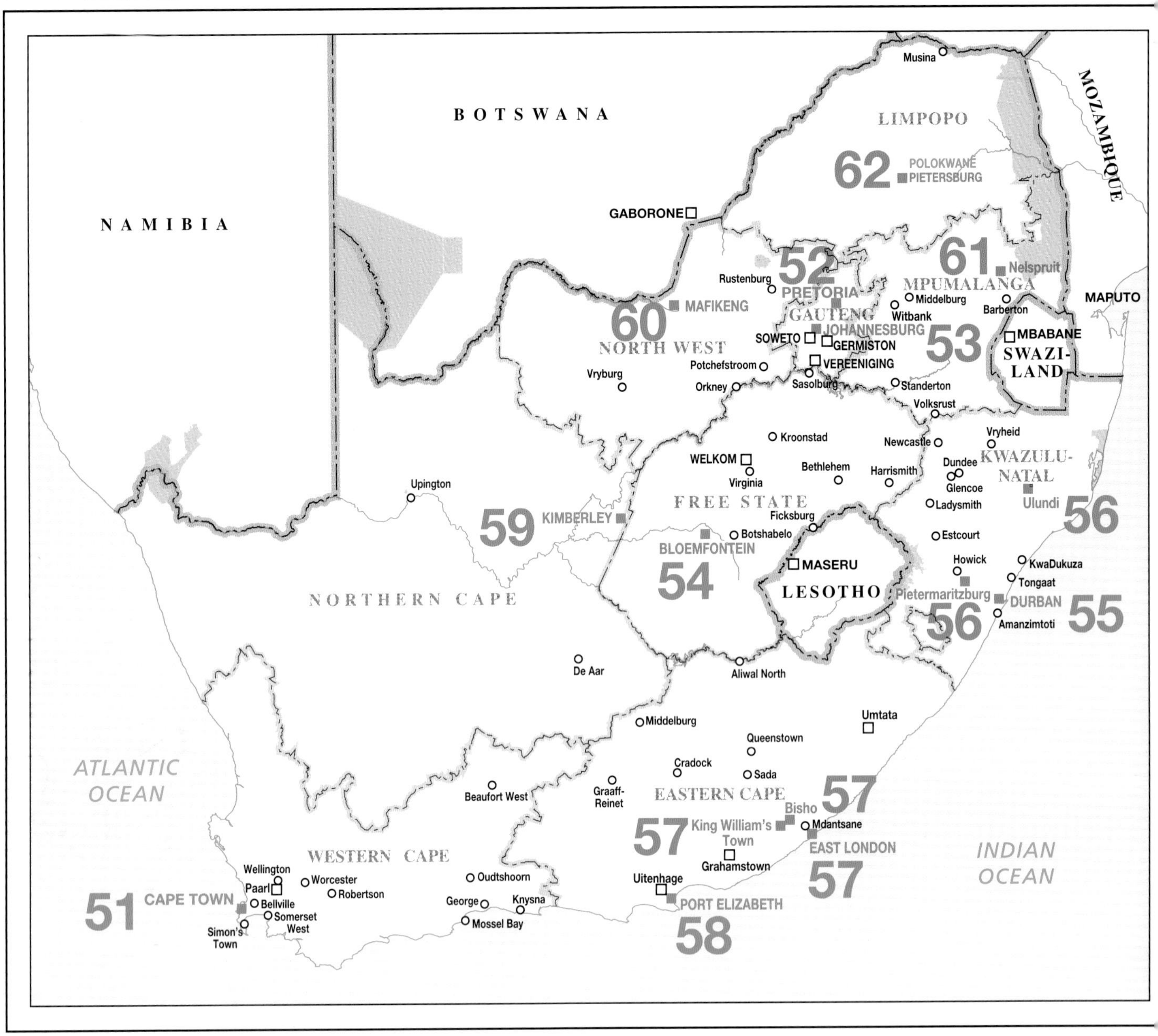

KEY

Motorway		Park		Hospital – 24 hr	
National road		Rugby ground		Hospital/clinic	
Main road		Soccer ground		Bus terminus	
Other road		Cricket ground		Hotel	H
National route number	N7	Tennis court		Library	
Route numbers	R 29 R302	National monument building		Place of worship	W
Metropolitan road number	M 46	Monument/memorial		International airport	
One-way street		Swimming pool		Airport and airfield	
Bridge over		Information centre	i	Lighthouse	
Railway and station		Parking	P	Toll road	T
Pedestrian mall		Police station		Shopping centre	
Built-up area		Place of interest			

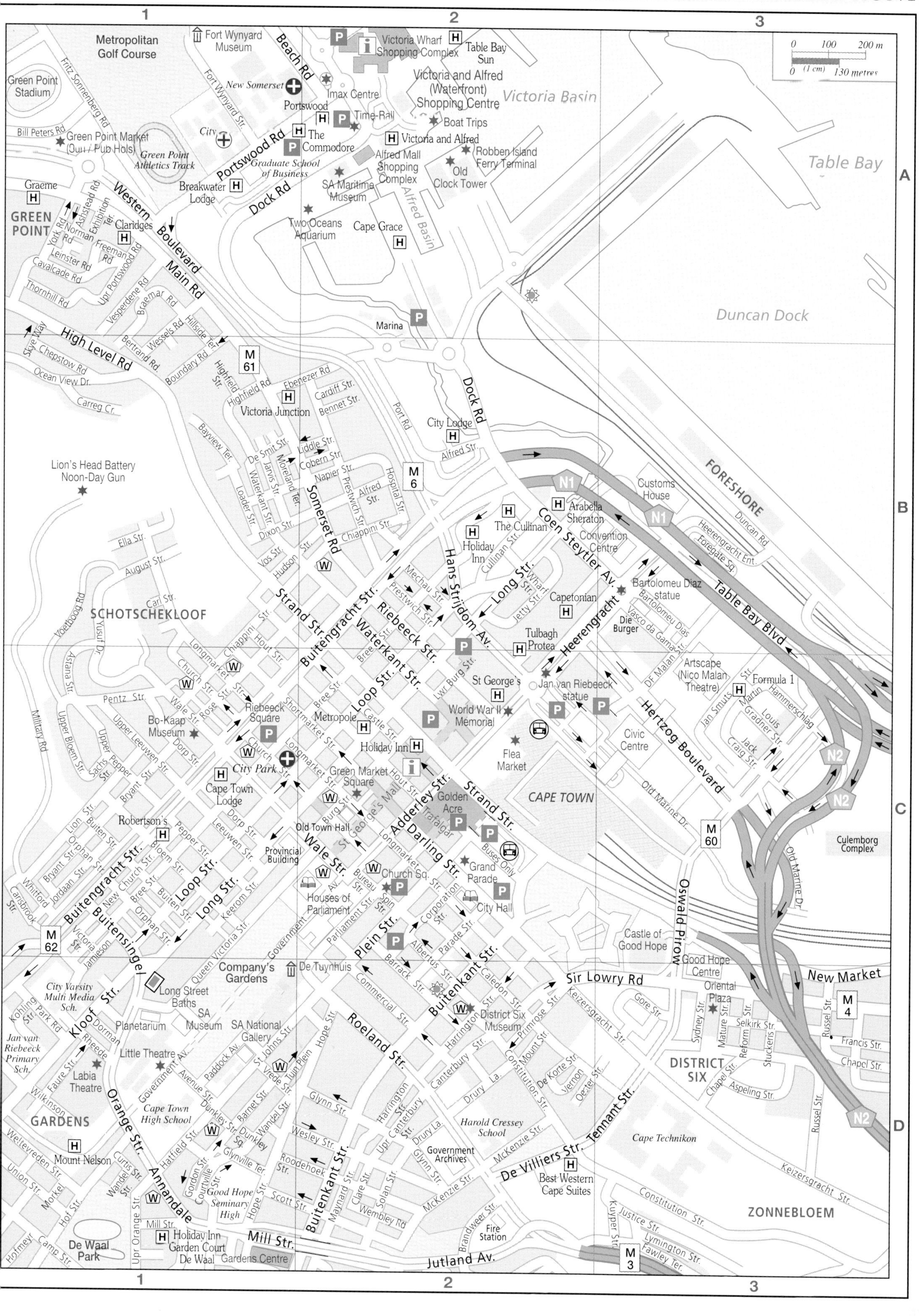
Metropolitan Golf Course
Green Point Stadium
Fort Wynyard Museum
Beach Rd
Victoria Wharf Shopping Complex
Table Bay Sun
Victoria and Alfred (Waterfront) Shopping Centre
Victoria Basin
New Somerset
Imax Centre
Portswood
Time-Ball
Boat Trips
Fritz Sonnenberg Rd
Fort Wynyard Str.
City
The Commodore
Victoria and Alfred
Bill Peters Rd
Green Point Market (Sun / Pub Hols)
Green Point Athletics Track
Portswood Rd
Graduate School of Business
Alfred Mall Shopping Complex
Robben Island Ferry Terminal
Old Clock Tower
Table Bay
Graeme
Breakwater Lodge
Dock Rd
SA Maritime Museum
Alfred Basin
GREEN POINT
Claridges
Western Boulevard
Two Oceans Aquarium
Cape Grace
York Rd
Norman Rd
Freeman Rd
Leinster Rd
Cavalcade Rd
Thornhill Rd
Main Rd
Upr Portswood Rd
Vesperdene Rd
Braemar Rd
Duncan Dock
Marina
Skye Way
High Level Rd
Chepstow Rd
Ocean View Dr.
Carreg Cr.
Wessels Rd
Hillside Ter.
Bertrand Rd
Boundary Rd
Highfield Str.
Highfield Rd
Ebenezer Rd
Victoria Junction
Cardiff Str.
Bennet Str.
Port Rd
Dock Rd
City Lodge
Alfred Str.
Bayview Ter.
De Smit Str.
Liddle Str.
Cobern Str.
Moreland Ter.
Jarvis Str.
Napier Str.
Prestwich Str.
Alfred Str.
Hospital Str.
Lion's Head Battery Noon-Day Gun
Loader Str.
Waterkant Str.
Somerset Rd
Dixon Str.
Chiappini Str.
Customs House
FORESHORE
Arabella Sheraton
The Cullinan
Coen Steytler Av.
Convention Centre
Duncan Rd
Heerengracht Ext.
Foregate Sq.
Ella Str.
Vos Str.
Hudson Str.
Holiday Inn
Cullinan Str.
August Str.
Mechau Str.
Hans Strijdom Av.
Long Str.
Wharf Str.
Jetty Str.
Capetonian
Bartolomeu Diaz statue
Table Bay Blvd
Carl Str.
Voetboog Rd
SCHOTSCHEKLOOF
Yusuf Dr.
Strand Str.
Buitengracht Str.
Riebeeck Str.
Waterkant Str.
Prestwich Str.
Heerengracht
Die Burger
Vasco da Gama Str.
Tulbagh Protea
Bree Str.
Longmarket Str.
Chiappini Str.
Hout Str.
Lwr Burg Str.
St George's
DF Malan Str.
Artscape (Nico Malan Theatre)
Formula 1
Martin Hammerschlag
Astana Str.
Church Str.
Rose Str.
Jan van Riebeeck statue
Jan Smuts Str.
Pentz Str.
Wale Str.
Riebeeck Square
Bree Str.
Loop Str.
Shortmarket Str.
Metropole
Castle Str.
World War II Memorial
Hertzog Boulevard
Louis Gradner Str.
Military Rd
Upper Bloem Str.
Bo-Kaap Museum
Dorp Str.
Upper Leeuwen Str.
Church Str.
Holiday Inn
Civic Centre
Jack Craig Str.
Sachs Str.
Upper Pepper Str.
City Park
Longmarket Str.
Flea Market
Bryant Str.
Cape Town Lodge
Green Market Square
Hout Str.
Adderley Str.
Strand Str.
Golden Acre
CAPE TOWN
Old Marine Dr.
St George's Mall
Trafalgar
Burg Str.
Lion Str.
Buiten Str.
Robertson's
Dorp Str.
Old Town Hall
Darling Str.
M 60
Culemborg Complex
Bryant Str.
Orphan Str.
Pepper Str.
Leeuwen Str.
Provincial Building
Wale Str.
Longmarket Str.
Buses Only
Jordaan Str.
Buitengracht Str.
Bloem Str.
Loop Str.
Grand Parade
Whitford Str.
New Church Str.
Bree Str.
Buiten Str.
Long Str.
Keerom Str.
Bureau Str.
Church Sq.
Old Marine Dr.
Carisbrook Str.
Houses of Parliament
Parliament Str.
Spin Str.
Corporation Str.
City Hall
Oswald Pirow
Buitensingel
Orphan Str.
Queen Victoria Str.
Government Av.
Plein Str.
Parade Str.
Castle of Good Hope
M 62
Victoria Str.
Jameson Str.
Company's Gardens
De Tuynhuis
Albertus Str.
Buitenkant Str.
Good Hope Centre
Barrack Str.
Caledon Str.
Sir Lowry Rd
New Market
Commercial Str.
Oriental Plaza
M 4
City Varsity Multi Media Sch.
Kloof Str.
Long Street Baths
Keizersgracht Str.
Gore Str.
Kohling Str.
Park Rd
SA Museum
District Six Museum
Primrose Str.
Sydney Str.
Mature Str.
Reform Str.
Selkirk Str.
Russel Str.
Jan van Riebeeck Primary Sch.
Dorman Str.
Planetarium
SA National Gallery
Roeland Str.
Harrington Str.
Mount Str.
Stuckeris Str.
Francis Str.
Rheede Str.
Little Theatre
Paddock Av.
St Johns Str.
Hope Str.
Tuin Plein
Constitution Str.
De Korte Str.
DISTRICT SIX
Chapel Str.
Faure Str.
Labia Theatre
Government Av.
Avenue Str.
Vrede Str.
Canterbury Str.
Vernon Str.
Oester Str.
Aspeling Str.
Wilkinson Str.
Barnet Str.
Glynn Str.
Drury La.
GARDENS
Orange Str.
Cape Town High School
Dunkley Str.
Dunkley Sq.
Wandel Str.
Wesley Str.
Harrington Str.
Upr Canterbury Str.
Harold Cressey School
Tennant Str.
Cape Technikon
Russel Str.
N2
Hatfield Str.
Glynville Ter.
Roodehoek Str.
Buitenkant Str.
Drury La.
Government Archives
McKenzie Str.
Mount Nelson
Weltevreden Str.
Curtis Str.
Annandale
Gordon Str.
Courtville Str.
Good Hope Seminary High
Scott Str.
Maynard Str.
Clare Str.
Solan Str.
Glynn Str.
McKenzie Str.
De Villiers Str.
Best Western Cape Suites
Keizersgracht Str.
Union Str.
Morkel Str.
Wandel Str.
Hope Str.
Wembley Rd
Brandweer Str.
Constitution Str.
ZONNEBLOEM
Hof Str.
Upr Orange Str.
Mill Str.
Holiday Inn Garden Court De Waal
Mill Str.
Fire Station
Kuyper Str.
Justice Str.
Lymington Str.
Fawley Ter.
Hofmeyr Str.
Camp Str.
De Waal Park
Gardens Centre
Jutland Av.
M 3
M 61
M 6
N1
0 100 200 m
0 (1 cm) 130 metres
1
2
3
A
B
C
D

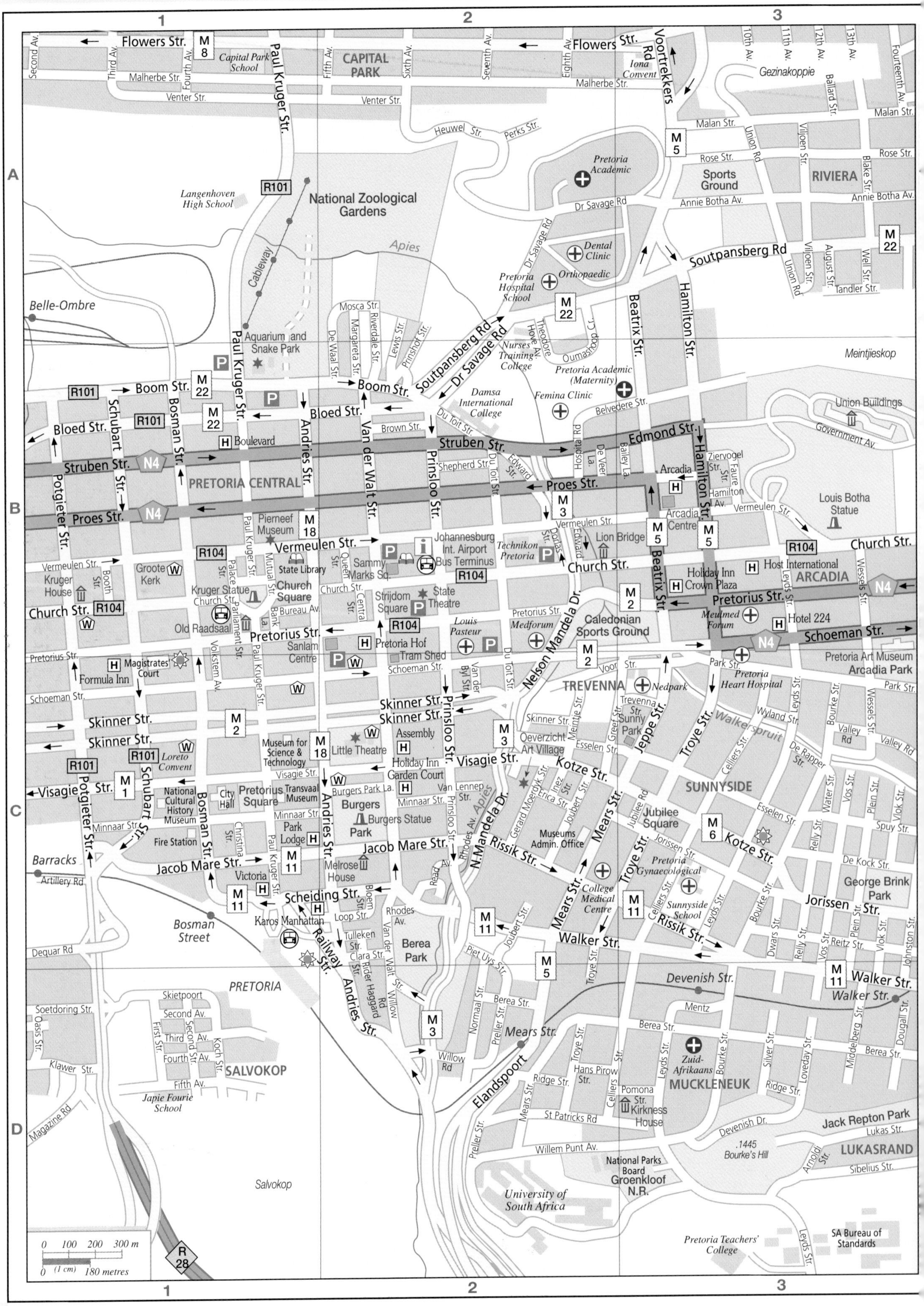

1
2
3
A
B
C
D
Flowers Str.
M 8
Capital Park School
Paul Kruger Str.
CAPITAL PARK
Second Av.
Third Av.
Fourth Av.
Fifth Av.
Sixth Av.
Seventh Av.
Eighth Av.
Malherbe Str.
Venter Str.
Iona Convent
Voortrekkers Rd
10th Av.
11th Av.
12th Av.
13th Av.
Fourteenth Av.
Gezinakoppie
Ballard Str.
Malan Str.
Heuwel Str.
Perks Str.
M 5
Union Rd
Viljoen Str.
Rose Str.
Pretoria Academic
Sports Ground
RIVIERA
Blake Str.
R101
Langenhoven High School
National Zoological Gardens
Dr Savage Rd
Annie Botha Av.
M 22
Apies
Cableway
Dental Clinic
Orthopaedic
Soutpansberg Rd
August Str.
Well Str.
Tandler Str.
Belle-Ombre
Pretoria Hospital School
Hamilton Str.
Beatrix Str.
Mosca Str.
De Waal Str.
Margareta Str.
Riverdale Str.
Lewis Str.
Prinshof Str.
Theodore Str.
Howe Av.
Nurses Training College
Oumashoop
Aquarium and Snake Park
Meintjieskop
Pretoria Academic (Maternity)
Boom Str.
Damsa International College
Femina Clinic
Union Buildings
Government Av.
Belvedere Str.
Bloed Str.
Schubart Str.
Bosman Str.
Andries Str.
Van der Walt Str.
Prinsloo Str.
Brown Str.
Du Toit Str.
Boulevard
Struben Str.
N4
Edmond Str.
Shepherd Str.
Edward Str.
Hospital Rd
De Veer La.
Bailey La.
Zeirvogel Str.
Faure Str.
Arcadia
Hamilton Av.
Louis Botha Statue
PRETORIA CENTRAL
Proes Str.
M 3
Vermeulen Str.
Potgieter Str.
Pierneef Museum
M 18
Johannesburg Int. Airport Bus Terminus
Technikon Pretoria
Dorlas Str.
Lion Bridge
Arcadia Centre
R104
Church Str.
Groote Kerk
Kruger House
Booth Str.
State Library
Sammy Marks Sq.
Palace Str.
Mutual Str.
Queen Str.
Holiday Inn Crown Plaza
Host International
ARCADIA
Leyds Str.
Wessels Str.
Kruger Statue
Church Square
Church Str.
Central Str.
Strijdom Square
State Theatre
Nelson Mandela Dr.
M 2
Caledonian Sports Ground
Pretorius Str.
Medforum
Mediomed Forum
Hotel 224
Bureau Av.
Bank La.
Parliament Str.
Old Raadsaal
Sanlam Centre
Pretoria Hof
Louis Pasteur
Schoeman Str.
Tram Shed
Magistrates' Court
Formula Inn
Volkstem Av.
Van der Byl Str.
Voor Str.
Park Str.
Pretoria Heart Hospital
Pretoria Art Museum
Arcadia Park
TREVENNA
Nedpark
Skinner Str.
Trevenna Str.
Sunny Park
Jeppe Str.
Troye Str.
Walkerspruit
Wyland Str.
Bourke Str.
Valley Rd
Valley Str.
Museum for Science & Technology
Little Theatre
Assembly
Oeverzicht Art Village
Meintje Str.
Greef Str.
Esselen Str.
Kotze Str.
Celliers Str.
De Rapper Str.
Loreto Convent
Holiday Inn Garden Court
Visagie Str.
M 1
National Cultural History Museum
City Hall
Pretorius Square
Transvaal Museum
Burgers Park La.
Van Lennep Str.
Gerard Moerdijk Str.
Inez Str.
Erica Str.
Joubert Str.
Mears Str.
Jubilee Rd
Jubilee Square
SUNNYSIDE
M 6
Water Str.
Vos Str.
Plein Str.
Vlok Str.
Spuy Str.
Minnaar Str.
Christina Str.
Park Lodge
Burgers Park
Burgers Statue
Rhodes Av.
N. Mandela Dr.
Museums Admin. Office
Jorissen Str.
Relly Str.
Fire Station
Jacob Mare Str.
M 11
Rissik Str.
Melrose House
Pretoria Gynaecological
De Kock Str.
Barracks
Artillery Rd
Victoria
Scheiding Str.
Bloem Str.
Read Av.
College Medical Centre
George Brink Park
Bosman Street
Karos Manhattan
Loop Str.
Tulleken Str.
Clara Str.
Berea Park
Sunnyside School
Dwars Str.
Reitz Str.
Johnston Str.
Dequar Rd
Railway Str.
Rider Haggard Rd
Willow Str.
Piet Uys Str.
Walker Str.
PRETORIA
Devenish Str.
Skietpoort
Second Av.
Soetdoring Str.
Oasis Str.
First Str.
Third Av.
Koch Str.
Fourth Av.
Fifth Av.
SALVOKOP
Klawer Str.
Normaal Str.
Preller Str.
Berea Str.
Mentz
Middelberg Str.
Dougall Str.
Loveday Str.
Silver Str.
Willow Rd
Hans Pirow Str.
Zuid-Afrikaans
Elandspoort
Ridge Str.
Pomona Str.
Kirkness House
MUCKLENEUK
Japie Fourie School
Magazine Rd
St Patricks Rd
Jack Repton Park
Lukas Str.
Devenish Dr.
.1445 Bourke's Hill
LUKASRAND
Arnold Str.
Sibelius Str.
Willem Punt Av.
National Parks Board
Groenkloof N.R.
Salvokop
University of South Africa
Pretoria Teachers' College
SA Bureau of Standards
0 100 200 300 m
0 (1 cm) 180 metres
R 28

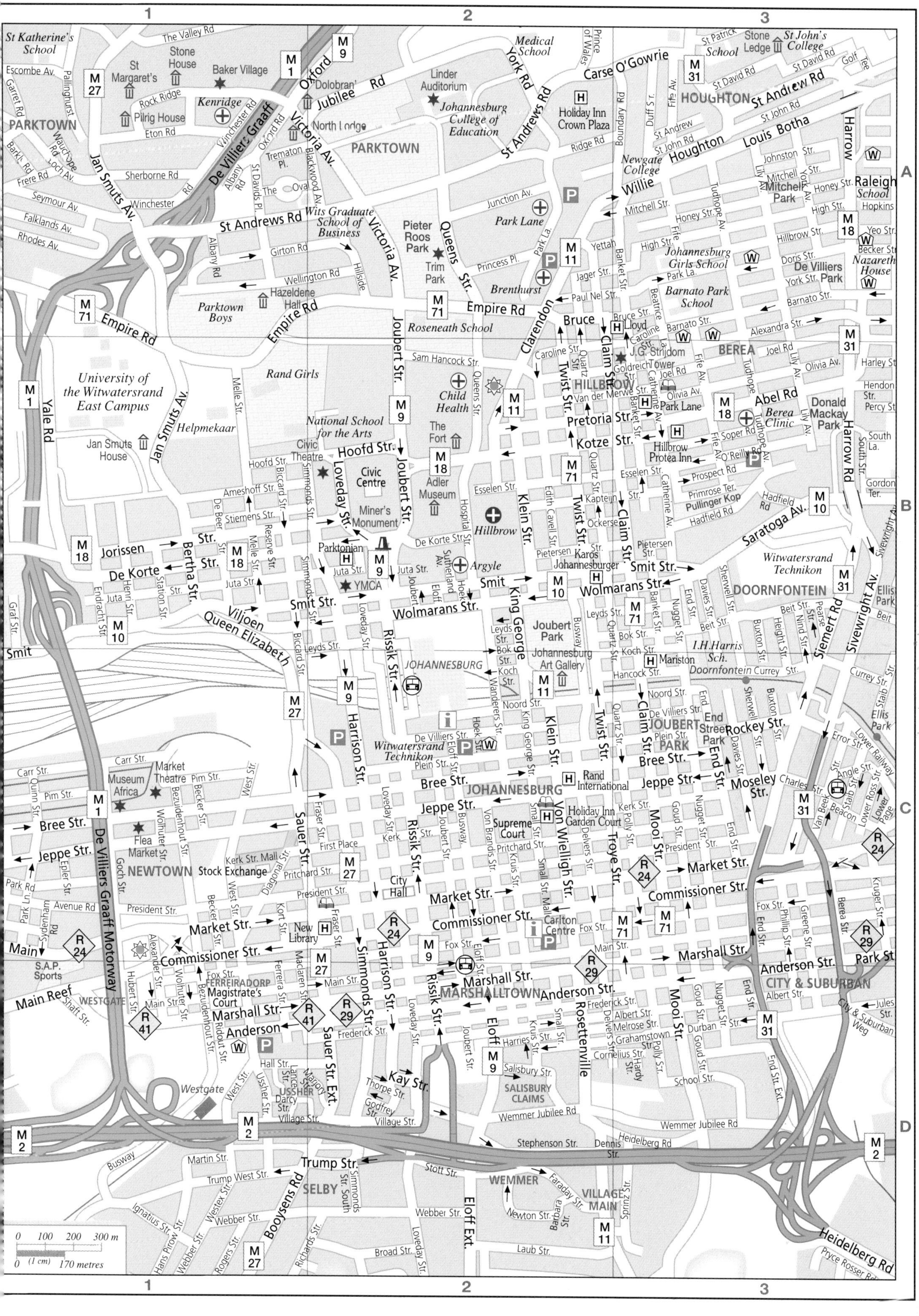
1
2
3
A
B
C
D
St Katherine's School
The Valley Rd
Stone House
Baker Village
St Margaret's
Escombe Av.
Garret Rd
Pallinghurst
Rock Ridge
Kenridge
Pilrig House
Eton Rd
PARKTOWN
Winchester Rd
Oxford Rd
De Villiers Graaff
Oxford
'Dolobran'
Jubilee Rd
Victoria Av.
North Lodge
Linder Auditorium
Johannesburg College of Education
Medical School
York Rd
Prince of Wales
Carse O'Gowrie
St Andrews Rd
Holiday Inn Crown Plaza
Ridge Rd
Boundary Rd
St Patrick School
Stone Ledge
St John's College
St David Rd
Golf Tee
HOUGHTON
St Andrew Rd
St John Rd
Louis Botha
Houghton
Newgate College
Harrow
Johnston Str.
Mitchell Str.
Mitchell Park
Raleigh School
Hopkins
Honey Str.
High Str.
Yeo Str.
Becker Str.
Nazareth House
De Villiers Park
York Str.
Doris Str.
Barnato Str.
Hillbrow Str.
Jan Smuts Av.
Sherborne Rd
Frere Rd
Seymour Av.
Falklands Av.
Rhodes Av.
Winchester
Trematon Pl.
Albany Rd
St Davids Pl.
The Oval
Blackwood Av.
PARKTOWN
Wits Graduate School of Business
St Andrews Rd
Girton Rd
Wellington Rd
Hillside
Hazeldene Hall
Parktown Boys
Empire Rd
Pieter Roos Park
Trim Park
Queens Str.
Junction Av.
Park Lane
Princess Pl.
Park La.
Brenthurst
Jager Str.
Yettah
Willie
Paul Nel Str.
Banket Str.
Johannesburg Girls School
Park La.
Barnato Park School
Fife
Tudhope Av.
Empire Rd
Roseneath School
Clarendon
Bruce
Bruce Str.
Lloyd
Caroline Str.
Alexandra Str.
BEREA
Joel Rd
Olivia Av.
Harley Str.
Hendon Str.
Percy Str.
University of the Witwatersrand East Campus
Yale Rd
Melle Str.
Rand Girls
Sam Hancock Str.
Joubert Str.
Child Health
J.G. Strijdom Tower
HILLBROW
Goldreich Str.
Van der Merwe Str.
Twist Str.
Claim Str.
Pretoria Str.
Kotze Str.
Park Lane
Abel Rd
Berea Clinic
Donald Mackay Park
Harrow Rd
South La.
Soper Rd
O'Reilly Rd
Hillbrow Protea Inn
Helpmekaar
Jan Smuts House
National School for the Arts
The Fort
Civic Theatre
Hoofd Str.
Civic Centre
Adler Museum
Miner's Monument
Loveday Str.
Esselen Str.
Hospital Str.
Hillbrow
Klein Str.
Edith Cavell Str.
Kapteijn Str.
Ockerse Str.
Prospect Rd
Primrose Ter.
Pullinger Kop
Hadfield Rd
Saratoga Av.
Gordon Ter.
Ameshoff Str.
Biccard Str.
De Beer Str.
Stiemens Str.
Reserve Str.
Simmonds Str.
Jorissen Str.
Bertha Str.
De Korte Str.
Parktonian
De Korte Str.
Sutherland Av.
Argyle
Pietersen Str.
Karos Johannesburger
Smit Str.
Witwatersrand Technikon
Sivewright Av.
Juta Str.
YMCA
Hoek Str.
Smit
Wolmarans Str.
DOORNFONTEIN
Endracht Str.
Henri Str.
Station Str.
Viljoen
Queen Elizabeth
Wolmarans Str.
King George
Joubert Park
Leyds Str.
Bok Str.
Koch Str.
Johannesburg Art Gallery
Buxton Str.
Beit Str.
Height Str.
Nind Str.
Siemert Rd
Pearse Str.
I.H.Harris Sch.
Mariston
Doornfontein
Currey Str.
Graf Str.
Smit
Leyds Str.
Rissik Str.
JOHANNESBURG
Wanderers Str.
Noord Str.
Hancock Str.
Noord Str.
De Villiers Str.
JOUBERT PARK
End Street Park
Rockey Str.
Staib Str.
Ellis Park
Lower Railway
Error Str.
Harrison Str.
Witwatersrand Technikon
De Villiers Str.
Plein Str.
Bree Str.
Rand International
Jeppe Str.
Moseley Str.
Charles Str.
Angle Str.
Carr Str.
Market Theatre
Museum Africa
Quinn Str.
Pim Str.
Bezuidenhout Str.
Becker Str.
West Str.
Bree Str.
Jeppe Str.
Sauer Str.
Fraser Str.
Loveday Str.
Jeppe Str.
Busway
JOHANNESBURG
Holiday Inn Garden Court
Kerk Str.
Polly Str.
Mooi Str.
Troye Str.
Von Wielligh Str.
Supreme Court
Von Brandis Str.
Pritchard Str.
Kruis Str.
Van Beek Str.
Beacon
Lower Ross Str.
Lower Page
Flea Market
Wolhuter Str.
Epler Str.
Park Rd
NEWTOWN
Stock Exchange
Kerk Str. Mall
Diagonal Str.
First Place
President Str.
Market Str.
Commissioner Str.
Kruger Str.
Berea Str.
Avenue Rd
Sydenham Rd
Park Ln.
Goch Str.
President Str.
City Hall
Market Str.
Commissioner Str.
Carlton Centre
Fox Str.
Greene Str.
Phillip Str.
Main
S.A.P. Sports
Alexander Str.
Commissioner Str.
Market Str.
New Library
Maclaren Str.
Ferreira Str.
Main Str.
Marshall Str.
Park Str.
Anderson Str.
CITY & SUBURBAN
Albert Str.
Jules Str.
City & Suburban Weg
Main Reef
Shaft Str.
WESTGATE
Hubert Str.
FERREIRADORP
Magistrate's Court
Marshall Str.
Anderson
Ridout Str.
Marshall Str.
MARSHALLTOWN
Anderson Str.
Frederick Str.
Albert Str.
Melrose Str.
Grahamstown Str.
Cornelius Str.
Hardy Str.
Rosettenville
Durban Str.
Goud Str.
Nugget Str.
End St. Ext.
School Str.
Hall Str.
Lance Str.
Marlory Str.
Sauer Str. Ext.
Harries Str.
Salisbury Str.
SALISBURY CLAIMS
Eloff
Kay Str.
Thorpe Str.
Godfrey Str.
Village Str.
USSHER
Darcy Str.
Westgate
West Str.
Ussher Str.
Wemmer Jubilee Rd
Wemmer Jubilee Rd
Stephenson Str.
Dennis Str.
Heidelberg Rd
De Villiers Graaff Motorway
Busway
Martin Str.
Trump Str.
Trump West Str.
Stott Str.
Westex Str.
SELBY
Simmonds Str. South
Booysens Rd
WEMMER
Faraday Str.
VILLAGE MAIN
Sprinz Str.
Barbara Str.
Newton Str.
Webber Str.
Eloff Ext.
Ignatius Str.
Hans Prow Str.
Webber Str.
Rogers Str.
Richards Str.
Broad Str.
Loveday Str.
Laub Str.
Heidelberg Rd
Pryce Rosser Rd
M 1
M 2
M 9
M 10
M 11
M 18
M 27
M 31
M 71
R 24
R 29
R 41
0 100 200 300 m
0 (1 cm) 170 metres

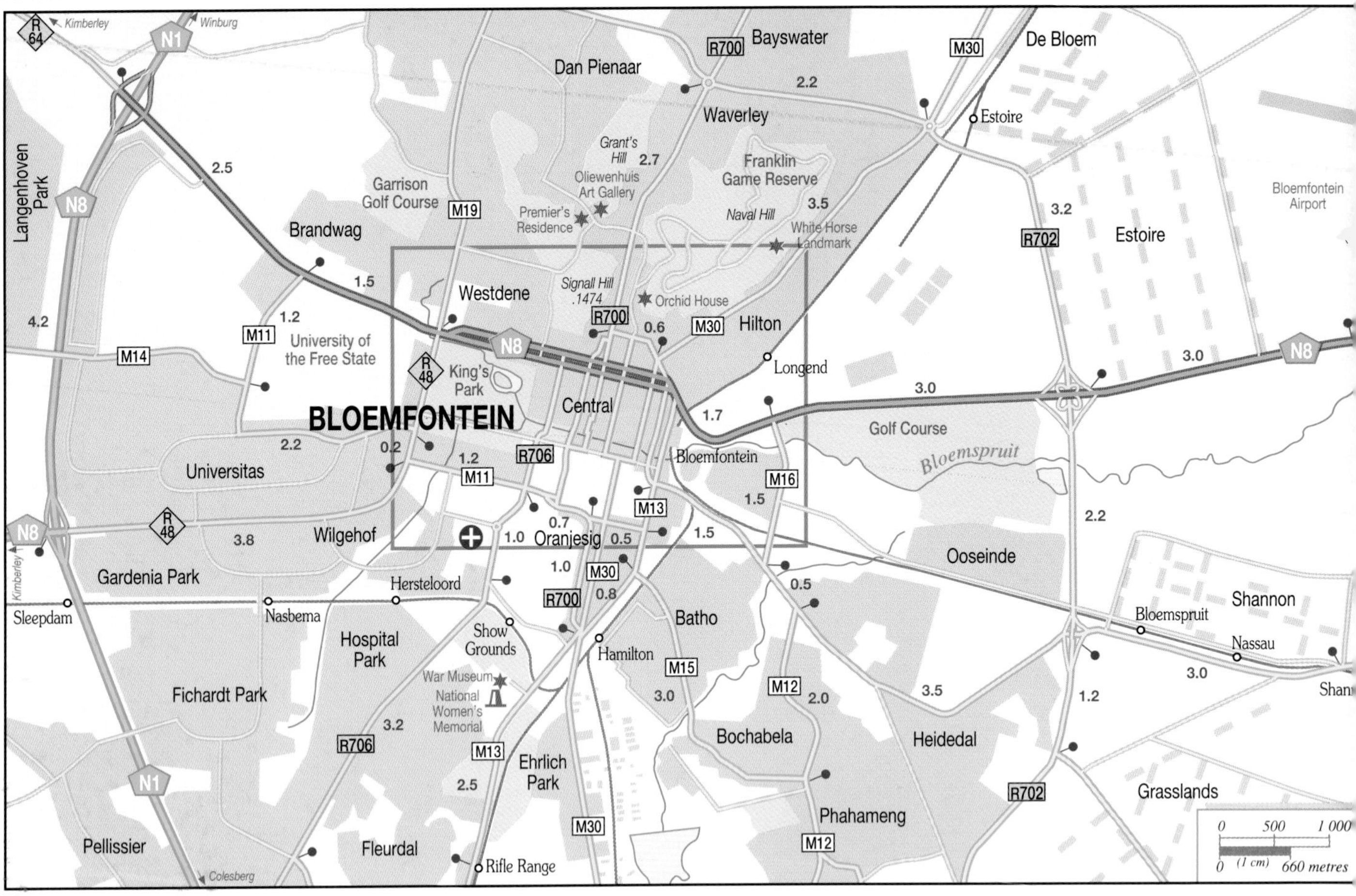

Kimberley
Winburg
N1
R64
Dan Pienaar
R700
Bayswater
M30
De Bloem
Estoire
Waverley
2.2
Grant's Hill
2.7
Oliewenhuis Art Gallery
Franklin Game Reserve
Langenhoven Park
2.5
Garrison Golf Course
M19
Premier's Residence
Naval Hill
3.5
White Horse Landmark
Bloemfontein Airport
3.2
R702
Estoire
N8
Brandwag
1.5
Westdene
Signall Hill .1474
Orchid House
4.2
1.2
M11
University of the Free State
R700
0.6
M30
Hilton
M14
R48
King's Park
Longend
3.0
BLOEMFONTEIN
Central
1.7
Golf Course
2.2
0.2
1.2
R706
Bloemfontein
Bloemspruit
Universitas
M11
M16
1.5
M13
2.2
R48
3.8
Wilgehof
0.7
1.0
Oranjesig
0.5
1.5
Gardenia Park
Hersteloord
1.0
M30
0.8
0.5
Ooseinde
Sleepdam
Nasbema
R700
Shannon
Bloemspruit
Nassau
Hospital Park
Show Grounds
Hamilton
Batho
War Museum
National Women's Memorial
M15
3.0
Fichardt Park
M12
2.0
3.5
1.2
Shan
3.2
R706
Bochabela
Heidedal
M13
Ehrlich Park
2.5
R702
Grasslands
N1
Phahameng
M30
Pellissier
Fleurdal
Rifle Range
M12
Colesberg
0 500 1 000
0 (1 cm) 660 metres

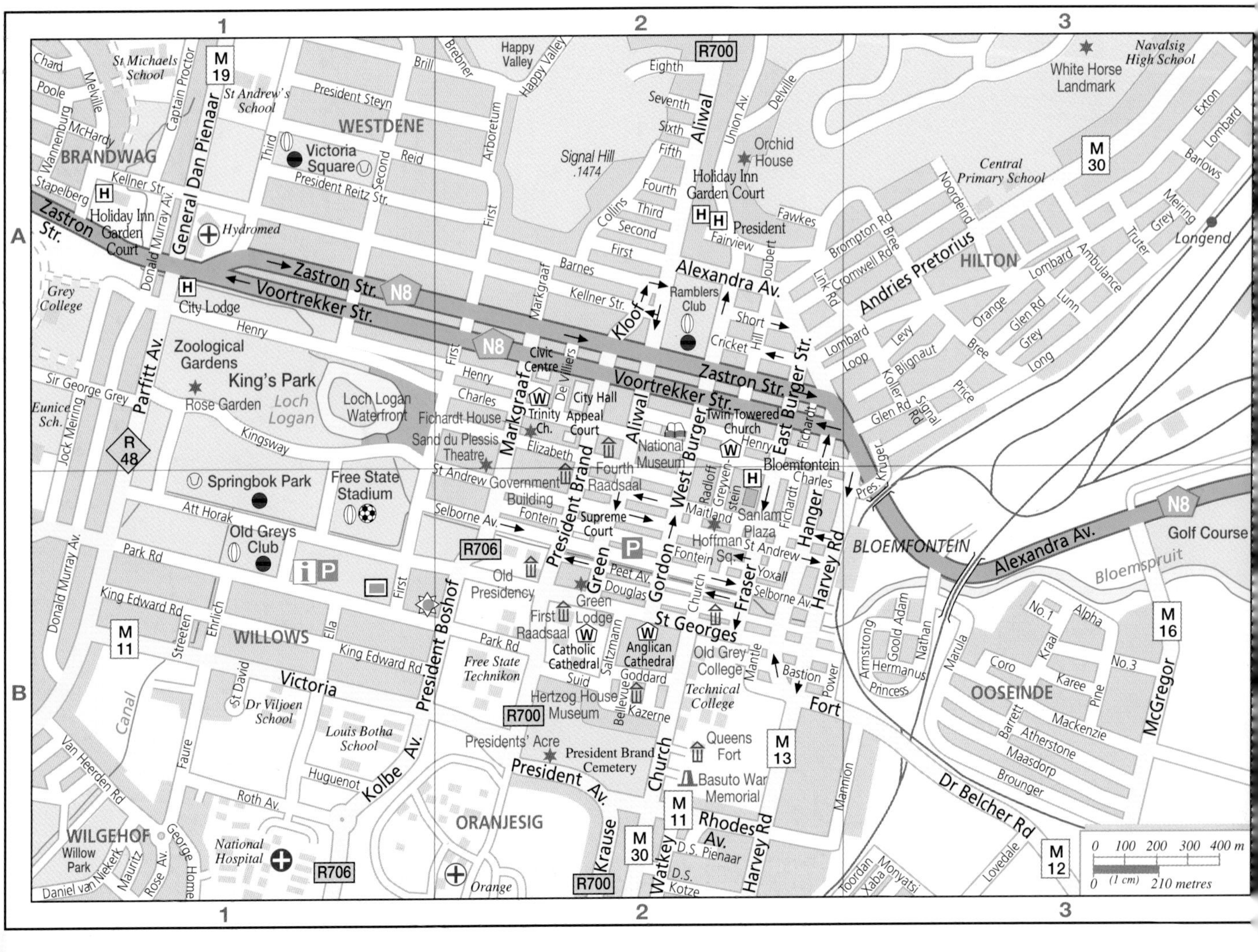

1
2
3
A
B
Chard
Poole
St Michaels School
M19
St Andrew's School
President Steyn
Brill
Happy Valley
R700
Eighth
Seventh
Sixth
Fifth
Navalsig High School
White Horse Landmark
WESTDENE
BRANDWAG
Victoria Square
President Reitz Str.
Signal Hill .1474
Orchid House
Holiday Inn Garden Court
Central Primary School
M30
Kellner Str.
Holiday Inn Garden Court
General Dan Pienaar
Hydromed
Zastron Str.
Voortrekker Str.
N8
City Lodge
Grey College
Barnes
Kellner Str.
Kloof
Ramblers Club
Alexandra Av.
President
Fairview
Andries Pretorius
HILTON
Longend
Zoological Gardens
King's Park
Rose Garden
Loch Logan
Loch Logan Waterfront
Parfitt Av.
Sir George Grey
Eunice Sch.
R48
Civic Centre
City Hall
Appeal Court
Trinity Ch.
Fichardt House
Sand du Plessis Theatre
National Museum
Twin Towered Church
Bloemfontein
East Burger Str.
Springbok Park
Free State Stadium
Government Building
Raadsaal
Supreme Court
Att Horak
Old Greys Club
Park Rd
R706
Old Presidency
Sanlam Plaza
Hoffman Sq.
BLOEMFONTEIN
Alexandra Av.
N8
Golf Course
Bloemspruit
King Edward Rd
M11
WILLOWS
King Edward Rd
First Raadsaal
Green Lodge
Catholic Cathedral
Anglican Cathedral
Old Grey College
St Georges
Free State Technikon
Victoria
President Boshof
Technical College
Bastion
Fort
OOSEINDE
M16
McGregor
Dr Viljoen School
R700
Hertzog House Museum
Kazerne
Louis Botha School
Presidents' Acre
President Brand Cemetery
Queens Fort
M13
Basuto War Memorial
Dr Belcher Rd
Kolbe Av.
President Av.
ORANJESIG
Rhodes Av.
WILGEHOF
Willow Park
National Hospital
R706
Orange
R700
M30
M11
D.S. Pienaar
D.S. Kotze
Harvey Rd
M12
0 100 200 300 400 m
0 (1 cm) 210 metres

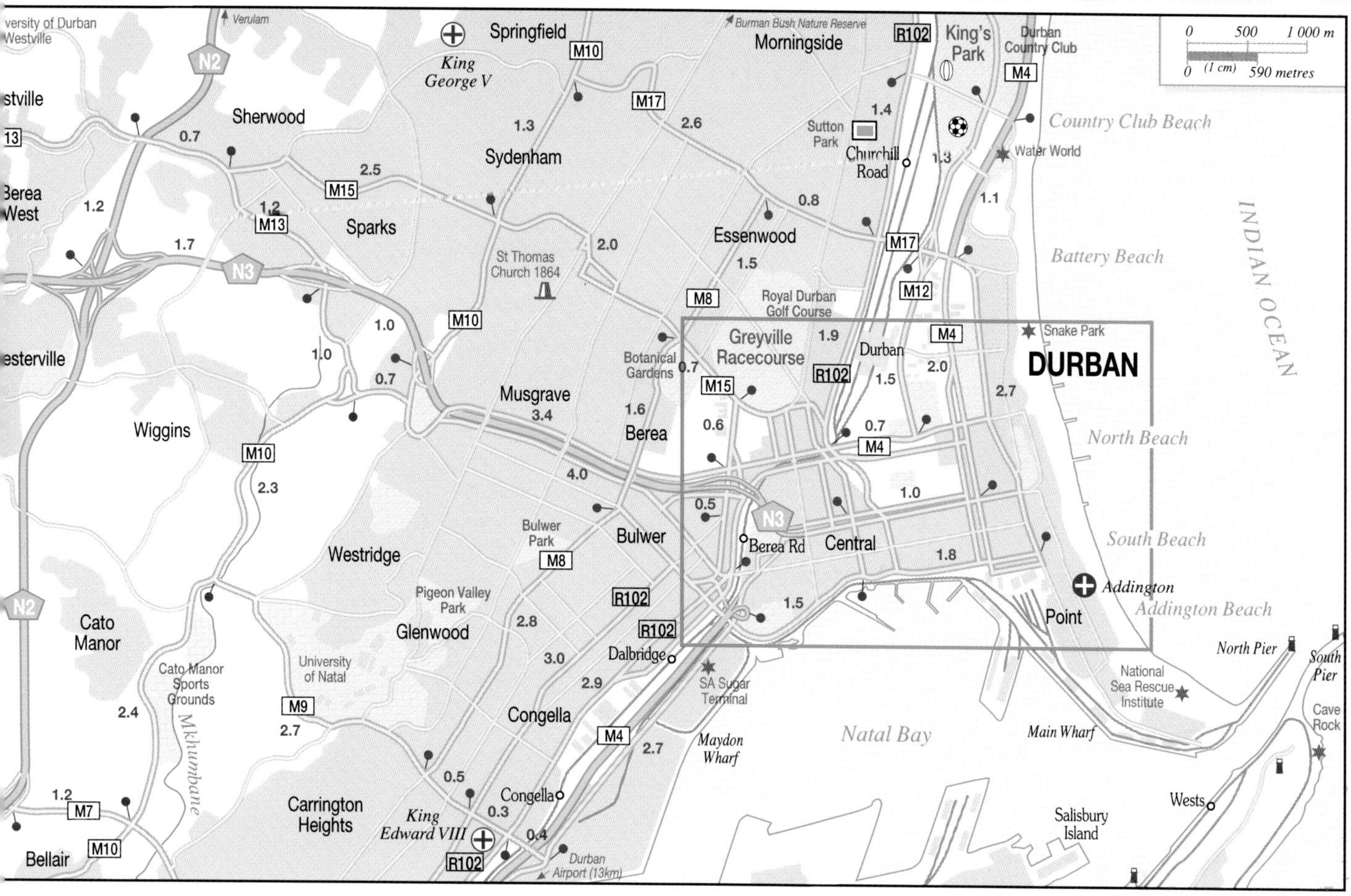

versity of Durban Westville
Verulam
N2
Springfield
King George V
M10
Burman Bush Nature Reserve
Morningside
R102
King's Park
Durban Country Club
M4
0 500 1 000 m
0 (1 cm) 590 metres
stville
13
Sherwood
0.7
1.3
M17
2.6
Sutton Park
1.4
Country Club Beach
Churchill Road
1.3
Water World
Sydenham
Berea West
1.2
2.5
M15
1.2
M13
Sparks
0.8
1.1
INDIAN OCEAN
1.7
N3
St Thomas Church 1864
2.0
Essenwood
M17
1.5
M12
Battery Beach
M8
Royal Durban Golf Course
1.0
M10
Snake Park
M4
Greyville Racecourse
1.9
Durban
esterville
1.0
0.7
Botanical Gardens
0.7
R102
1.5
2.0
DURBAN
Musgrave
3.4
M15
2.7
Wiggins
1.6
Berea
0.6
0.7
North Beach
M10
M4
2.3
4.0
1.0
0.5
N3
Bulwer Park
Bulwer
Berea Rd
Central
South Beach
M8
1.8
Westridge
Addington
Pigeon Valley Park
R102
1.5
Addington Beach
N2
Cato Manor
Glenwood
2.8
R102
Point
Dalbridge
North Pier
South Pier
Cato Manor Sports Grounds
University of Natal
3.0
SA Sugar Terminal
National Sea Rescue Institute
2.9
Cave Rock
2.4
Mkhumbane
M9
Congella
2.7
Natal Bay
Main Wharf
M4
2.7
Maydon Wharf
0.5
Congella
Wests
1.2
M7
Carrington Heights
0.3
King Edward VIII
Salisbury Island
0.4
Bellair
M10
R102
Durban Airport (13km)

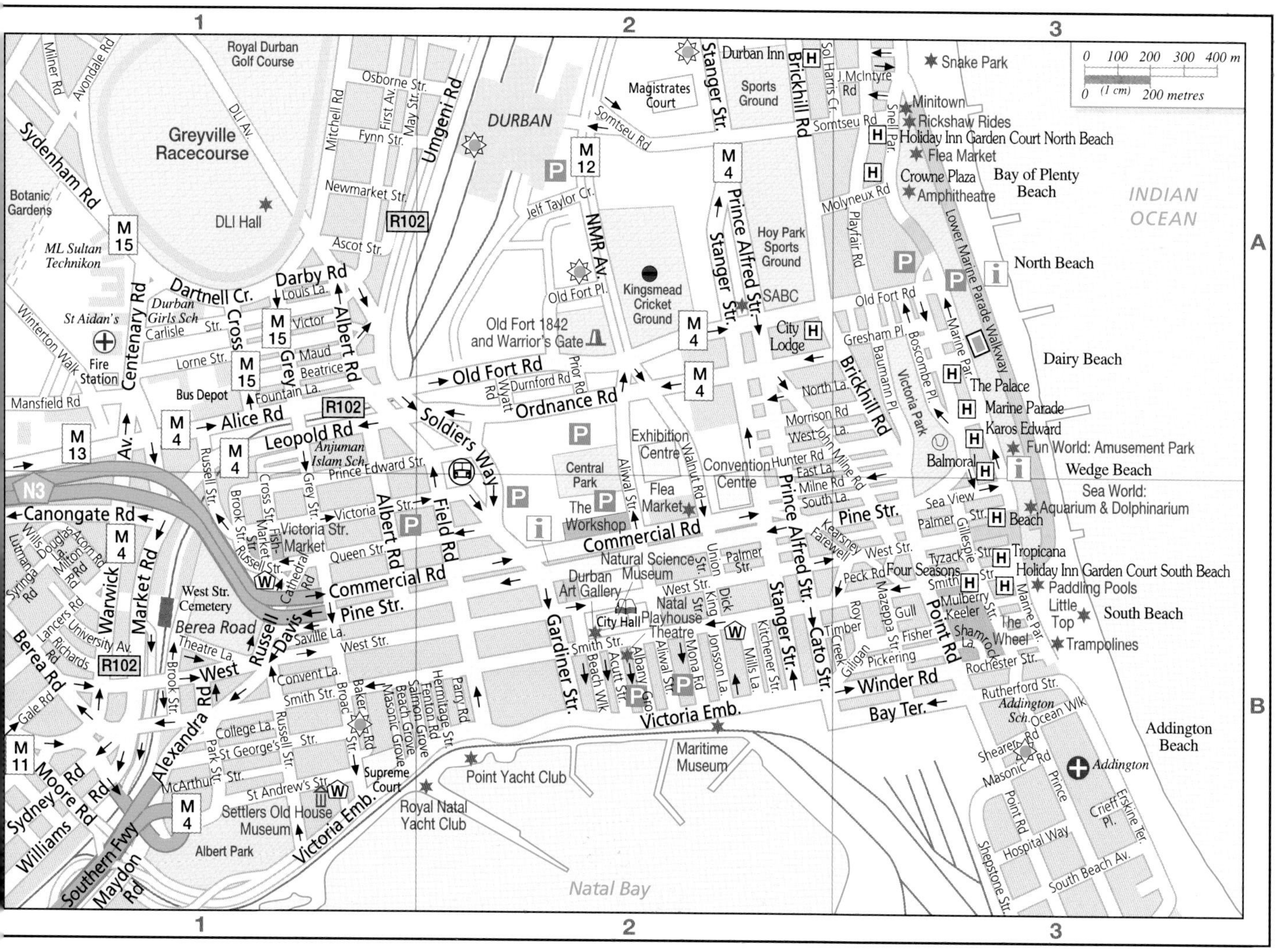

1
2
3
Royal Durban Golf Course
Milner Rd
Avondale Rd
DLI Av.
Osborne Str.
Mitchell Rd
First Av.
May Str.
Umgeni Rd
Magistrates Court
Durban Inn
Stanger Str.
Brickhill Rd
Sports Ground
Sol Harris Cr.
J.McIntyre Rd
Snake Park
0 100 200 300 400 m
0 (1 cm) 200 metres
Greyville Racecourse
Sydenham Rd
Fynn Str.
DURBAN
Somtseu Rd
Somtseu Rd
Snell Par.
Minitown
Rickshaw Rides
Holiday Inn Garden Court North Beach
M 12
M 4
Flea Market
Newmarket Str.
Jelf Taylor Cr.
Crowne Plaza
Bay of Plenty Beach
Botanic Gardens
DLI Hall
R102
Molyneux Rd
Amphitheatre
INDIAN OCEAN
M 15
Ascot Str.
NMR Av.
Prince Alfred Str.
Hoy Park Sports Ground
Playfair Rd
Lower Marine Parade Walkway
A
ML Sultan Technikon
Kingsmead Cricket Ground
North Beach
Darby Rd
Dartnell Cr.
Louis La.
Old Fort Pl.
Stanger Str.
SABC
Old Fort Rd
Durban Girls Sch
Victor
Centenary Rd
Carlisle Str.
Cross Str.
M 15
Albert Rd
Old Fort 1842 and Warrior's Gate
M 4
City Lodge
Gresham Pl.
Marine Par.
St Aidan's
Winterton Walk
Maud
Beatrice
Lorne Str.
Grey Str.
Baumann Pl.
Boscombe Pl.
Dairy Beach
M 15
Old Fort Rd
Durnford Rd
Prior Rd
Wyatt Rd
M 4
Brickhill Rd
Victoria Park
The Palace
Fire Station
Fountain La.
North La.
Mansfield Rd
Bus Depot
Ordnance Rd
Marine Parade
R102
Morrison Rd
Karos Edward
M 4
M 13
Alice Rd
Leopold Rd
Soldiers Way
Exhibition Centre
West La.
John Milne Rd
Fun World: Amusement Park
Av.
Anjuman Islam Sch.
Walnut Rd
Hunter Rd
Balmoral
Wedge Beach
M 4
Prince Edward Str.
Central Park
Convention Centre
East La.
N3
Russell Str.
Cross Str.
Grey Str.
Milne Rd
Sea World: Aquarium & Dolphinarium
Canongate Rd
Brook Str.
Victoria
Str.
Field Rd
Aliwal Str.
Flea Market
South La.
Prince Alfred Str.
Sea View Str.
Beach
Wills Rd
Douglas La.
Acorn Rd
Milton Rd
Lutman Rd
Syringa Rd
Victoria Str.
Fish Market
The Workshop
Pine Str.
Palmer
M 4
Market Rd
Russell Str.
Albert Rd
Commercial Rd
Kearsney Farewell
Gillespie Str.
Tropicana
Warwick
Queen Str.
Cathedral Rd
Natural Science Museum
Palmer Str.
West Str.
Tyzack
Holiday Inn Garden Court South Beach
West Str. Cemetery
Durban Art Gallery
Union Str.
Peck Rd
Four Seasons
Smith Str.
Marine Par.
Paddling Pools
Commercial Rd
West Str.
King Str.
Dick Str.
Mazeppa Str.
Little Top
South Beach
Lancers Rd
University Av.
Pine Str.
Natal Playhouse Theatre
Roy
Gull
Mulberry
Keeler
Point Rd
The Wheel
Berea Road
Davis
City Hall
Timber
Fisher
Shamrock La.
Trampolines
Richards
Saville La.
Jonsson La.
Kitchener Str.
Creek
Theatre La.
West Str.
Smith Str.
Mona Rd
Mills La.
Cato Str.
Gilligan
Pickering
Rochester Str.
Berea Rd
R102
West
Gardiner Str.
Beach Wlk
Acutt Str.
Aliwal Str.
Albany Gro
Stanger Str.
Convent La.
Smith Str.
Broad
Baker Str.
Beach Grove
Salmon Grove
Masonic Grove
Hermitage Str.
Fenton Rd
Parry Rd
Winder Rd
Rutherford Str.
Addington Sch.
B
Gale Rd
Brook Str.
Alexandra Rd
Bay Ter.
Ocean Wlk
Addington Beach
College La.
Victoria Emb.
Russell Str.
St George's Str.
Maritime Museum
M 11
Park Str.
Shearer Rd
Moore Rd
McArthur Str.
Masonic Rd
Addington
St Andrew's Str.
Supreme Court
Point Yacht Club
Sydney Rd
M 4
Settlers Old House Museum
Prince
Crieff Pl.
Erskine Ter.
Williams Rd
Victoria Emb.
Royal Natal Yacht Club
Point Rd
Hospital Way
Southern Fwy
Albert Park
Shepstone Str.
Maydon Rd
Natal Bay
South Beach Av.

PIETERMARITZBURG and ULUNDI

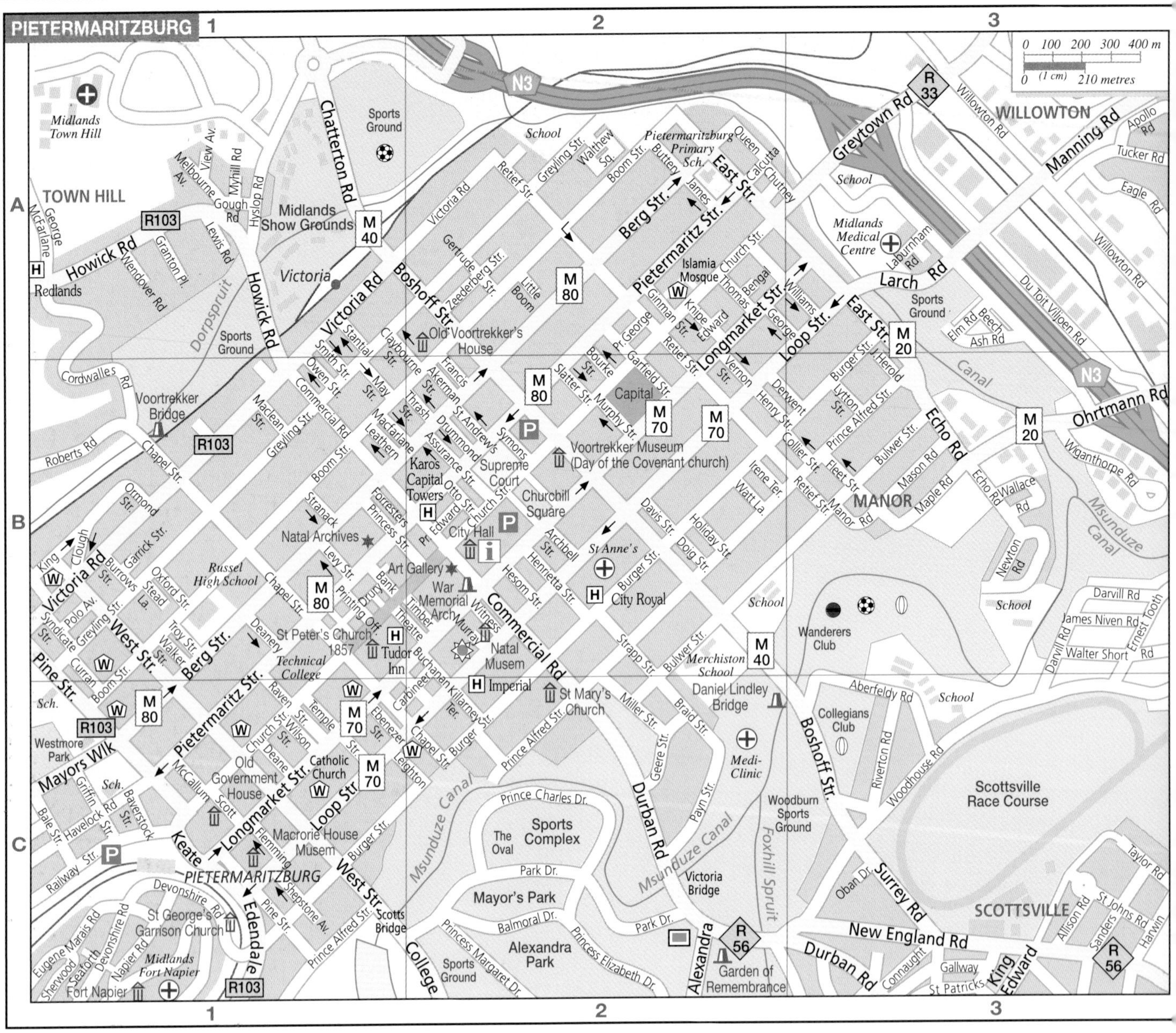

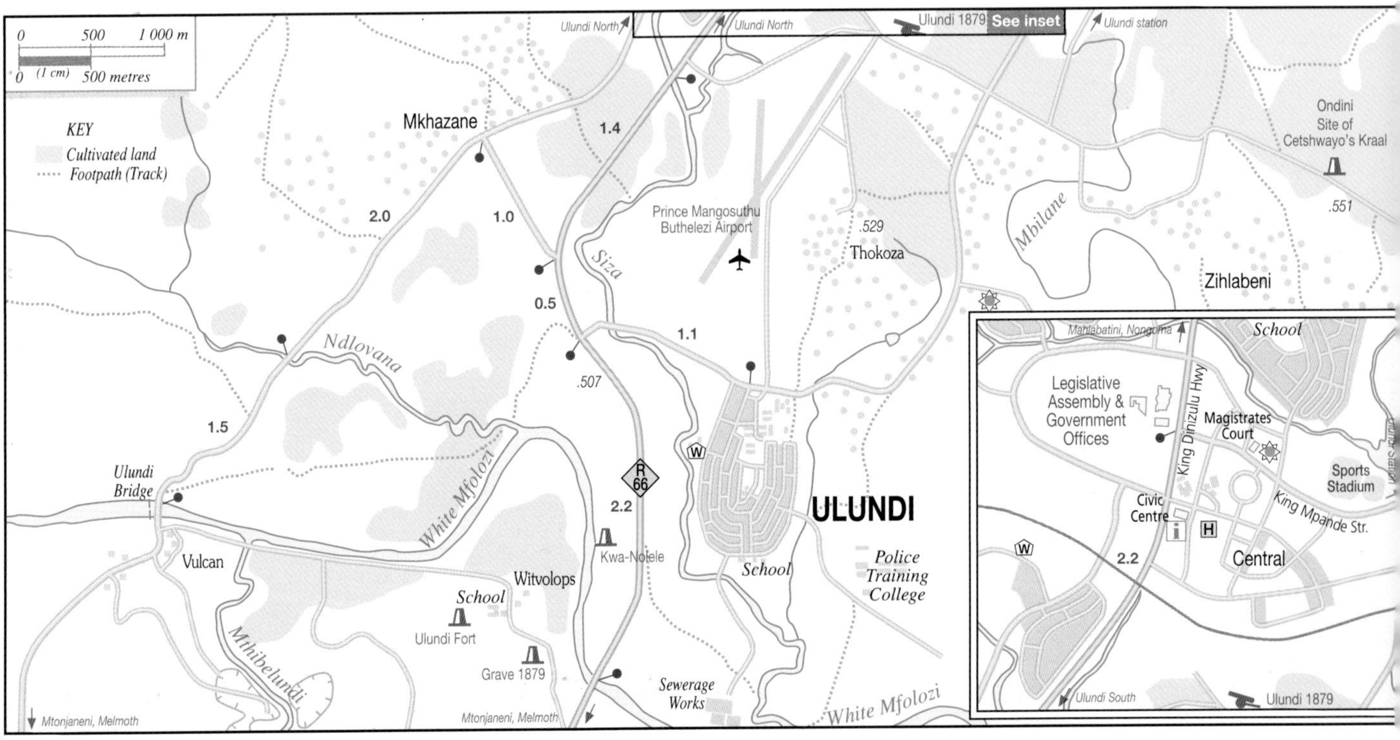

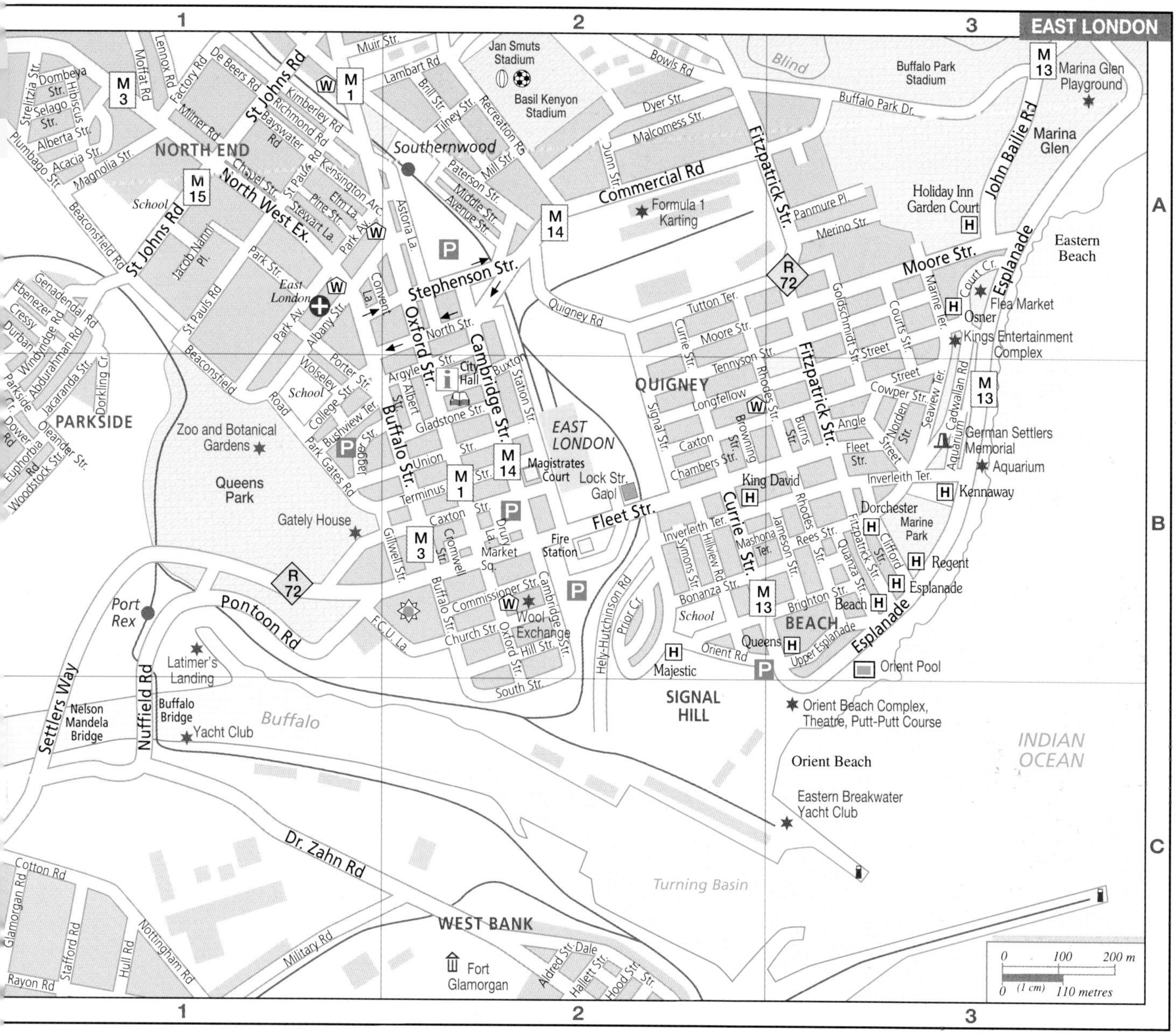
EAST LONDON
NORTH END
PARKSIDE
Queens Park
Zoo and Botanical Gardens
Gately House
Southernwood
Jan Smuts Stadium
Basil Kenyon Stadium
Buffalo Park Stadium
Marina Glen Playground
Marina Glen
Holiday Inn Garden Court
Eastern Beach
Formula 1 Karting
Commercial Rd
Fitzpatrick Str.
Moore Str.
Esplanade
Flea Market
Osner
Kings Entertainment Complex
QUIGNEY
German Settlers Memorial
Aquarium
Kennaway
Dorchester
Marine Park
Regent
Esplanade
Beach
BEACH
Queens
Majestic
Orient Pool
SIGNAL HILL
Orient Beach Complex, Theatre, Putt-Putt Course
Orient Beach
Eastern Breakwater Yacht Club
INDIAN OCEAN
Turning Basin
WEST BANK
Fort Glamorgan
Dr. Zahn Rd
Military Rd
Buffalo
Yacht Club
Buffalo Bridge
Nelson Mandela Bridge
Latimer's Landing
Port Rex
Pontoon Rd
Settlers Way
Nuffield Rd
EAST LONDON
Magistrates Court
Lock Str. Gaol
Fire Station
Fleet Str.
Market Sq.
Wool Exchange
City Hall
Oxford Str.
Cambridge Str.
Buffalo Str.
Stephenson Str.
St Johns Rd
North West Ex.
East London
School
Blind
0 100 200 m
0 (1 cm) 110 metres

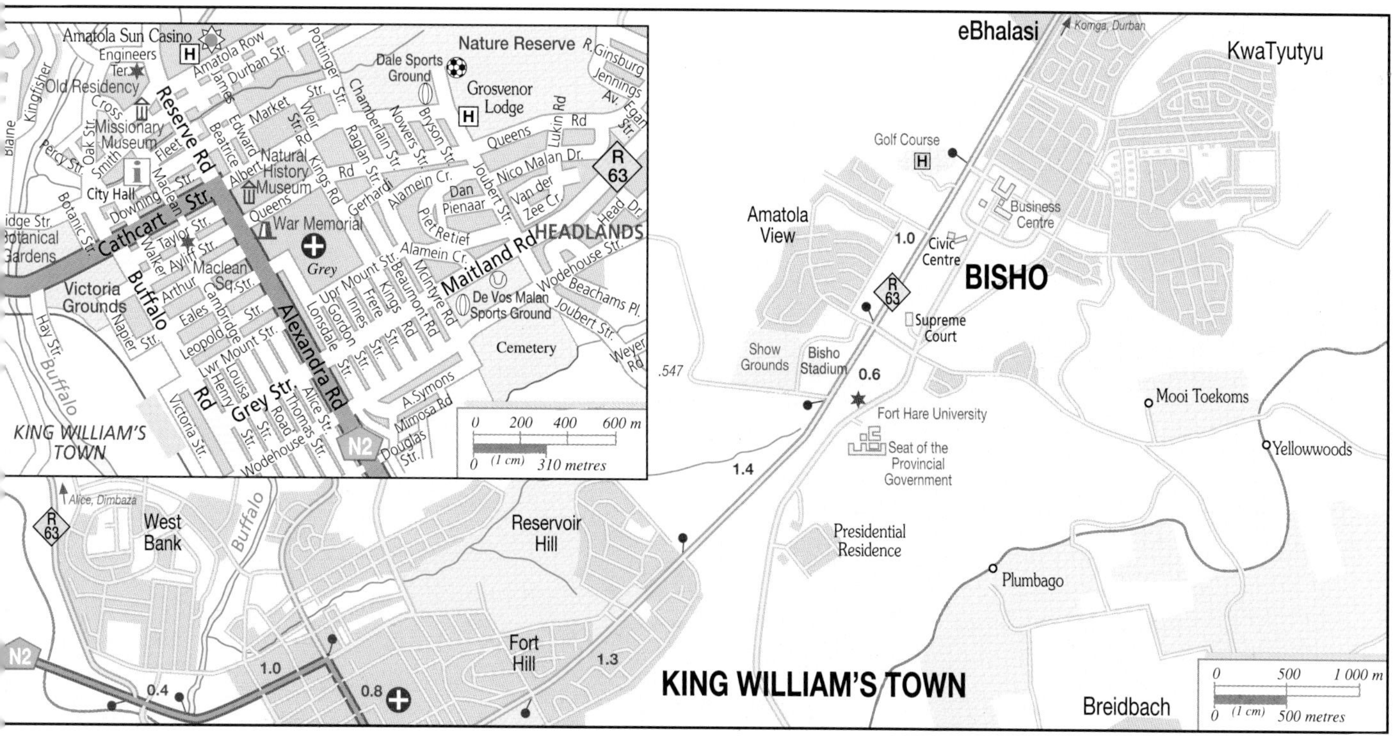
Amatola Sun Casino
Engineers Ter.
Old Residency
Missionary Museum
City Hall
Natural History Museum
War Memorial
Grey
Nature Reserve
Dale Sports Ground
Grosvenor Lodge
Botanical Gardens
Victoria Grounds
Reserve Rd
Cathcart Str.
Alexandra Rd
Maitland Rd
HEADLANDS
De Vos Malan Sports Ground
Cemetery
Buffalo
KING WILLIAM'S TOWN
0 200 400 600 m
0 (1 cm) 310 metres
eBhalasi
Komga, Durban
KwaTyutyu
Golf Course
Business Centre
Amatola View
Civic Centre
BISHO
Supreme Court
Show Grounds
Bisho Stadium
Fort Hare University
Seat of the Provincial Government
Mooi Toekoms
Yellowwoods
Presidential Residence
Plumbago
Alice, Dimbaza
West Bank
Reservoir Hill
Fort Hill
KING WILLIAM'S TOWN
Breidbach
0 500 1 000 m
0 (1 cm) 500 metres

PORT ELIZABETH and ENVIRONS

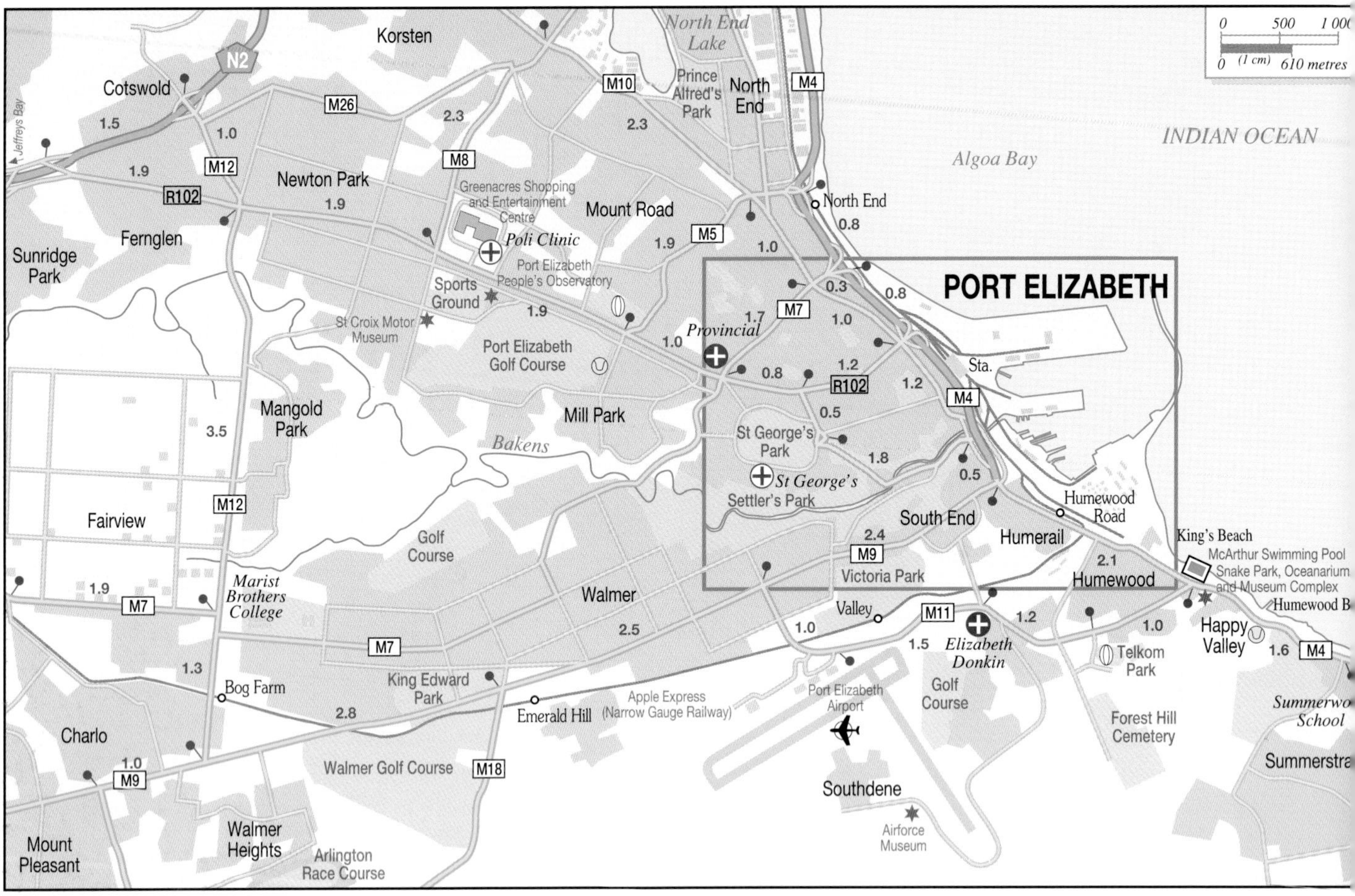

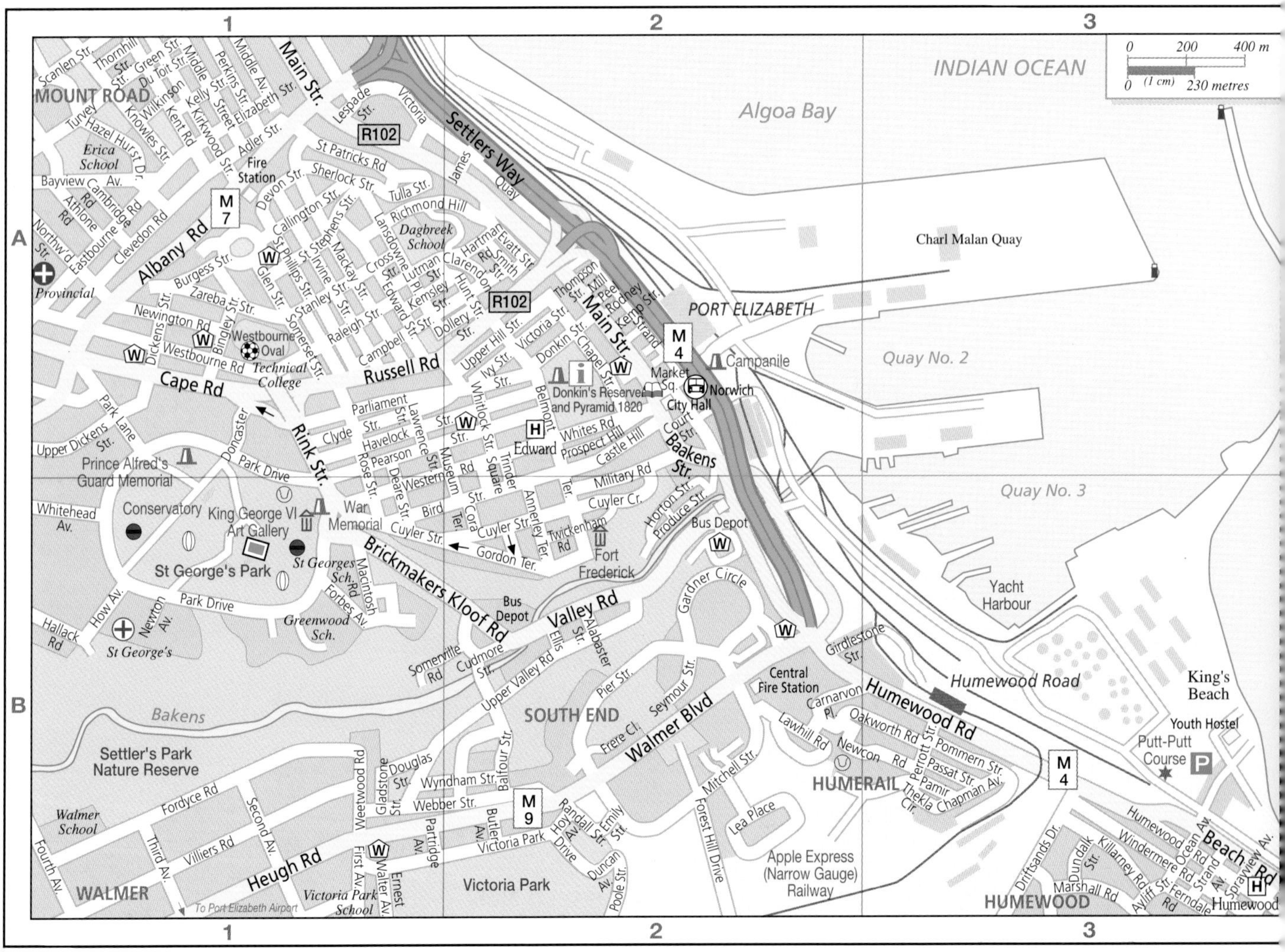

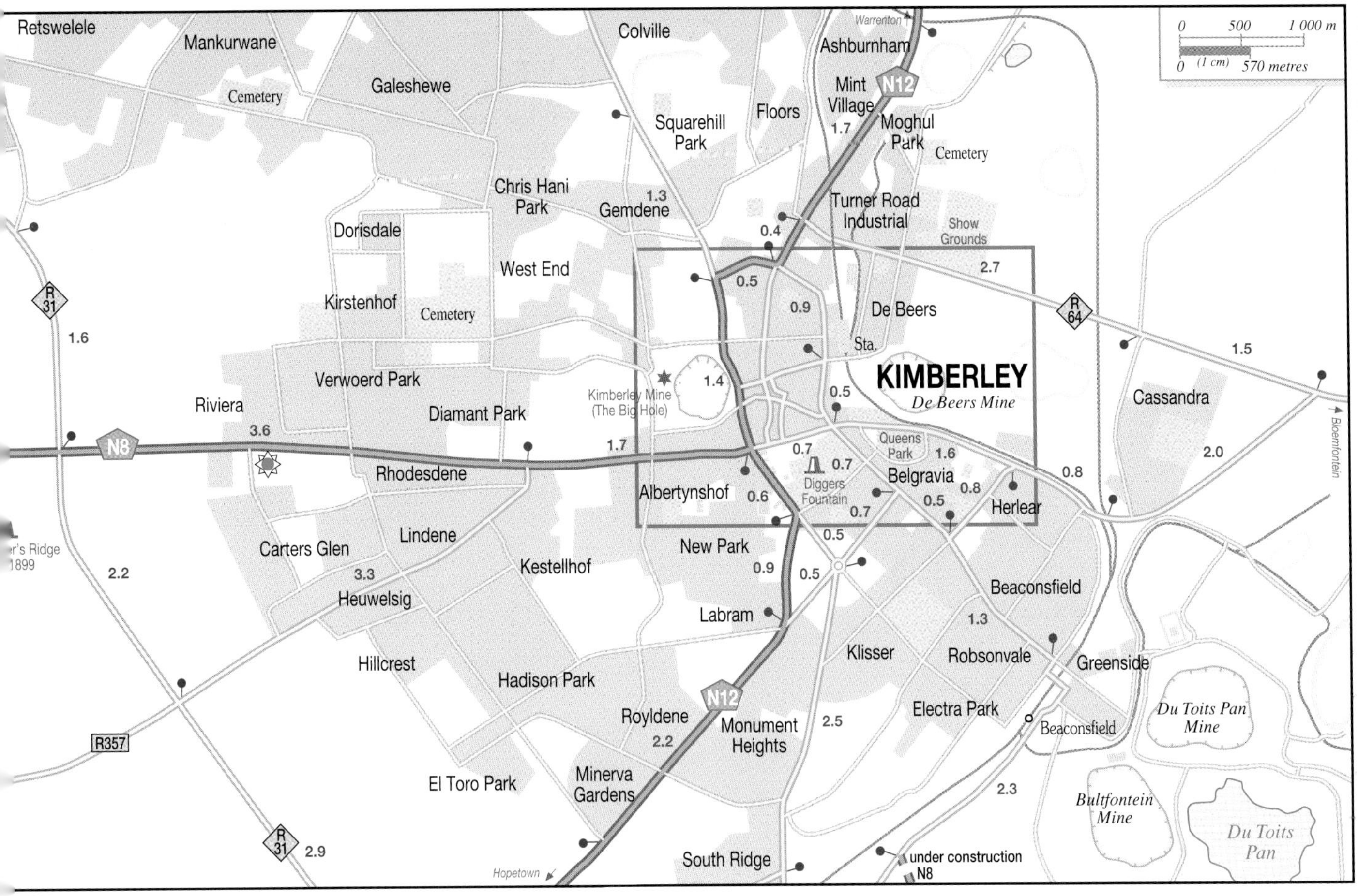
0 500 1 000 m
0 (1 cm) 570 metres
Retswelele
Mankurwane
Galeshewe
Cemetery
Colville
Warrenton
Ashburnham
Mint Village
N12
Moghul Park
Cemetery
Squarehill Park
Floors
Chris Hani Park
Gemdene
Dorisdale
West End
Turner Road Industrial
Show Grounds
Kirstenhof
Cemetery
De Beers
Sta.
R 31
R 64
Verwoerd Park
KIMBERLEY
De Beers Mine
Riviera
Diamant Park
Kimberley Mine (The Big Hole)
Cassandra
Bloemfontein
N8
Rhodesdene
Queens Park
Belgravia
Diggers Fountain
Albertynshof
Herlear
Carters Glen
Lindene
Kestellhof
New Park
Heuwelsig
Beaconsfield
Labram
Hillcrest
Klisser
Robsonvale
Greenside
Hadison Park
Royldene
Monument Heights
Electra Park
Beaconsfield
Du Toits Pan Mine
R357
El Toro Park
Minerva Gardens
Bultfontein Mine
Du Toits Pan
South Ridge
Hopetown
under construction N8
r's Ridge 1899

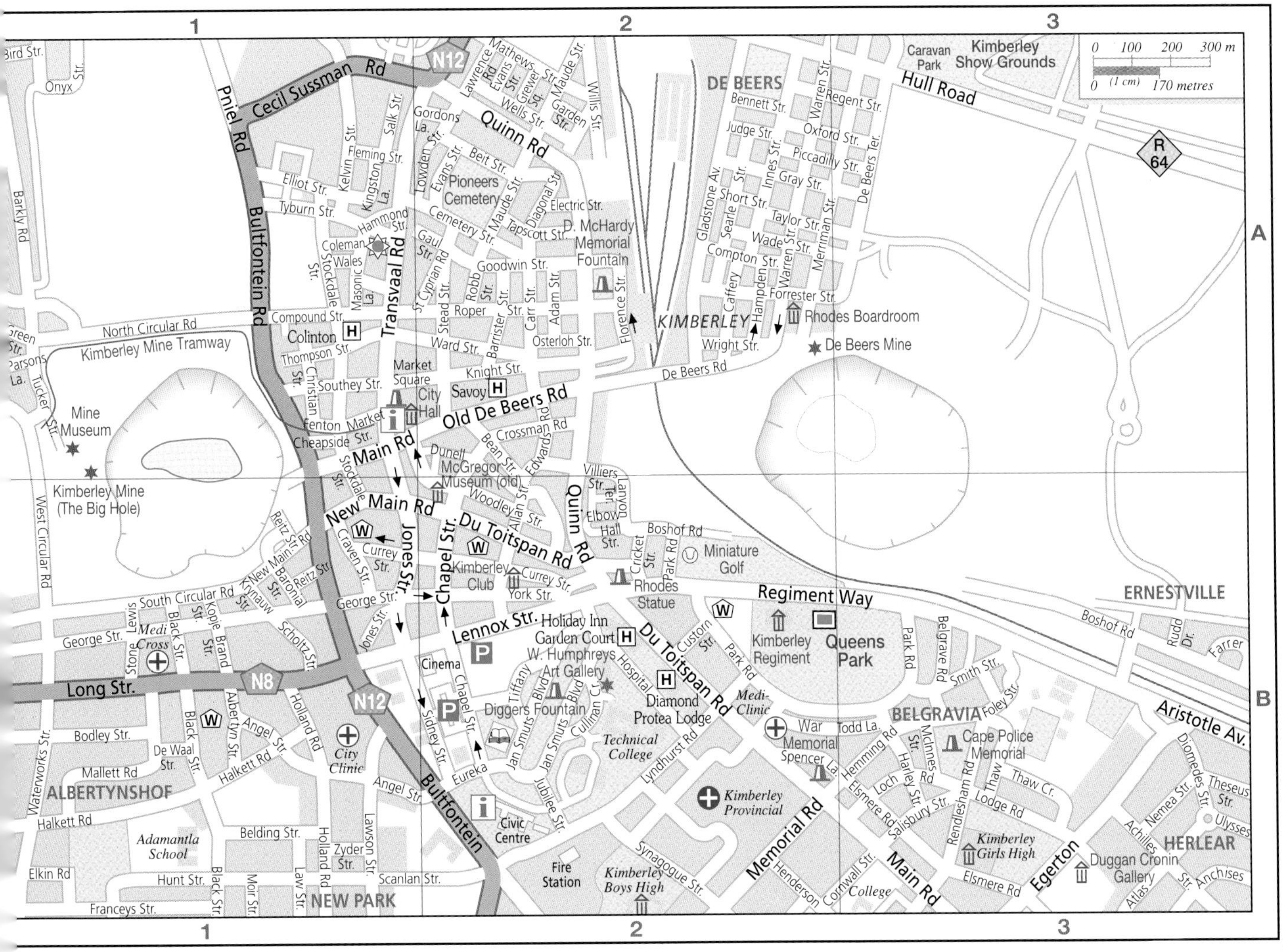
1 2 3
A B
0 100 200 300 m
0 (1 cm) 170 metres
Caravan Park
Kimberley Show Grounds
Hull Road
R 64
DE BEERS
Cecil Sussman Rd
N12
Pniel Rd
Quinn Rd
Pioneers Cemetery
D. McHardy Memorial Fountain
Bultfontein Rd
Transvaal Rd
North Circular Rd
Kimberley Mine Tramway
Colinton
KIMBERLEY
Rhodes Boardroom
De Beers Mine
De Beers Rd
Market Square
City Hall
Savoy
Old De Beers Rd
Mine Museum
Kimberley Mine (The Big Hole)
Main Rd
New Main Rd
McGregor Museum (old)
Du Toitspan Rd
Jones Str.
Chapel Str.
Kimberley Club
Miniature Golf
Rhodes Statue
Regiment Way
Kimberley Regiment
Queens Park
ERNESTVILLE
Holiday Inn Garden Court
Cinema
W. Humphreys Art Gallery
Diggers Fountain
Diamond Protea Lodge
Medi-Clinic
Technical College
War Memorial
BELGRAVIA
Cape Police Memorial
Aristotle Av.
Long Str.
N8
Medi Cross
City Clinic
ALBERTYNSHOF
Adamantia School
Civic Centre
Fire Station
Kimberley Boys High
Kimberley Provincial
Memorial Rd
Main Rd
Kimberley Girls High
Duggan Cronin Gallery
HERLEAR
NEW PARK
Egerton Rd

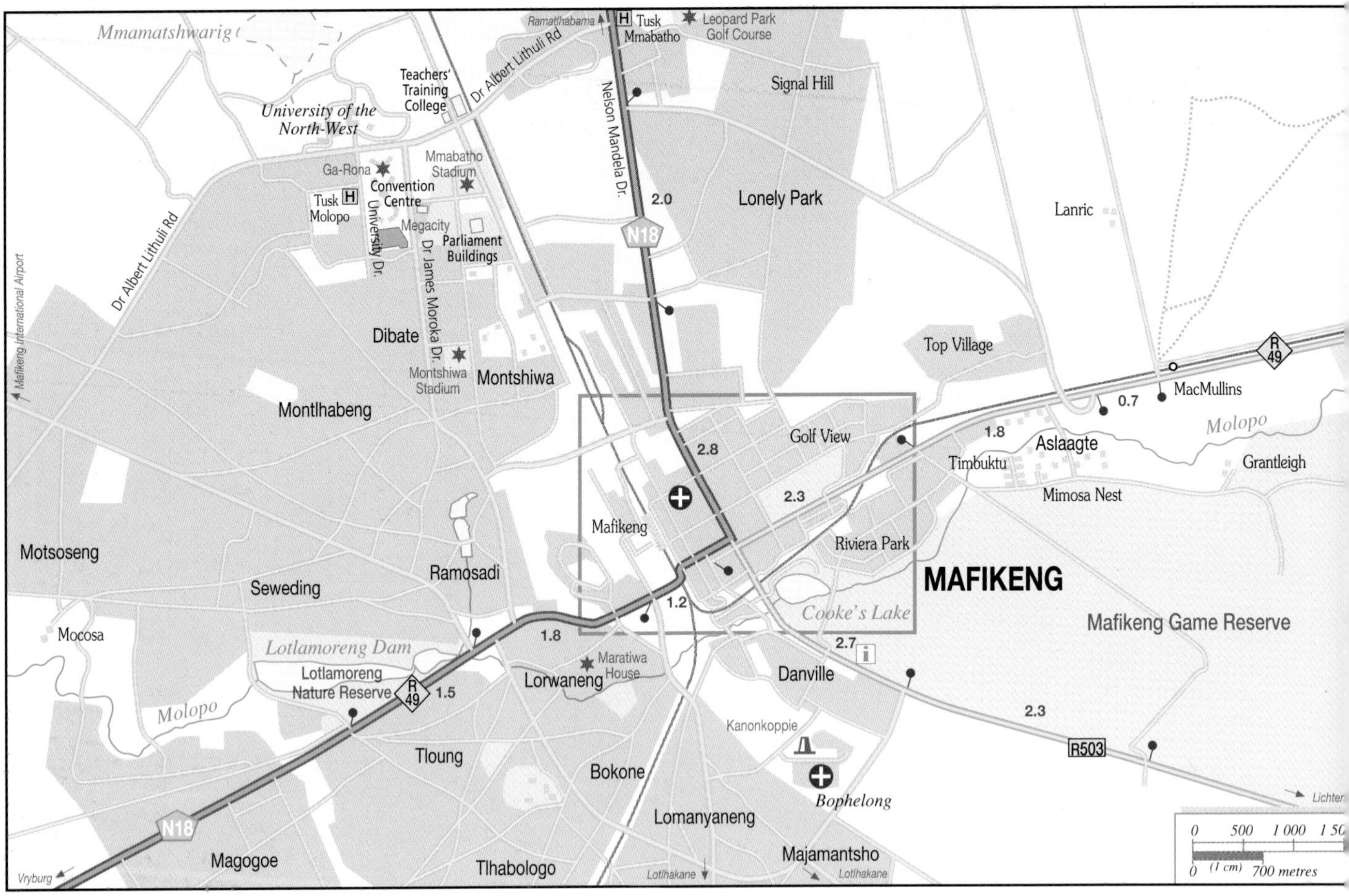
Mmamatshwarig
Ramatlhabama
Tusk Mmabatho
Leopard Park Golf Course
Teachers' Training College
Dr Albert Lithuli Rd
University of the North-West
Signal Hill
Nelson Mandela Dr.
Ga-Rona
Convention Centre
Mmabatho Stadium
Tusk Molopo
University Dr.
Megacity
Parliament Buildings
Dr James Moroka Dr.
Lonely Park
Lanric
Dr Albert Lithuli Rd
Mafikeng International Airport
Dibate
Montshiwa Stadium
Montshiwa
Top Village
Montlhabeng
MacMullins
0.7
1.8
Aslaagte
Molopo
Grantleigh
Golf View
Timbuktu
Mimosa Nest
2.8
2.3
2.0
Mafikeng
Riviera Park
Motsoseng
Seweding
Ramosadi
MAFIKENG
1.2
Cooke's Lake
Mafikeng Game Reserve
Mocosa
1.8
Lotlamoreng Dam
Maratiwa House
2.7
Lotlamoreng Nature Reserve
1.5
Lorwaneng
Danville
Molopo
Kanonkoppie
2.3
R503
Tloung
Bokone
Bophelong
Lomanyaneng
Lichtenburg
0 500 1 000 1 500
0 (1 cm) 700 metres
Magogoe
Tlhabologo
Majamantsho
Vryburg
Lotlhakane
Lotlhakane

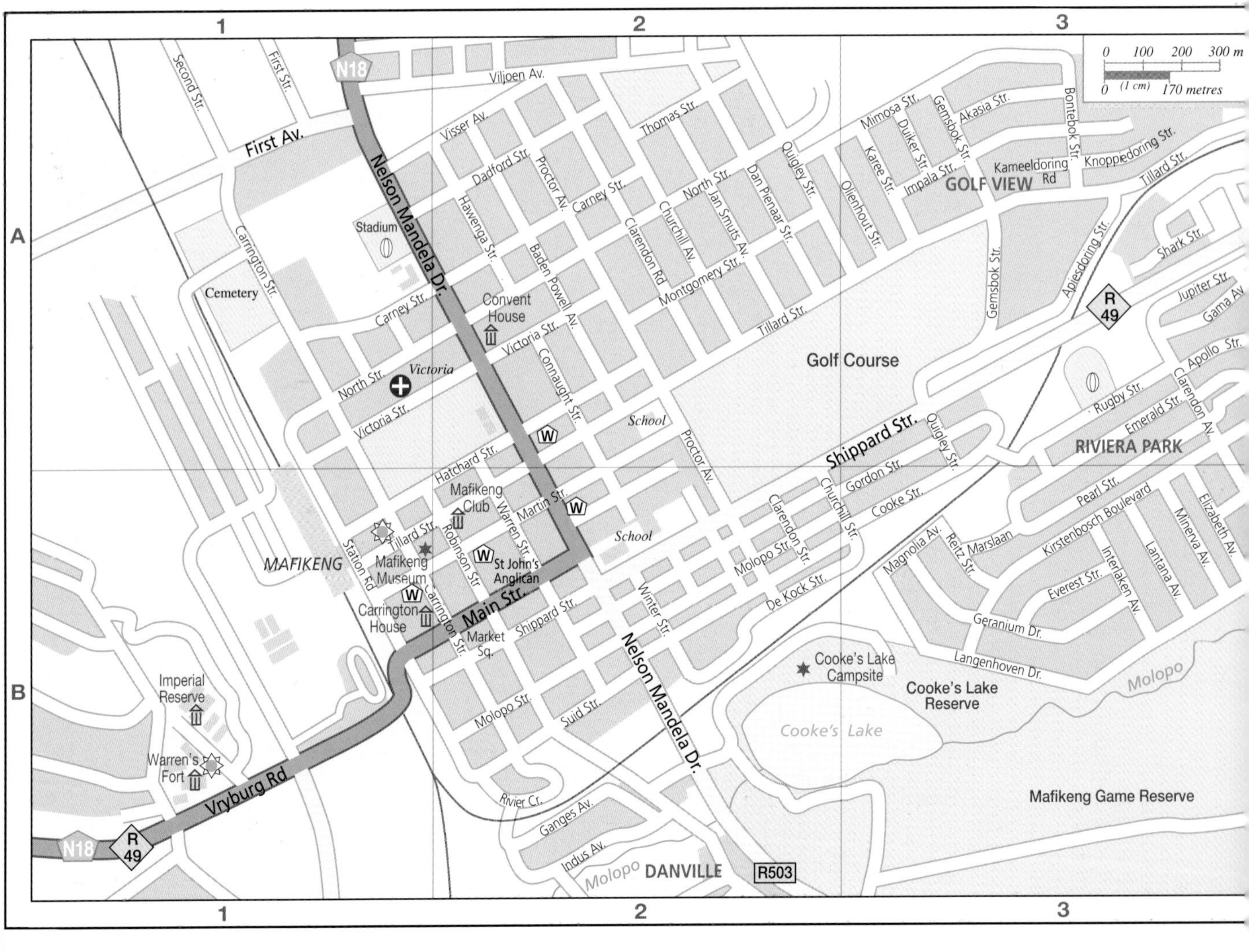
1
2
3
A
B
0 100 200 300 m
0 (1 cm) 170 metres
Second Str.
First Str.
N18
Viljoen Av.
First Av.
Visser Av.
Thomas Str.
Mimosa Str.
Gemsbok Str.
Akasia Str.
Bontebok Str.
Duiker Str.
Dadford Str.
Karee Str.
Impala Str.
Kameeldoring Rd
Knoppiedoring Str.
Tillard Str.
GOLF VIEW
Nelson Mandela Dr.
Proctor Av.
Carney Str.
North Str.
Jan Smuts Av.
Dan Pienaar Str.
Quigley Str.
Olienhout Str.
Hawenga Str.
Clarendon Rd
Churchill Av.
Stadium
Carrington Str.
Baden Powell Av.
Montgomery Str.
Gemsbok Str.
Apiesdoring Str.
Shark Str.
Cemetery
Convent House
Carney Str.
Tillard Str.
Jupiter Str.
Gama Av.
Victoria Str.
Connaught Str.
Golf Course
Apollo Str.
North Str.
Victoria
Victoria Str.
Rugby Str.
Clarendon Av.
Emerald Str.
School
Proctor Av.
Shippard Str.
Quigley Str.
RIVIERA PARK
Hatchard Str.
Gordon Str.
Mafikeng Club
Martin Str.
Warren Str.
Cooke Str.
Pearl Str.
Tillard Str.
Robinson Str.
School
Clarendon Str.
Churchill Str.
Kirstenbosch Boulevard
MAFIKENG
Station Rd
Mafikeng Museum
St John's Anglican
Molopo Str.
Magnolia Av.
Reitz Str.
Marslaan
Lantana Av.
Minerva Av.
Elizabeth Av.
Carrington Str.
Main Str.
De Kock Str.
Everest Str.
Interlaken Av.
Carrington House
Shippard Str.
Winter Str.
Market Sq.
Geranium Dr.
Langenhoven Dr.
Imperial Reserve
Cooke's Lake Campsite
Cooke's Lake Reserve
Molopo
Molopo Str.
Suid Str.
Nelson Mandela Dr.
Cooke's Lake
Warren's Fort
Vryburg Rd
Mafikeng Game Reserve
Rivier Cr.
Ganges Av.
N18
R 49
Indus Av.
Molopo
DANVILLE
R503

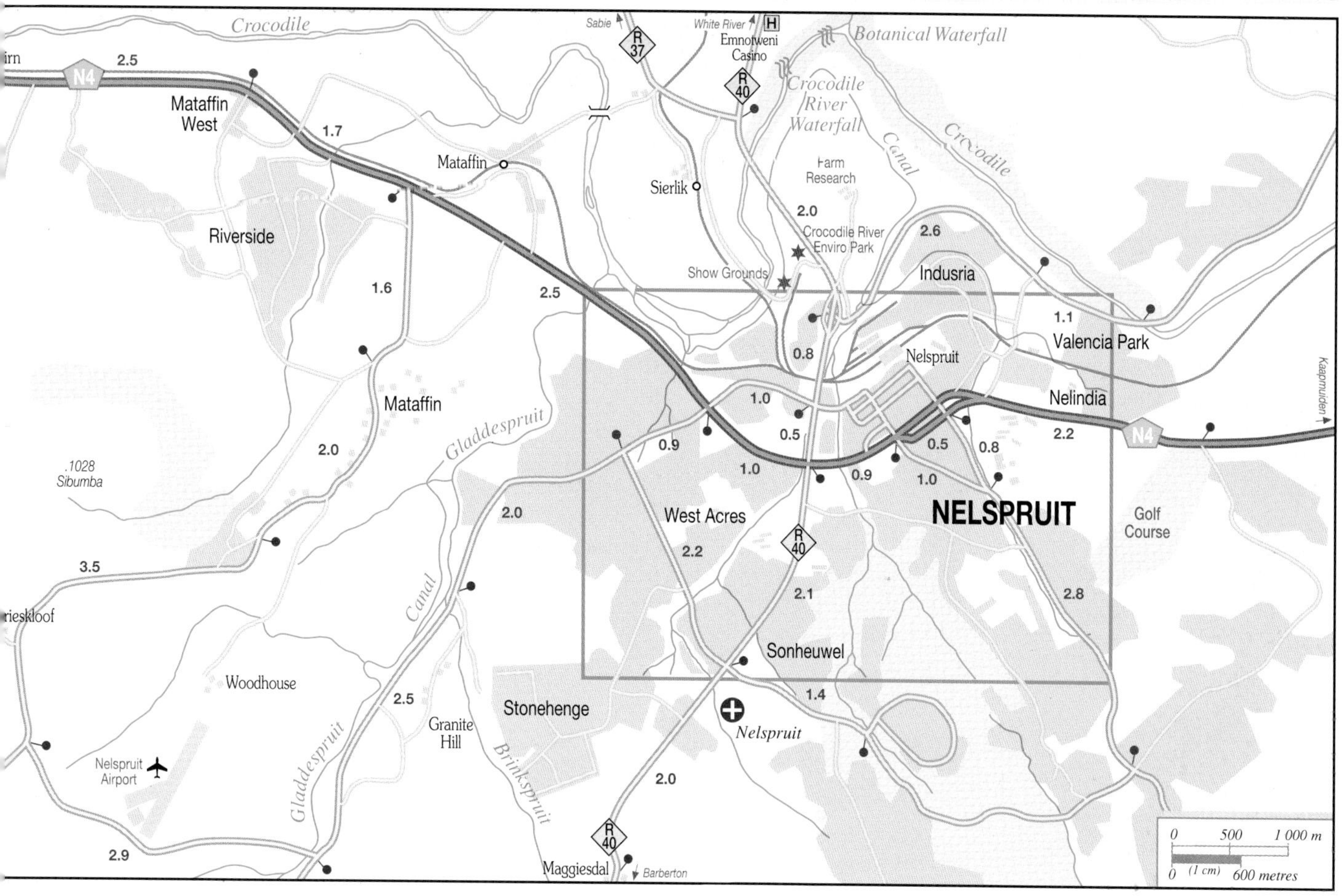
Crocodile
N4
2.5
Mataffin West
1.7
Mataffin
Riverside
1.6
2.5
Sabie
R 37
White River
Emnotweni Casino
R 40
Botanical Waterfall
Crocodile River Waterfall
Canal
Crocodile
Sierlik
Farm Research
2.0
Crocodile River Enviro Park
Show Grounds
2.6
Indusria
1.1
Valencia Park
Nelspruit
Nelindia
Kaapmuiden
2.2
0.8
1.0
0.5
0.9
1.0
0.9
0.5
0.8
1.0
Mataffin
2.0
1028 Sibumba
Gladdespruit
2.0
West Acres
2.2
NELSPRUIT
Golf Course
3.5
Canal
2.1
2.8
Sonheuwel
Woodhouse
2.5
Granite Hill
Stonehenge
1.4
Nelspruit
Nelspruit Airport
Gladdespruit
Brinkspruit
2.0
2.9
Maggiesdal
Barberton
0
500
1 000 m
(1 cm)
600 metres

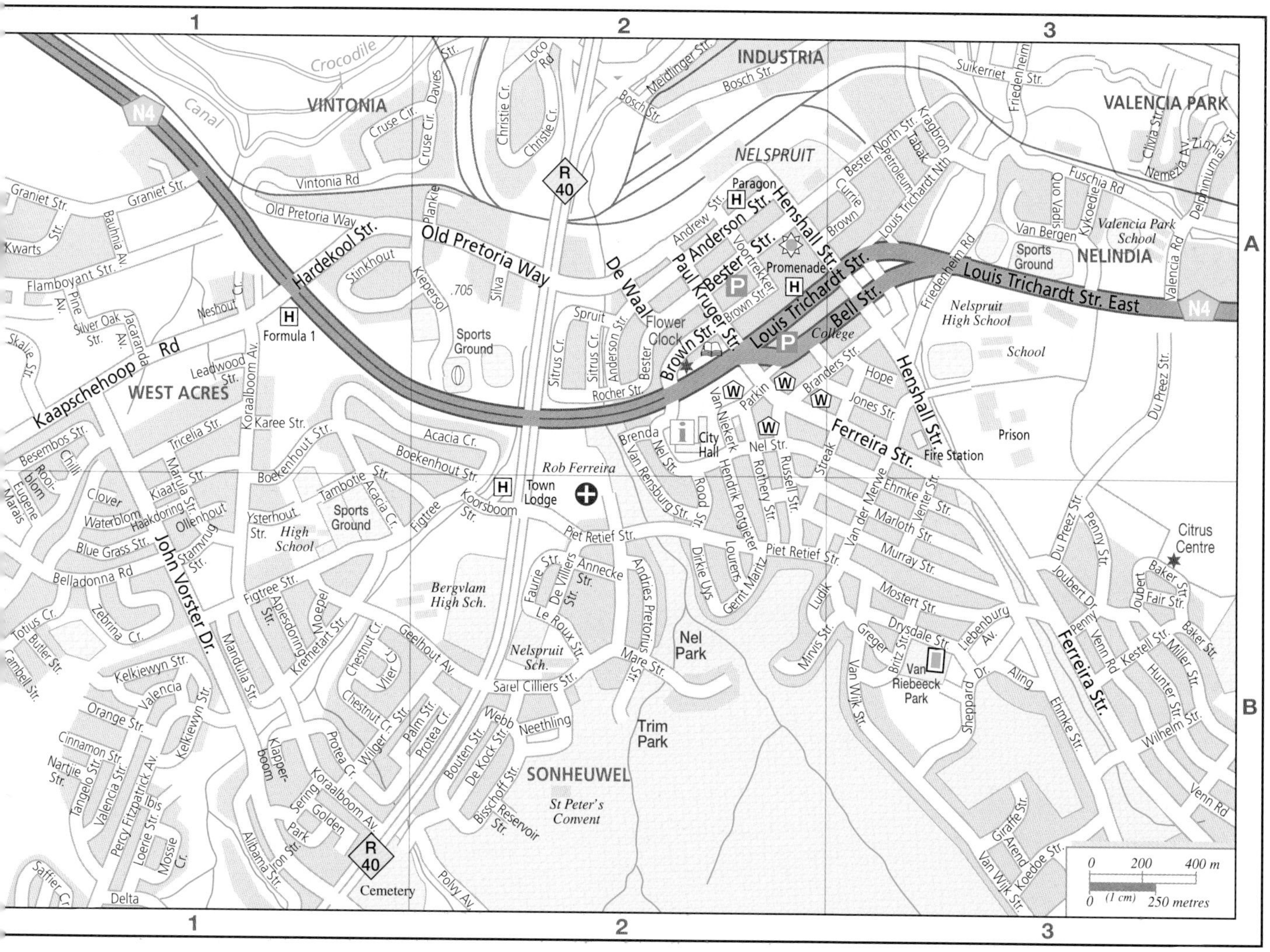
1
2
3
Crocodile
Canal
N4
VINTONIA
INDUSTRIA
Bosch Str.
Meidlinger Str.
Suikerriet Str.
Friedenheim
VALENCIA PARK
Cruse Cir.
Cruse Cir.
Davies
Christie Cr.
Christie Cr.
Loco Rd
R 40
NELSPRUIT
Paragon
Bester North Str.
Kraaibron
Tabak
Petroleum
Louis Trichardt Nth
Fuschia Rd
Quo Vadis
Kykoedie
Valencia Park School
Clivia Str.
Zinnia Str.
Nemezia Av.
Delphinium Str.
Vintonia Rd
Graniet Str.
Graniet Str.
Old Pretoria Way
Kwarts
Bauhinia Av.
Hardekool Str.
Old Pretoria Way
Plankie
De Waal
Andrew Str.
Anderson Str.
Henshall Str.
Currie
Brown
Van Bergen
Sports Ground
NELINDIA
A
Flamboyant Str.
Pine Av.
Stinkhout
Kiepersol
Silva
705
Paul Kruger Str.
Bester Str.
Voortrekker
Promenade
Friedenheim Rd
Louis Trichardt Str. East
Valencia Rd
N4
Silver Oak Str.
Jacaranda Av.
Neshout Cr.
Formula 1
Spruit
Flower Clock
Brown Str.
Louis Trichardt Str.
Bell Str.
College
Nelspruit High School
School
Skalie Str.
Kaapschehoop Rd
Leadwood Str.
Koraalboom Av.
Sports Ground
Sitrus Cr.
Sitrus Cr.
Anderson Str.
Bester
Rocher Str.
Van Niekerk
Parkin
Branders Str.
Hope
Henshall Str.
Du Preez Str.
WEST ACRES
Karee Str.
Besembos Str.
Chilli
Tricelia Str.
Boekenhout Str.
Acacia Cr.
Brenda
City Hall
Nel Str.
Jones Str.
Ferreira Str.
Fire Station
Prison
Rooiblom
Eugene Marais
Marula Str.
Kiaat Str.
Boekenhout Str.
Tambotie Str.
Acacia Cr.
Figtree
Koorsboom Str.
Rob Ferreira
Town Lodge
Van Rensburg Str.
Rood Str.
Hendrik Potgieter
Rothery Str.
Russell Str.
Streak
Ehmke Str.
Venter Str.
Marloth Str.
Du Preez Str.
Penny Str.
Citrus Centre
Clover
Waterblom
Haakdoring Str.
Ollenhout
Ysterhout Str.
Sports Ground
High School
Piet Retief Str.
Piet Retief Str.
Van der Merwe
Murray Str.
Blue Grass Str.
John Vorster Dr.
Stamvrug Str.
Faurie Str.
De Villiers Str.
Annecke Str.
Andries Pretorius Str.
Dirkie Uys
Lourens
Gerrit Maritz
Mostert Str.
Joubert Dr.
Joubert
Baker Str.
Belladonna Rd
Fair Str.
Bergvlam High Sch.
Ludik
Totius Cr.
Zebrina Cr.
Figtree Str.
Apiesdoring Str.
Moepel
Kremetart Str.
Chestnut Cr.
Vlier Cr.
Geelhout Av.
Le Roux Str.
Nel Park
Drysdale Str.
Liebenburg Av.
Penny
Venn Rd
Kestell Str.
Miller Str.
Baker Str.
Butler Str.
Cambell Str.
Kelkiewyn Str.
Mandulia Str.
Nelspruit Sch.
Mare Str.
Mirvis Str.
Greger
Britz Str.
Van Riebeeck Park
Sheppard
Dr.
Aling
Ferreira Str.
Hunter Str.
B
Valencia
Orange Str.
Kelkiewyn Str.
Chestnut Cr.
Wilger Str.
Palm Str.
Protea Cr.
Sarel Cilliers Str.
Webb
Neethling
Trim Park
Van Wijk Str.
Ehmke Str.
Wilhelm Str.
Cinnamon Str.
Nartjie Str.
Tangelo Str.
Valencia Str.
Percy Fitzpatrick Av.
Ibis
Klapperboom
Protea Cr.
Bouten Str.
De Kock Str.
SONHEUWEL
Bischoff Str.
Reservoir Str.
St Peter's Convent
Venn Rd
Loerie Str.
Mossie Cr.
Sering
Koraalboom Av.
Golden
Park
Albama Str.
Iron Str.
R 40
Cemetery
Polvy Av.
Giraffe Str.
Arend
Koedoe Str.
Van Wijk Str.
Saffier Cr.
Delta
0
200
400 m
(1 cm)
250 metres

POLOKWANE (PIETERSBURG) and ENVIRONS

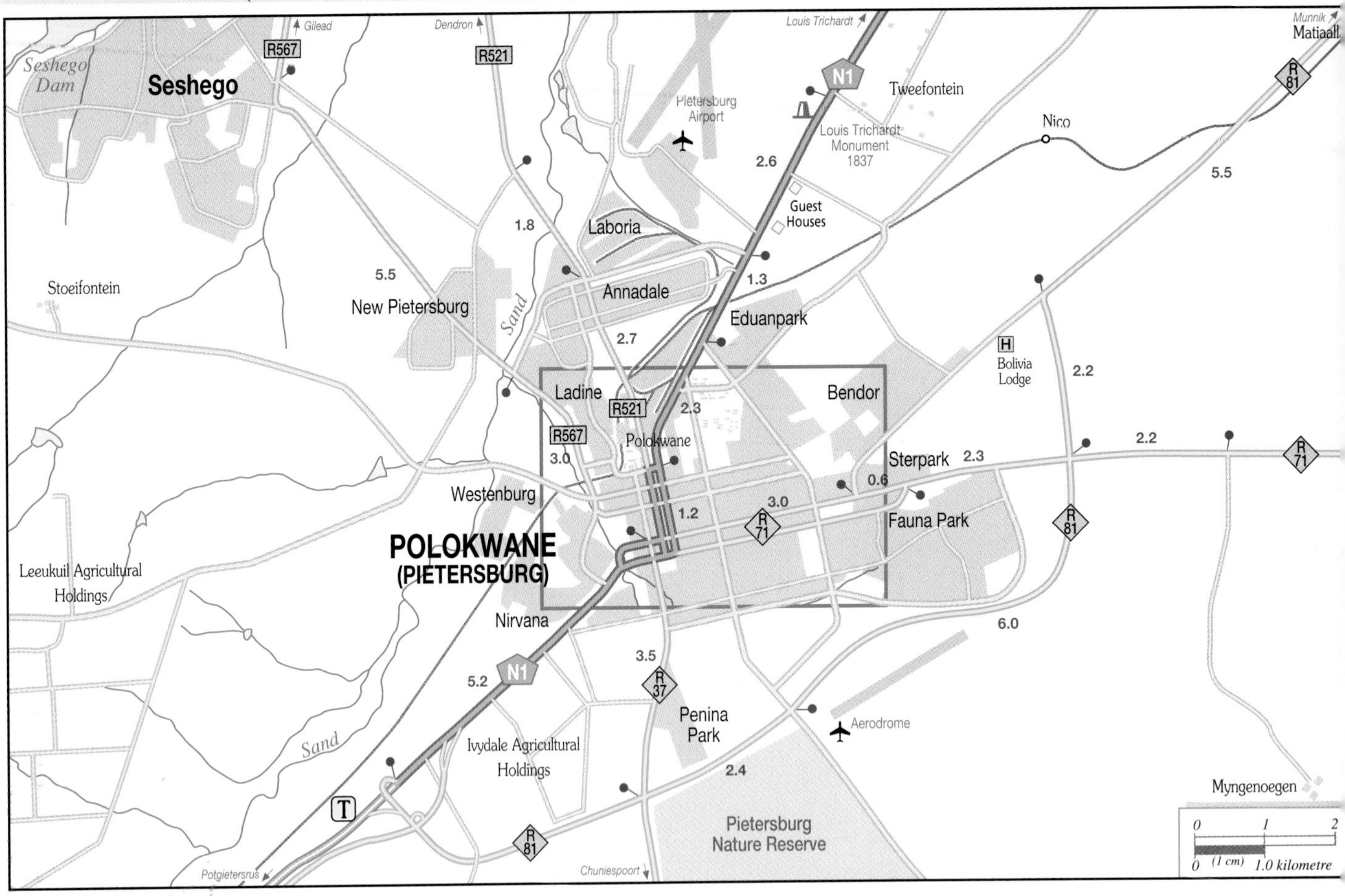

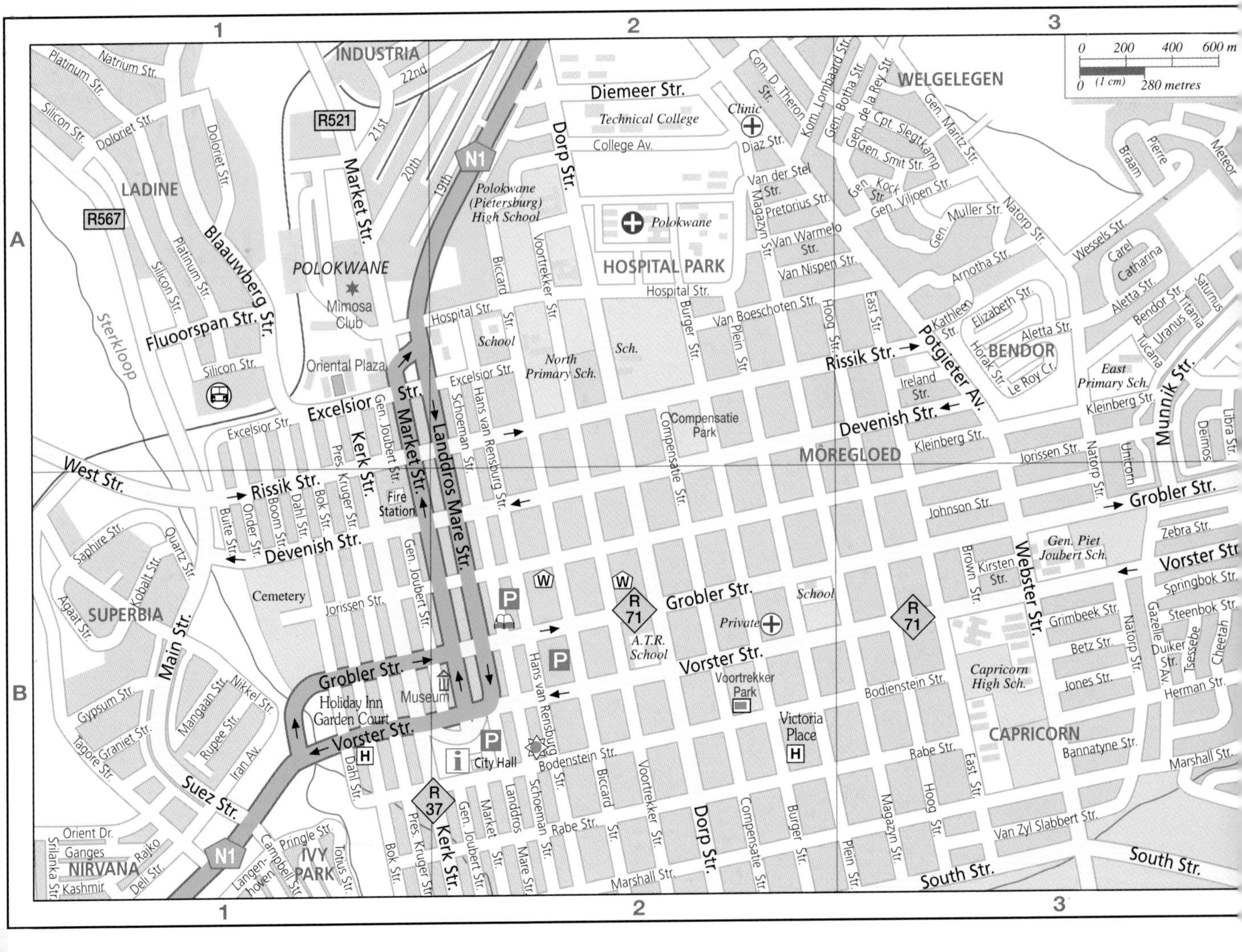

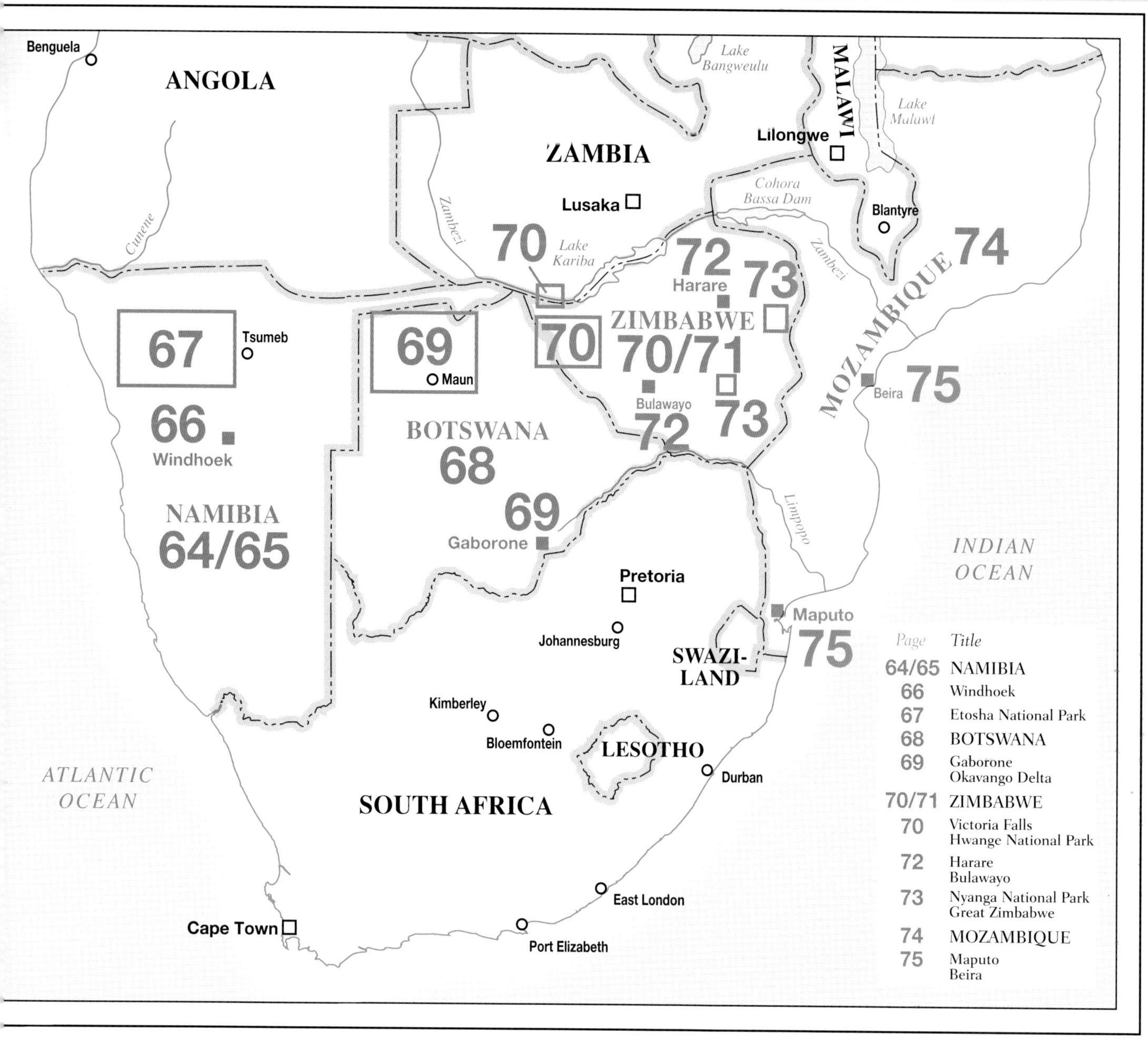

KEY

Motorway		Railway		National airport	
National road		International boundary		Airport and airfield	
Main road		Nature reserve		Chalet/holiday resort	
Secondary road		City with built-up area		Hotel	
Route numbers	B1 C28 D620	City		Border crossing	Vioolsdrif
4x4 track		Major town		Place of interest	Picnic area
Distance in kilometres	6	Secondary town		Monument	
Trail		Large village		Waterfall	
River, marsh and dam		Village		Camping ground	
Information centre		Small village or station		Parking	

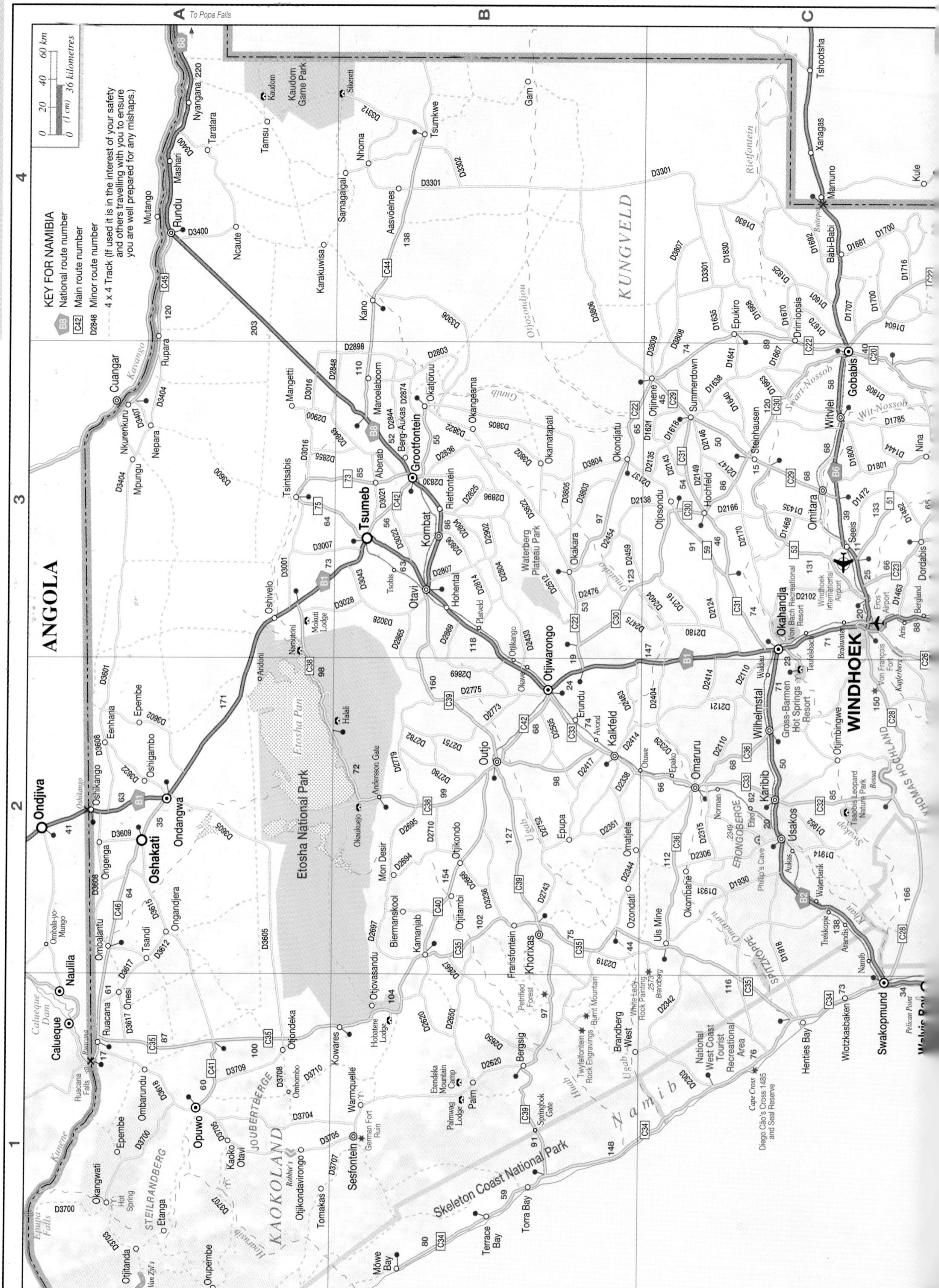
KEY FOR NAMIBIA
B8 National route number
C42 Main route number
D2848 Minor route number
4 x 4 Track (If used it is in the interest of your safety and others travelling with you to ensure you are well prepared for any mishaps.)
0 20 40 60 km
0 (1 cm) 36 kilometres
To Popa Falls
ANGOLA
KUNGVELD
KAOKOLAND
Etosha National Park
Etosha Pan
Skeleton Coast National Park
Namib
Waterberg Plateau Park
Kaudom Game Park
National West Coast Tourist Recreational Area
Diego Cão's Cross 1485 and Seal Reserve
Tsaobis Leopard Nature Park
Von Bach Recreational Resort
Gross-Barmen Hot Springs Resort
Windhoek International Airport
Eros Airport
WINDHOEK
Okahandja
Gobabis
Swakopmund
Tsumeb
Grootfontein
Otjiwarongo
Otavi
Outjo
Khorixas
Omaruru
Karibib
Usakos
Rundu
Ondangwa
Oshakati
Ondjiva
Opuwo
Calueque
Ruacana
Tsumkwe
Henties Bay
Wlotzkasbaken
Torra Bay
Terrace Bay
Möwe Bay
Uis Mine
Kamanjab
Sesfontein
Witvlei
Omitara
Seeis
Wilhelmstal
Kalkfeld
Kombat
Mashari
Nyangana
Cuangar
Rupara
Mangetti
Steinhausen
Epukiro
Otjinene
Summerdown
Hochfeld
Okakarara
Brandberg West
Springbok Gate
Cape Cross
ERONGOBERGE
SPITZKOPPE
JOUBERTBERGE
STEILRANDBERG
KHOMAS HOCHLAND

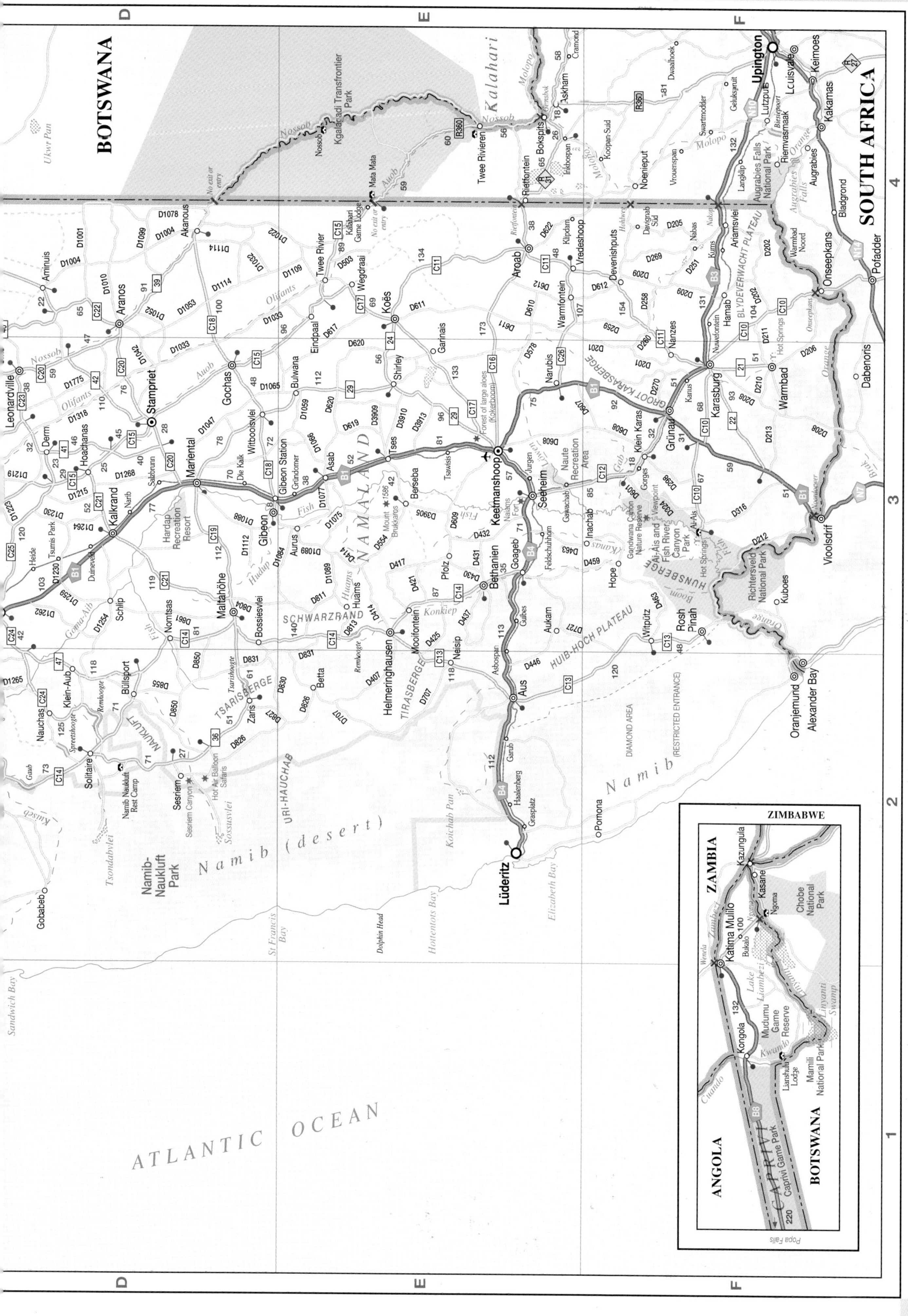
BOTSWANA
SOUTH AFRICA
ATLANTIC OCEAN
Kalahari
Namib (desert)
Kgalagadi Transfrontier Park
Namib-Naukluft Park
Ai-Ais and Fish River Canyon Park
Richtersveld National Park
Augrabies Falls National Park
Gondwana Cañon Nature Reserve
Hardap Recreation Resort
Naute Recreation Area
NAMALAND
SCHWARZRAND
TSARISBERGE
TIRASBERGE
HUNSBERGE
HUIB-HOCH PLATEAU
GROOT KARASBERGE
BLYDEVERWACHT PLATEAU
URI-HAUCHAB
NAUKLUFT
DIAMOND AREA (RESTRICTED ENTRANCE)
Lüderitz
Keetmanshoop
Mariental
Upington
Aus
Bethanien
Seeheim
Karasburg
Grünau
Gibeon
Kalkrand
Stampriet
Gochas
Aranos
Koës
Aroab
Helmeringhausen
Maltahöhe
Rosh Pinah
Oranjemund
Alexander Bay
Noordoewer
Vioolsdrif
Warmbad
Sesriem
Solitaire
Gobabeb
Twee Rivieren
Rietfontein
Keimoes
Kakamas
Pofadder
Onseepkans
Augrabies
Leonardville
Aminuis
Berseba
Tses
Asab
Goageb
Witpütz
Kuboes
Sandwich Bay
Elizabeth Bay
Hottentots Bay
Dolphin Head
St Francis Bay
Pomona
Fish
Orange
Nossob
Auob
Molopo
ZIMBABWE
ZAMBIA
ANGOLA
BOTSWANA
Katima Mulilo
Kongola
Kasane
Kazungula
Chobe National Park
Mudumu Game Reserve
Mamili National Park
Caprivi Game Park
CAPRIVI
Popa Falls
Lake Liambezi
Linyanti Swamp

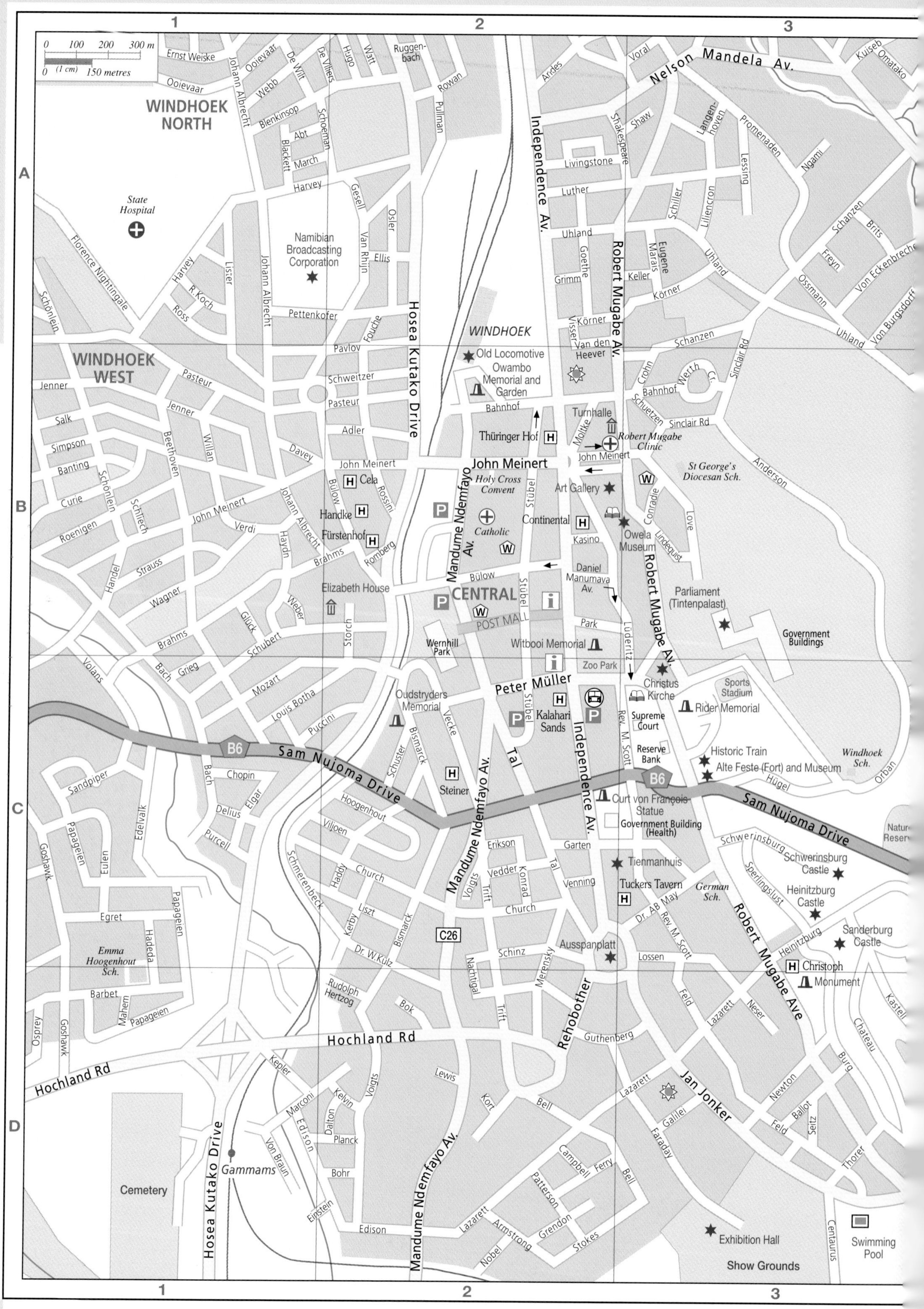
1
2
3
A
B
C
D
0 100 200 300 m
0 (1 cm) 150 metres
WINDHOEK NORTH
WINDHOEK WEST
WINDHOEK
CENTRAL
Ernst Weiske
Ooievaar
Johann Albrecht
Webb
De Wit
De Villiers
Hugo
Watt
Ruggenbach
Rowan
Pullman
Blenkinsop
Abt
Schoeman
Blackett
March
Harvey
Gesell
Osler
Van Rhijn
Ellis
State Hospital
Namibian Broadcasting Corporation
Florence Nightingale
Harvey
R.Koch
Ross
Lister
Schönlein
Pettenkofer
Fouche
Pavlov
Schweitzer
Pasteur
Adler
Hosea Kutako Drive
Jenner
Salk
Simpson
Banting
Curie
Roenigen
Beethoven
Willan
Davey
Schönlein
Schlech
John Meinert
Verdi
Cela
Bülow
Rossini
Handke
Fürstenhof
Romberg
Haydn
Brahms
Strauss
Handel
Wagner
Elizabeth House
Weber
Glück
Schubert
Storch
Brahms
Bach
Grieg
Volans
Mozart
Louis Botha
Puccini
B6
Sam Nujoma Drive
Sandpiper
Bach
Chopin
Delius
Elgar
Purcell
Edelvalk
Papageien
Eulen
Goshawk
Egret
Papageien
Hadeda
Emma Hoogenhout Sch.
Barbet
Mahem
Papageien
Osprey
Goshawk
Hochland Rd
Ardes
Voral
Nelson Mandela Av.
Kuiseb
Omatako
Independence Av.
Shaw
Shakespeare
Livingstone
Luther
Langenhoven
Promenaden
Lessing
Ngami
Schiller
Lilliencron
Uhland
Goethe
Robert Mugabe Av.
Keller
Eugene Marais
Grimm
Körner
Uhland
Schanzen
Brits
Freyn
Von Eckenbrecher
Ossmann
Von Burgsdorff
Visser
Körner
Van den Heever
Schanzen
Sinclair Rd
Uhland
Old Locomotive
Owambo Memorial and Garden
Bahnhof
Crohn
Bahnhof
Werth Cr.
Schuetzen
Sinclair Rd
Turnhalle
Thüringer Hof
Moltke
Robert Mugabe Clinic
John Meinert
St George's Diocesan Sch.
Anderson
Mandume Ndemfayo Av.
Holy Cross Convent
Stübel
Art Gallery
Conradie
Catholic
Continental
Kasino
Owela Museum
Lindequist
Love
Bülow
Daniel Manumava Av.
Stübel
Parliament (Tintenpalast)
POST MALL
Park
Government Buildings
Wernhill Park
Witbooi Memorial
Lüderitz
Zoo Park
Peter Müller
Christus Kirche
Sports Stadium
Oudstryders Memorial
Vecke
Kalahari Sands
Supreme Court
Rider Memorial
Schuster
Bismarck
Tal
Reserve Bank
Rev. M. Scott
Historic Train
Windhoek Sch.
Alte Feste (Fort) and Museum
Orban
Hügel
Steiner
Hoogenhout
Curt von François Statue
Government Building (Health)
Nature Reserve
Viljoen
Mandume Ndemfayo Av.
Erikson
Garten
Schwerinsburg
Schwerinsburg Castle
Sperlingslust
Heinitzburg Castle
Schmerenbeck
Haddy
Church
Vedder
Voigts
Triift
Konrad
Tal
Venning
Tienmanhuis
Tuckers Tavern
German Sch.
Dr. AB May
Rev. M. Scott
Kerby
Liszt
Bismarck
Church
C26
Schinz
Ausspanplatt
Lossen
Heinitzburg
Sanderburg Castle
Christoph
Monument
Dr. W.Külz
Nachtigal
Merensky
Rudolph Hertzog
Bok
Trift
Rehobother
Feld
Lazarett
Neser
Kastell
Guthenberg
Chateau
Robert Mugabe Ave
Hochland Rd
Kepler
Lewis
Burg
Voigts
Kelvin
Marconi
Kort
Bell
Lazarett
Jan Jonker
Newton
Galilei
Ballot
Edison
Dalton
Planck
Faraday
Feld
Seitz
Thorer
Von Braun
Gammams
Bohr
Campbell
Ferry
Bell
Cemetery
Patterson
Einstein
Lazarett
Grendon
Centaurus
Edison
Armstrong
Exhibition Hall
Swimming Pool
Nobel
Stokes
Show Grounds
Hosea Kutako Drive
Mandume Ndemfayo Av.

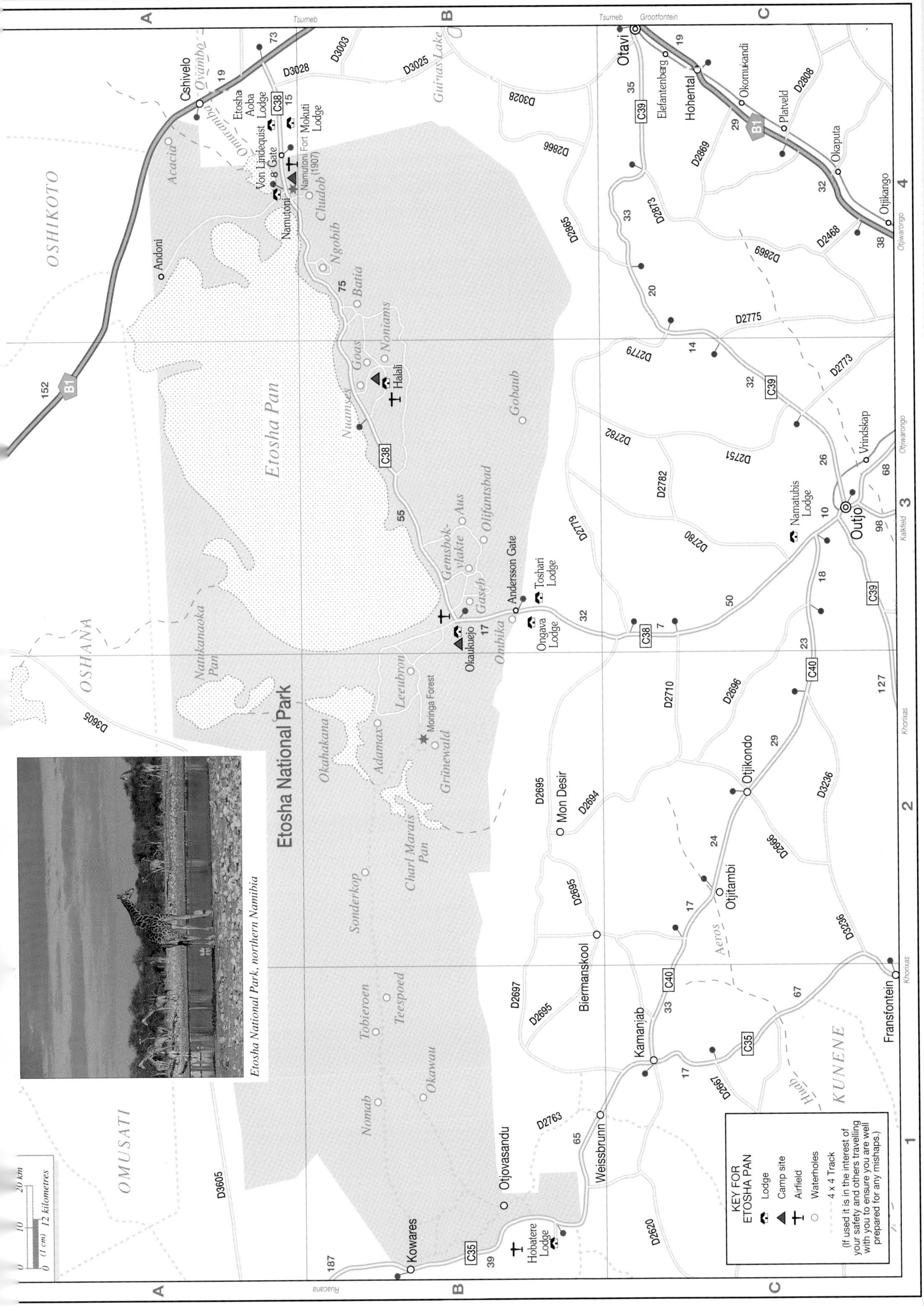

Etosha National Park, northern Namibia

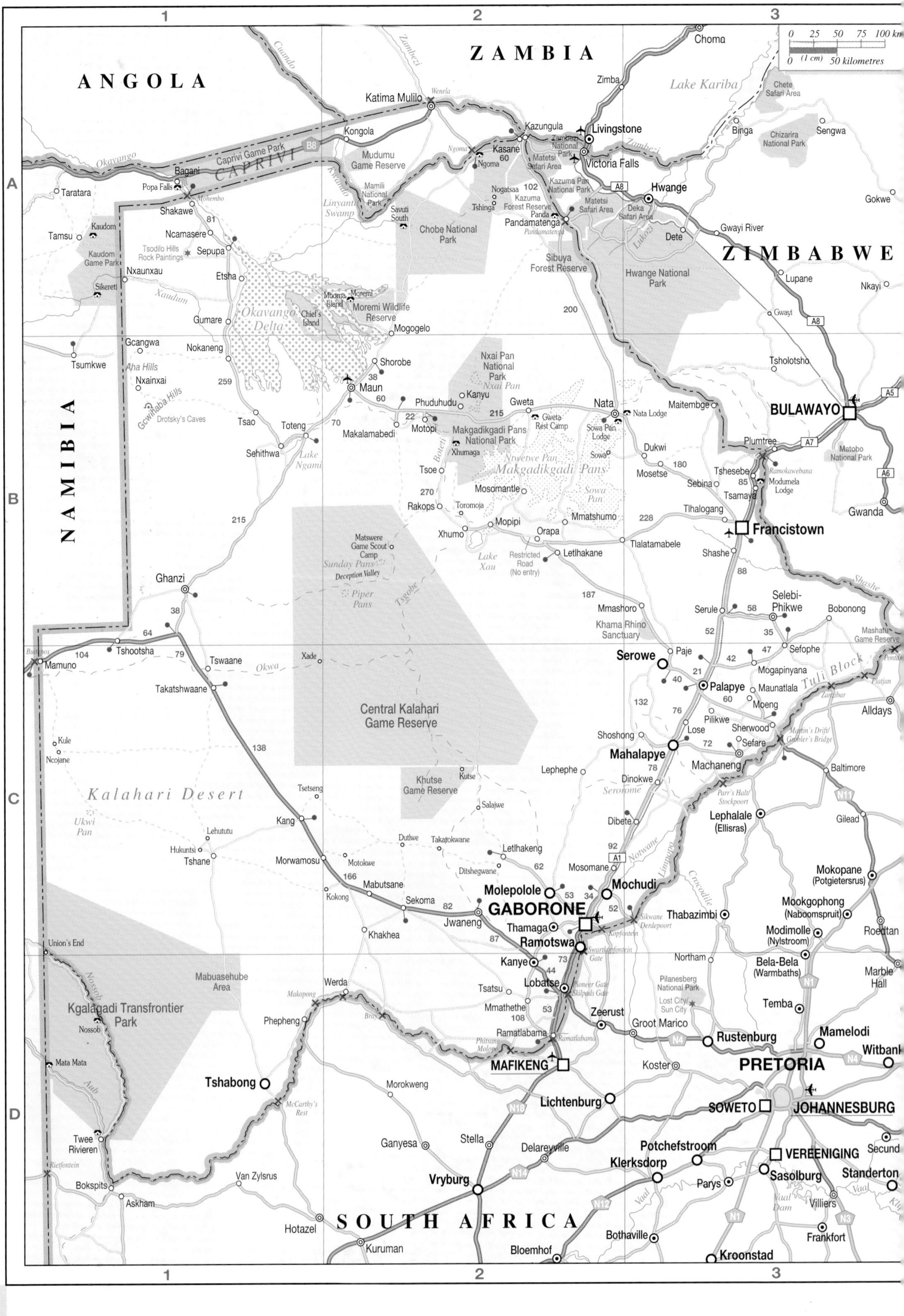

1
2
3
A
B
C
D
0 25 50 75 100 km
0 (1 cm) 50 kilometres
ANGOLA
ZAMBIA
ZIMBABWE
NAMIBIA
SOUTH AFRICA
Choma
Zimba
Lake Kariba
Chete Safari Area
Katima Mulilo
Wenela
Zambezi
Cuando
Kongola
Kazungula
Livingstone
Binga
Sengwa
Chizarira National Park
Caprivi Game Park
CAPRIVI
B8
Okavango
Mudumu Game Reserve
Ngoma
Kasane
Zambezi National Park
Matetsi Safari Area
Victoria Falls
Bagani
Popa Falls
Mohembo
Taratara
Mamili National Park
Kwando
Linyanti Swamp
Savuti South
Nogatsaa
Kazuma Forest Reserve
Tshinga
Kazuma Pan National Park
Matetsi Safari Area
A8
Hwange
Deka Safari Area
Gokwe
Shakawe
Panda
Pandamatenga
Chobe National Park
Dete
Gwayi River
Tamsu
Kaudom
Ncamasere
Kaudom Game Park
Tsodilo Hills Rock Paintings
Sepupa
Sibuya Forest Reserve
Hwange National Park
Lukosi
Nxaunxau
Etsha
Lupane
Nkayi
Sikereti
Xaudum
Mboma Island
Moremi
Moremi Wildlife Reserve
Chief's Island
Okavango Delta
Gumare
200
Gwayi
Mogogelo
Gcangwa
Nokaneng
Tsumkwe
Aha Hills
Nxainxai
Shorobe
Nxai Pan National Park
Nxai Pan
Tsholotsho
Maun
259
Gcwihaba Hills
Drotsky's Caves
Kanyu
Phuduhudu
Gweta
Nata
Nata Lodge
Maitembge
BULAWAYO
A5
Tsao
Toteng
Makalamabedi
Motopi
Gweta Rest Camp
Makgadikgadi Pans National Park
Sowa Pan Lodge
Plumtree
A7
Matobo National Park
Sehithwa
Lake Ngami
Xhumaga
Boteti
Ntwetwe Pan
Makgadikgadi Pans
Sowa
Dukwi
Ramokwebana
A6
Tsoe
Mosetse
Tshesebe
Sebina
Modumela Lodge
Mosomantle
Sowa Pan
Tsamaya
Rakops
Toromoja
Tlhalogang
Gwanda
Mmatshumo
Mopipi
Xhumo
Orapa
Francistown
Tlalatamabele
Matswere Game Scout Camp
Sunday Pans
Deception Valley
Lake Xau
Restricted Road (No entry)
Letlhakane
Shashe
Ghanzi
Piper Pans
Tsgobe
Selebi-Phikwe
Bobonong
Mmashoro
Serule
Khama Rhino Sanctuary
Mashatu Game Reserve
Buitepos
Mamuno
Tshootsha
Tswaane
Xade
Okwa
Serowe
Paje
Sefophe
Mogapinyana
Tuli Block
Pontdrif
Platjan
Takatshwaane
Palapye
Maunatlala
Zanzibar
Alldays
Central Kalahari Game Reserve
Moeng
Pilikwe
Sherwood
Martin's Drift/ Grobler's Bridge
Kule
Ncojane
Shoshong
Lose
Sefare
Mahalapye
Machaneng
Baltimore
Lephephe
Kutse
Khutse Game Reserve
Dinokwe
Serorome
Parr's Halt/ Stockpoort
Kalahari Desert
Tsetseng
N11
Salajwe
Lephalale (Ellisras)
Gilead
Ukwi Pan
Kang
Dibete
Lehututu
Dutlwe
Takatokwane
Notwane
Limpopo
Hukuntsi
Tshane
Letlhakeng
A1
Crocodile
Morwamosu
Motokwe
Ditshegwane
Mosomane
Mokopane (Potgietersrus)
Mabutsane
Mochudi
Kokong
Molepolole
Mookgophong (Naboomspruit)
Sekoma
GABORONE
Thabazimbi
Jwaneng
Sikwane
Derdepoort
Thamaga
Kopfontein
Khakhea
Modimolle (Nylstroom)
Roedtan
Union's End
Ramotswa
Swartkopfontein Gate
Kanye
Northam
Bela-Bela (Warmbaths)
Marble Hall
Nossob
Mabuasehube Area
Werda
Tsatsu
Lobatse
Pioneer Gate
Skilpads Gate
Pilanesberg National Park
N1
Kgalagadi Transfrontier Park
Makopong
Lost City/ Sun City
Temba
Nossob
Phepheng
Bray
Mmathethe
Zeerust
Groot Marico
Ramatlabama
Phitsane Molopo
Mamelodi
Rustenburg
N4
Witbank
Mata Mata
MAFIKENG
Koster
PRETORIA
Auob
Tshabong
Morokweng
McCarthy's Rest
Lichtenburg
SOWETO
JOHANNESBURG
N18
Twee Rivieren
Stella
Ganyesa
Delareyville
Potchefstroom
VEREENIGING
Secunda
Rietfontein
Klerksdorp
Standerton
Sasolburg
Vryburg
Van Zylsrus
N14
Parys
Vaal
Bokspits
Askham
N12
Vaal Dam
Villiers
N3
Hotazel
Bothaville
Frankfort
Kuruman
Bloemhof
Kroonstad

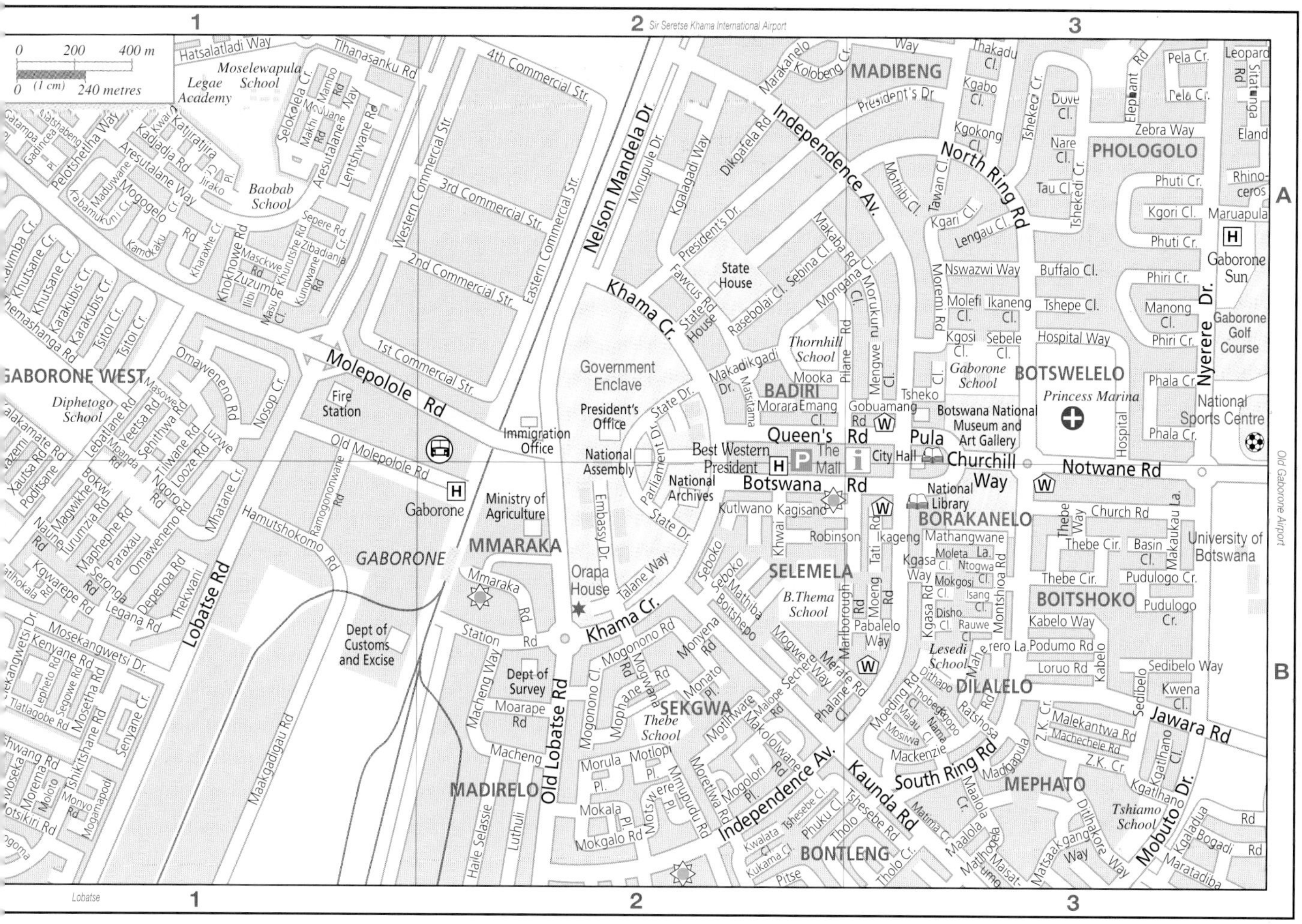

0 200 400 m
0 (1 cm) 240 metres
Sir Seretse Khama International Airport
MADIBENG
PHOLOGOLO
GABORONE WEST
BADIRI
BOTSWELELO
MMARAKA
GABORONE
BORAKANELO
SELEMELA
BOITSHOKO
SEKGWA
DILALELO
MADIRELO
MEPHATO
BONTLENG
Legae Academy
Moselewapula School
Baobab School
Diphetogo School
State House
Thornhill School
Gaborone School
Princess Marina Hospital
Government Enclave
President's Office
National Assembly
National Archives
Immigration Office
Fire Station
Gaborone
Ministry of Agriculture
Dept of Customs and Excise
Dept of Survey
Orapa House
Best Western President
The Mall
City Hall
Botswana National Museum and Art Gallery
National Library
Gaborone Sun
Gaborone Golf Course
National Sports Centre
University of Botswana
B.Thema School
Thebe School
Lesedi School
Tshiamo School
Molepolole Rd
Old Molepolole Rd
Nelson Mandela Dr.
Independence Av.
North Ring Rd
Khama Cr.
Queen's Rd
Botswana Rd
Churchill Way
Notwane Rd
Lobatse Rd
Old Lobatse Rd
Kaunda Rd
South Ring Rd
Jawara Rd
Mobuto Dr.
Nyerere Dr.
Western Commercial Str.
Eastern Commercial Str.
1st Commercial Str.
2nd Commercial Str.
3rd Commercial Str.
4th Commercial Str.
Old Gaborone Airport
Lobatse

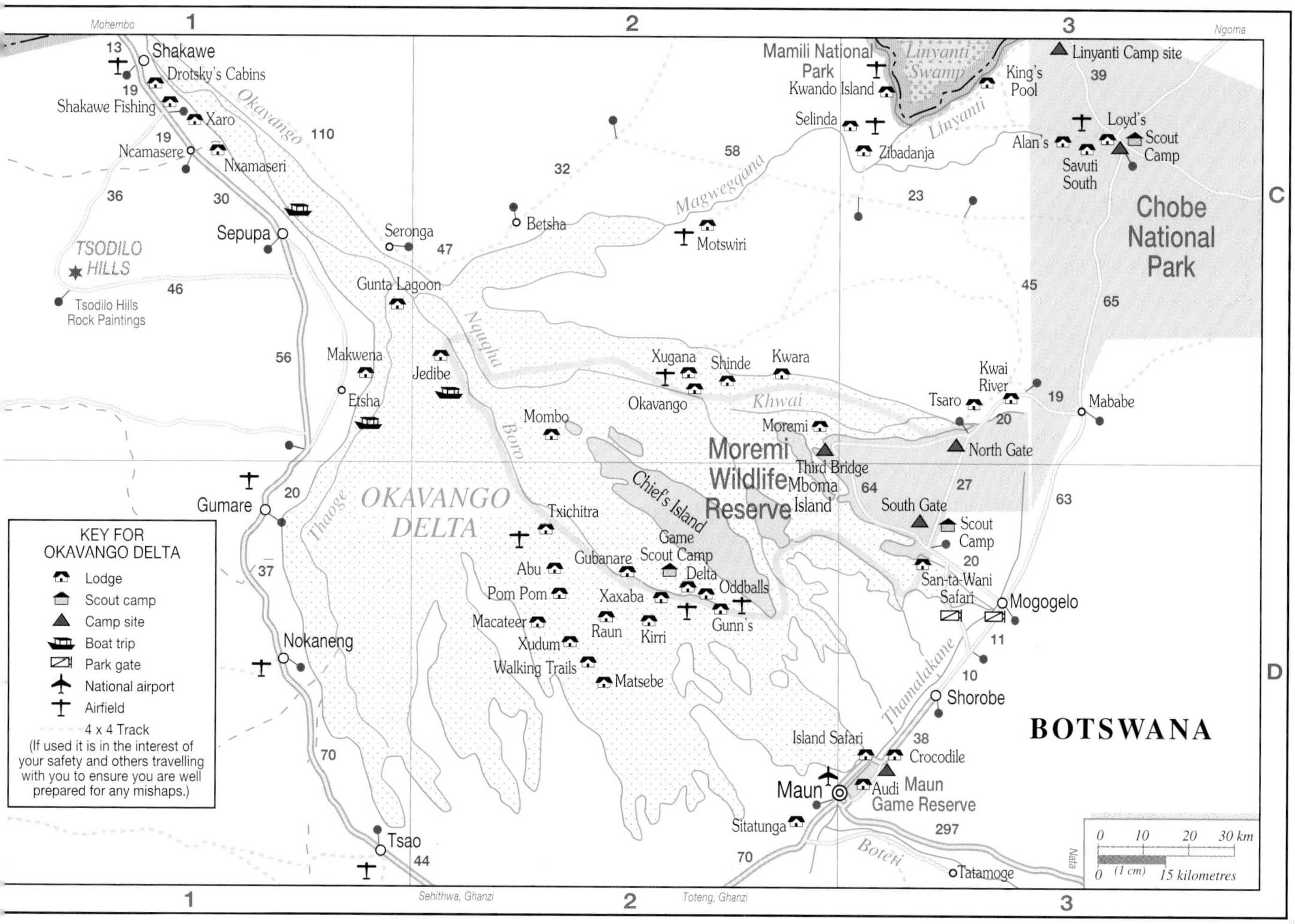

Mohembo
Ngoma
Shakawe
Drotsky's Cabins
Shakawe Fishing
Xaro
Ncamasere
Nxamaseri
Okavango
Sepupa
TSODILO HILLS
Tsodilo Hills Rock Paintings
Seronga
Betsha
Gunta Lagoon
Makwena
Etsha
Jedibe
Gumare
Nokaneng
Tsao
Mamili National Park
Kwando Island
Linyanti Swamp
King's Pool
Linyanti Camp site
Selinda
Zibadanja
Loyd's
Alan's
Scout Camp
Savuti South
Chobe National Park
Magwegqana
Motswiri
Xugana
Shinde
Kwara
Okavango
Khwai
Tsaro
Kwai River
Mabababe
Moremi
North Gate
Moremi Wildlife Reserve
Third Bridge
Mboma Island
South Gate
Scout Camp
San-ta-Wani Safari
Mogogelo
Mombo
Boro
Nqoga
Chief's Island
Game Scout Camp
OKAVANGO DELTA
Thaoge
Txichitra
Abu
Gubanare
Delta
Oddballs
Pom Pom
Xaxaba
Gunn's
Macateer
Raun
Kirri
Xudum
Walking Trails
Matsebe
Thamalakane
Shorobe
Island Safari
Crocodile
Maun
Audi
Maun Game Reserve
Sitatunga
Boteti
Tatamoge
BOTSWANA
Sehithwa, Ghanzi
Toteng, Ghanzi
Nata
0 10 20 30 km
0 (1 cm) 15 kilometres
KEY FOR OKAVANGO DELTA
Lodge
Scout camp
Camp site
Boat trip
Park gate
National airport
Airfield
4 x 4 Track
(If used it is in the interest of your safety and others travelling with you to ensure you are well prepared for any mishaps.)

ZIMBABWE – VICTORIA FALLS and HWANGE NATIONAL PARK

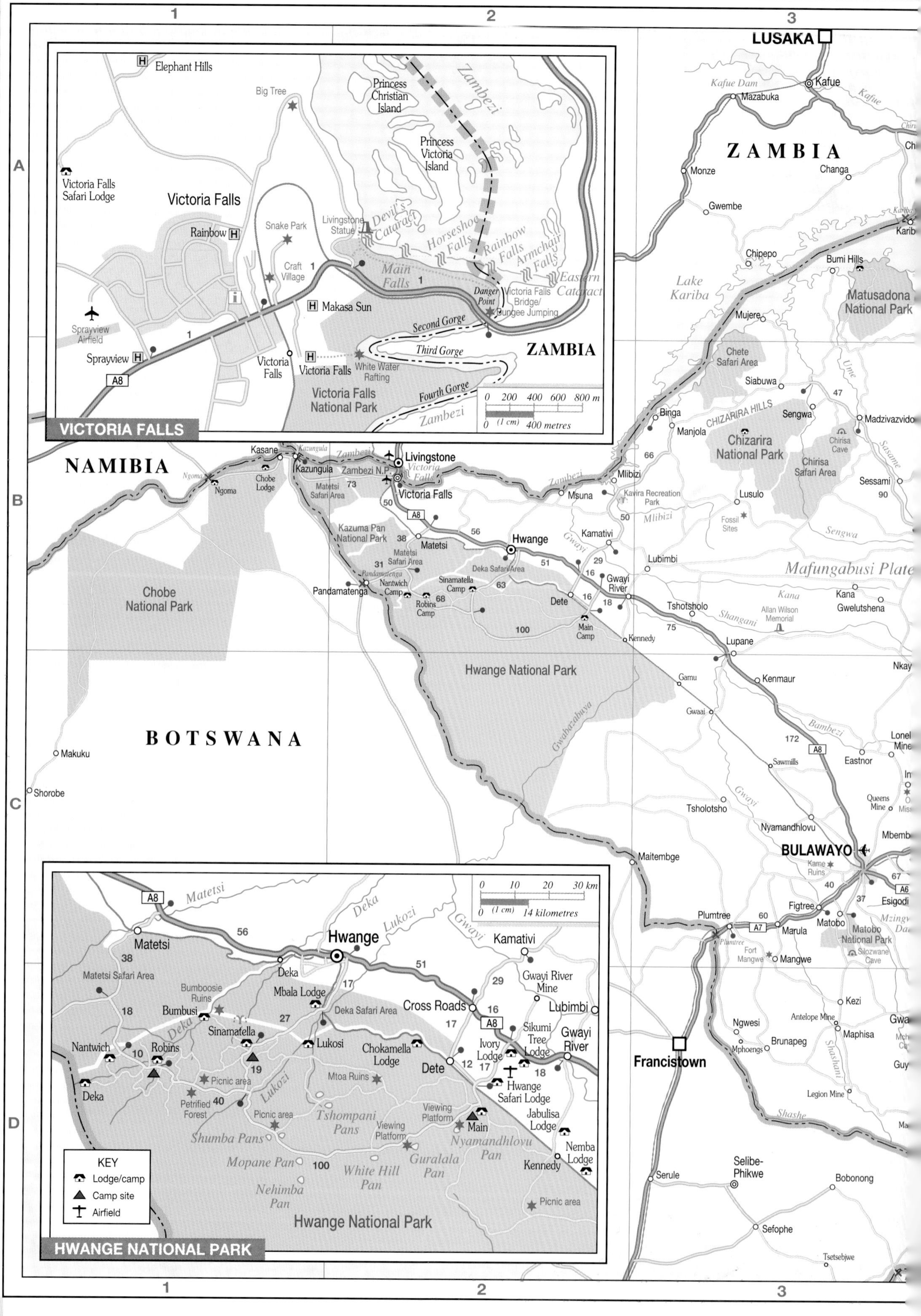

4
5
6
A
B
C
D
0 15 30 45 60 km
0 (1 cm) 30 kilometres
MOZAMBIQUE
MOZAMBIQUE
SOUTH AFRICA
HARARE
Lake Cahora Bassa
Zambezi
Mana Pools
Mana Pools National Park
Sapi Safari Area
Chewore Safari Area
Dande Safari Area
Luangwa
Kanyemba
Zumbo
Cahora Bassa
Songa
Chinhanda
Tete
Moatize
Rukomechi
ESCARPMENT
RUKOVAKUONA MOUNTAINS
Mushumbi Pools
Makuti
Vuti
Doma Safari Area
Muzarabani
Mukumbura
Mekumbura
St Alberts
MAVURADONHA MOUNTAINS
Rushinga
Marymount
Chioco
Guruve
Centenary
Karoi
Magunje
Madadzi
Mhangura
Portuguese Forts
Raffingora
Mvurwi
Mount Darwin
Mutepatepa
Umfurudzi Safari Area
Chitsungo
Nyamapanda
Kotwa
Changara
Chidamoyo
Mutorashanga
Mazowe
Ruya
Mupfurudzi Dam
Chimusimbe
Zave
Lions Den
Chinhoyi
Chinhoyi Caves
Mazwikadei Dam
Kildonan
Mwenje Dam
Bindura
Shamva
Elephant Cave
Suskwe
Makosa
Makaha Fort
Mungari
Banket
Gresham
Concession
Glendale
Domboshawa
Ewanrigg Botanical Gardens
Murehwa Cave
Mutoko
Ruins
Guro
Darwendale
Lake Manyame Rec. Park
Murewa
Arcturus
Ruwangwe
Elim
Norton
Makwiro
Lake Chivero Rec. Park
Goromonzi
Ruwa
Chitungwiza
Bromley
Mayo
Nyamaropa
Macossa
Gadzema
Chakari
Selous
Fort Mhondoro
Chegutu
Golden Valley
Kadoma
Eiffel Flats
Umsweswe
Mubayira
Beatrice
Marondera
Macheke
Headlands
Nyahokwe Ruins
INYANGA MTS.
Catandica
Nyanga
Nyanga National Park
Juliasdale
Tea Plantation
Wilton
Empress Mine
Claw Dam
Battlefields
Ngezi Dam
Ngezi Rec. Park
Mhakwe Cave
Rusape
Munyati
Fort Charter
Hwedza
Mutasa
Honde
Watsomba
Nyazura
Osborne Dam
Featherstone
Gorongosa
Gorongosa National Park
Kwekwe
Redcliff
Silobela
Sebakwe Rec. Park
Sebakwe Dam
Chivhu
The Range
Sadza
Dorowa
BEPE HILLS
Odzi
Penhalonga
Forbes-Mutare / Machipanda
Mutare
Manica
Bandula
Chimoio
Gondola
Fort Ingwenya
Daramombe
Vumba Botanical Reserve
Bunga Forest Botanical Reserve
Chicamba Dam
Lalapanzi
Mvuma
Buhera
Murambinda
Mutowa Ruins
Nhamatanda
Gweru
Shangani Dam
Somabhula
Shurugwi
Chatsworth
Gutu
Ruti Dam
Matenderi Ruins
Hot Springs
Mutambara
Cashel / Rutanda
Cashel
Rutanda
Mavita
Nsiza
Shangani
Gwanoro Dam
Nalatale Ruins
Dhlodhlo Ruins
Fort Rixon
Nyanyadzi
Chimanimani
Birchenough Bridge
Chimanimani National Park
Nyika
Moodies
Bikita
Chibvumani Ruins
Dombe
Buzi
Mashava
Masvingo
Mushandike Sanctuary
Mutirikwi Rec. Park
Lake Mutirikwi
Tanganda
Junction Gate
Chipinge
Chipinge Safari Area
Lake Cunningham Recreational Park
Zvishavane
Great Zimbabwe National Monument
Zaka
Turwi
Chibabava
Pambuka
Chivi
Mberengwa
Jerera
Manjirenji Rec. Park
Lake MacDougal
Rupisi
Mt Selinda
Espungabera
Mt Selinda / Espungabera
Ngezi
Renco
Silalabuhwa Dam
Ngungubane
Matago
Ngundu
Bangala Dam
Tokwane Dam
Manyuchi Dam
Runde
Chisekera Hot Springs
Mkwasine
Chisumbanje
Chitobe
West Nicholson
Triangle
Nandi
Chiredzi
Rupangwana
Tamba
Rutenga
Chipinda Pools
Macobere
Taula
Makado
Mwenezi
Mbizi
Boli
Cavane
Mazunga
Bubi
Gonarezhou National Park
Massangena
Zinave National Park
Zhouhe Dam
Mzingwane
Tswiza
Mabalauta
Malapati Game Reserve
Malapati
Pioneer Memorial
Chamunange
Lutumba
Nulli
Matibi
Sango
Sango / Chicualacuala
Beitbridge
Diti
Limpopo
Messina
Chikwarakwara
Pafuri Gate
Machaila
Mabote
Save
Mupfure
Munyati
Sanyati
Manyame
Odzi
Ruenya
Nyagui
Mwarazi
Ruzawi
Runde
Tokwe
Mwenezi
Chiredzi
Luia
Luenha
A1
A2
A3
A4
A5
A6
A9
A10
A11
A13
A14
A15
A16
A17
A18
102
103
6
1

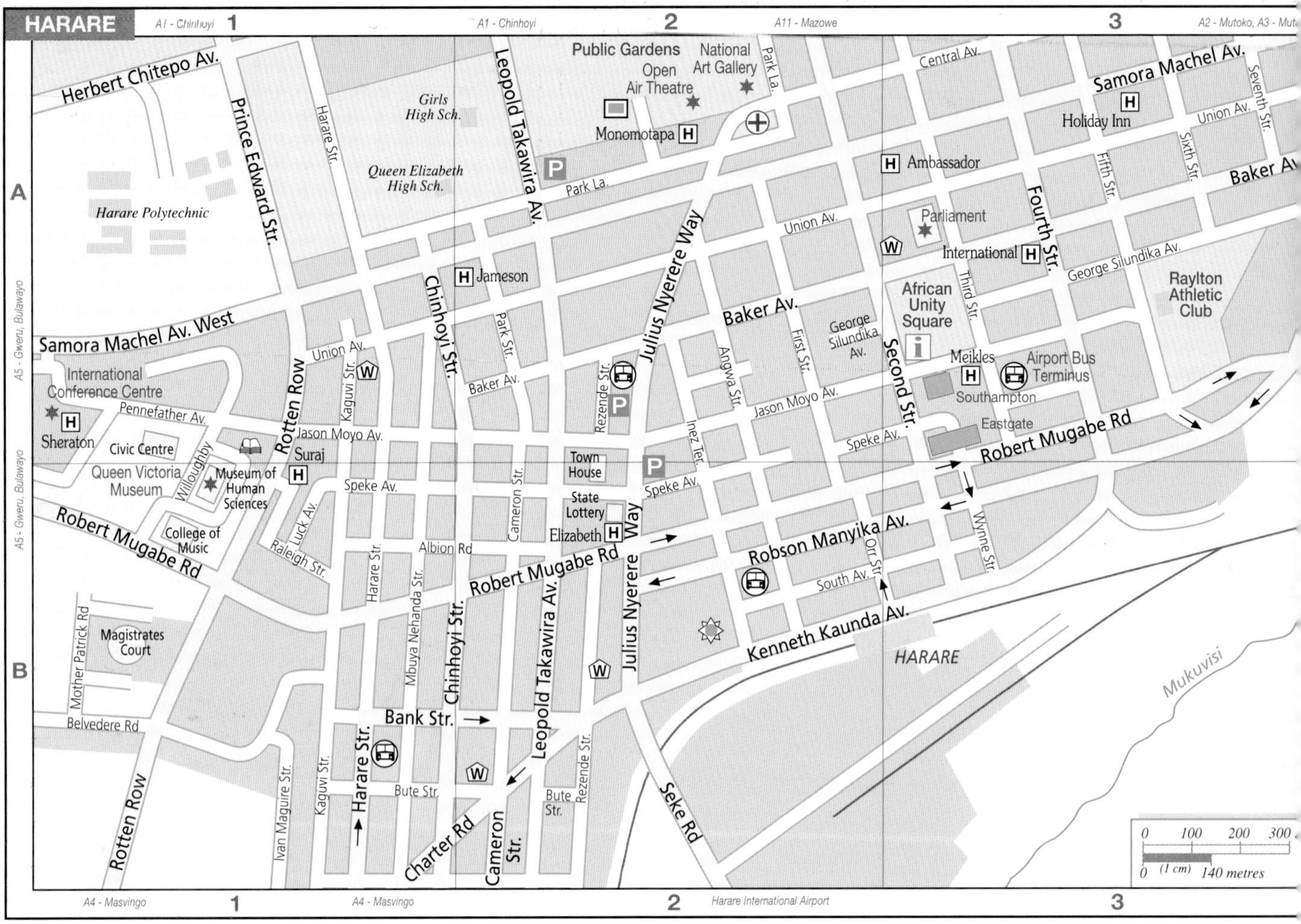
HARARE
A1 - Chinhoyi
A1 - Chinhoyi
A11 - Mazowe
A2 - Mutoko, A3 - Mutare
1
2
3
A
B
A5 - Gweru, Bulawayo
A5 - Gweru, Bulawayo
A4 - Masvingo
A4 - Masvingo
Harare International Airport
Herbert Chitepo Av.
Prince Edward Str.
Harare Str.
Girls High Sch.
Queen Elizabeth High Sch.
Leopold Takawira Av.
Public Gardens
Open Air Theatre
National Art Gallery
Park La.
Monomotapa
Central Av.
Samora Machel Av.
Holiday Inn
Union Av.
Seventh Str.
Sixth Str.
Fifth Str.
Baker Av.
Ambassador
Harare Polytechnic
Julius Nyerere Way
Union Av.
Parliament
Fourth Str.
International
George Silundika Av.
Jameson
Chinhoyi Str.
Park Str.
Baker Av.
African Unity Square
Third Str.
Raylton Athletic Club
Samora Machel Av. West
Union Av.
Kaguvi Str.
Rezende Str.
Angwa Str.
First Str.
George Silundika Av.
Second Str.
Meikles
Airport Bus Terminus
Southampton
International Conference Centre
Pennefather Av.
Sheraton
Civic Centre
Rotten Row
Jason Moyo Av.
Suraj
Jason Moyo Av.
Speke Av.
Eastgate
Robert Mugabe Rd
Queen Victoria Museum
Willoughby
Museum of Human Sciences
Speke Av.
Town House
Inez Ter.
Speke Av.
State Lottery
Cameron Str.
Luck Av.
College of Music
Robert Mugabe Rd
Raleigh Str.
Albion Rd
Elizabeth
Robson Manyika Av.
Wynne Str.
Harare Str.
Mbuya Nehanda Str.
Robert Mugabe Rd
Orr Str.
South Av.
Mother Patrick Rd
Magistrates Court
Kenneth Kaunda Av.
HARARE
Mukuvisi
Belvedere Rd
Bank Str.
Harare Str.
Kaguvi Str.
Ivan Maguire Str.
Bute Str.
Bute Str.
Rezende Str.
Seke Rd
Rotten Row
Charter Rd
Cameron Str.
0 100 200 300
0 (1 cm) 140 metres

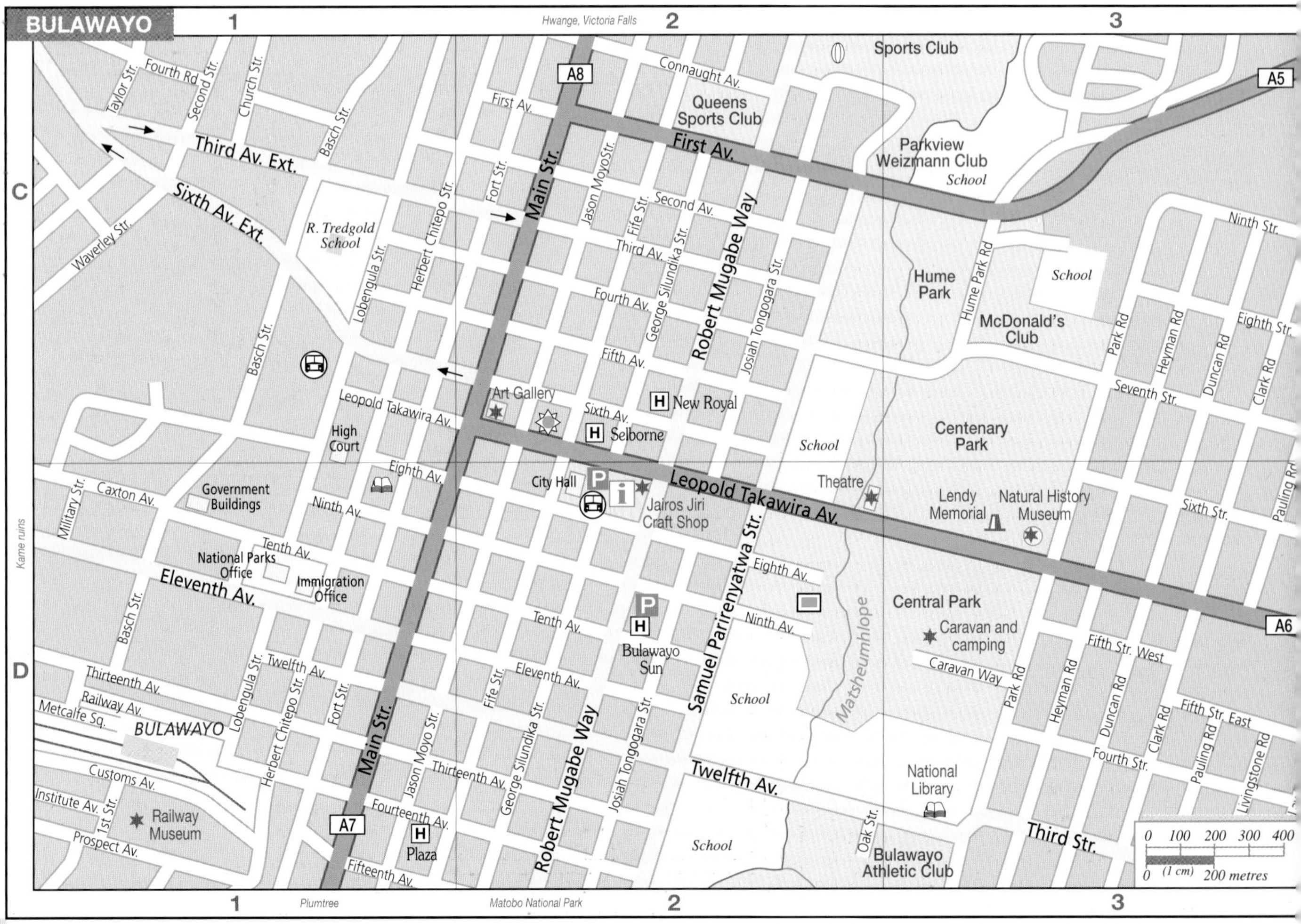
BULAWAYO
1
2
3
Hwange, Victoria Falls
C
D
Kame ruins
Plumtree
Matobo National Park
Taylor Str.
Fourth Rd
Second Str.
Church Str.
Basch Str.
A8
Connaught Av.
Sports Club
A5
First Av.
Queens Sports Club
Third Av. Ext.
First Av.
Parkview Weizmann Club
School
Sixth Av. Ext.
Waverley Str.
R. Tredgold School
Herbert Chitepo Str.
Fort Str.
Main Str.
Jason Moyo Str.
Fife Str.
Second Av.
Ninth Str.
Lobengula Str.
Third Av.
George Silundika Str.
Robert Mugabe Way
Josiah Tongogara Str.
Hume Park Rd
Hume Park
School
Fourth Av.
McDonald's Club
Park Rd
Heyman Rd
Duncan Rd
Clark Rd
Eighth Str.
Basch Str.
Fifth Av.
Seventh Str.
Leopold Takawira Av.
Art Gallery
Sixth Av.
New Royal
Selborne
High Court
School
Centenary Park
Eighth Av.
Government Buildings
Caxton Av.
Military Str.
City Hall
Jairos Jiri Craft Shop
Leopold Takawira Av.
Theatre
Lendy Memorial
Natural History Museum
Sixth Str.
Paulin Rd
Ninth Av.
Tenth Av.
National Parks Office
Immigration Office
Eleventh Av.
Samuel Parirenyatwa Str.
Eighth Av.
Matsheumhlope
Central Park
Caravan and camping
Tenth Av.
Ninth Av.
Basch Str.
Bulawayo Sun
A6
Twelfth Av.
Lobengula Str.
Fort Str.
Eleventh Av.
Fife Str.
Fifth Str. West
Caravan Way
Thirteenth Av.
Railway Av.
Metcalfe Sq.
BULAWAYO
Herbert Chitepo Str.
Jason Moyo Str.
School
Park Rd
Heyman Rd
Duncan Rd
Clark Rd
Fifth Str. East
Pauling Rd
Livingstone Rd
Fourth Str.
Customs Av.
Thirteenth Av.
George Silundika Str.
Robert Mugabe Way
Josiah Tongogara Str.
Twelfth Av.
National Library
Institute Av.
1st Str.
Railway Museum
Fourteenth Av.
A7
Plaza
Prospect Av.
Fifteenth Av.
School
Oak Str.
Bulawayo Athletic Club
Third Str.
0 100 200 300 400
0 (1 cm) 200 metres

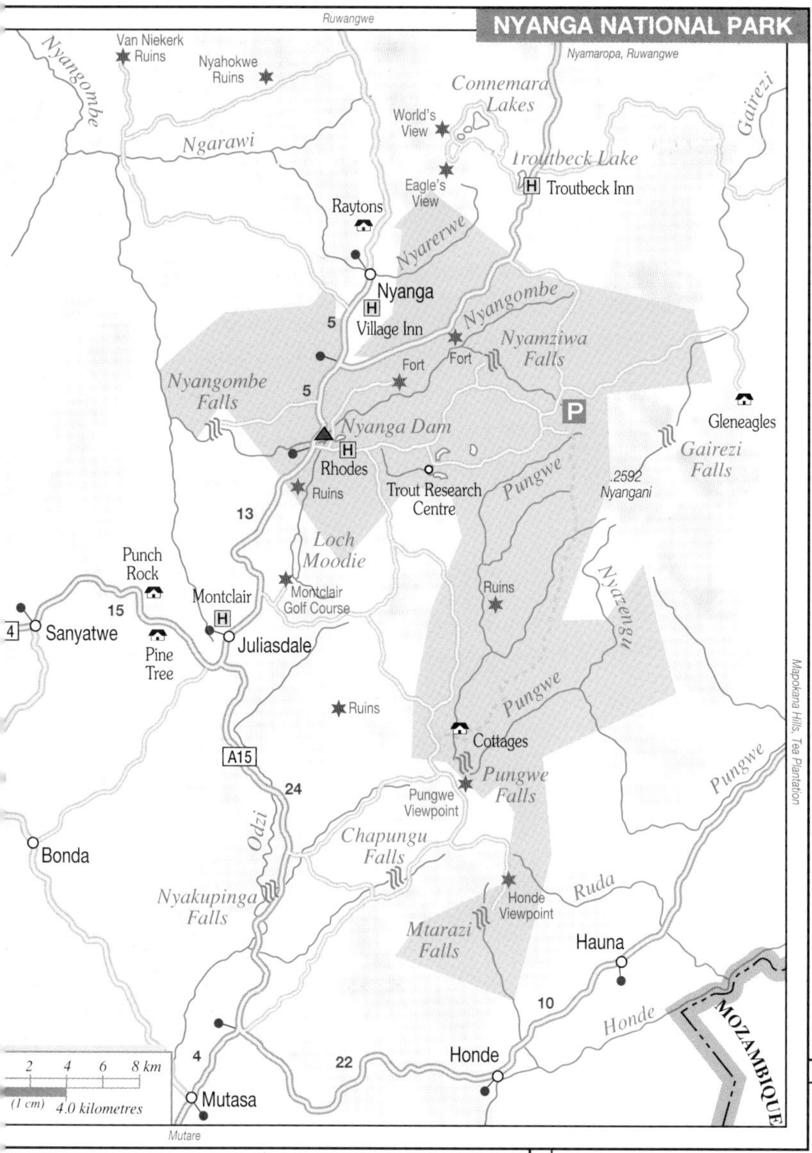

Mtarazi Falls in the Nyanga National Park, Eastern Highlands

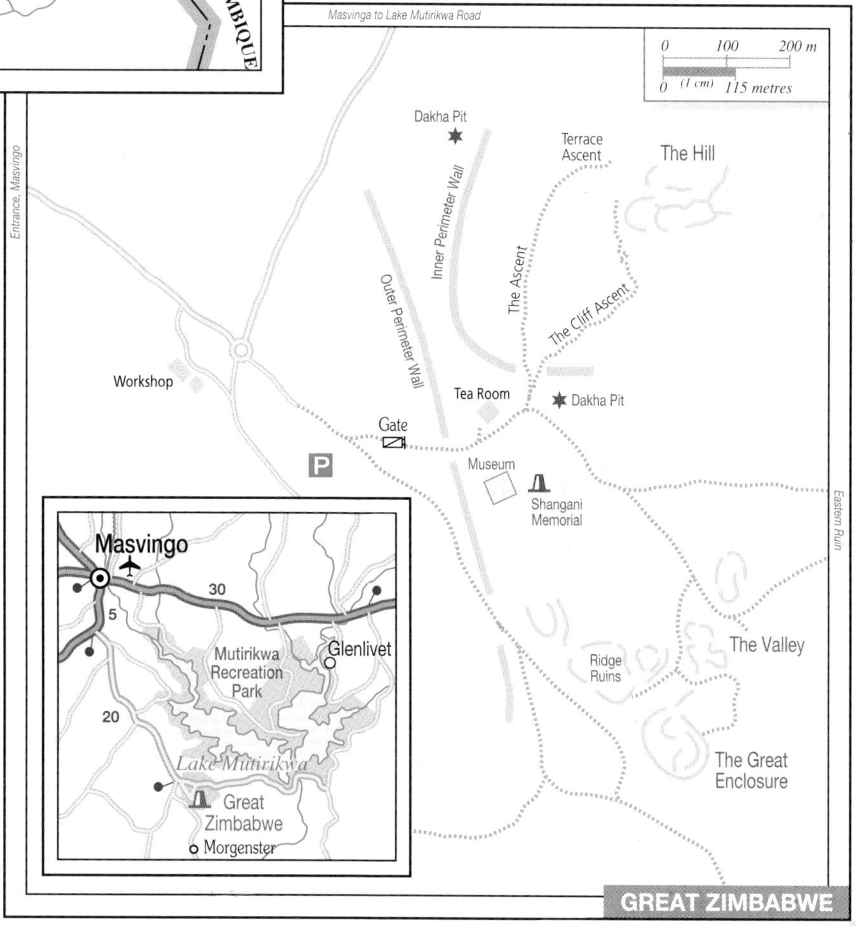

t Zimbabwe National Monument near Masvingo

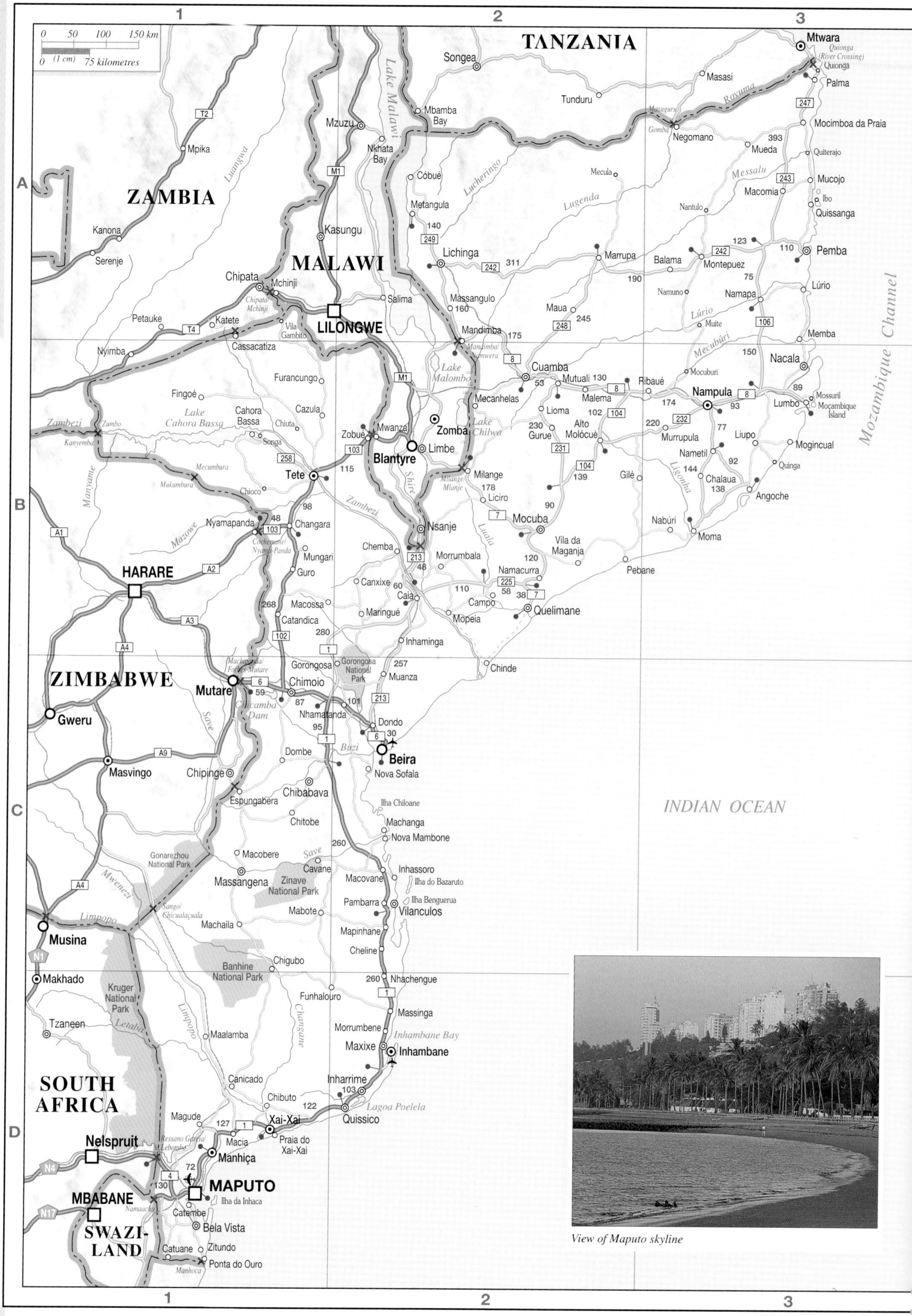

View of Maputo skyline

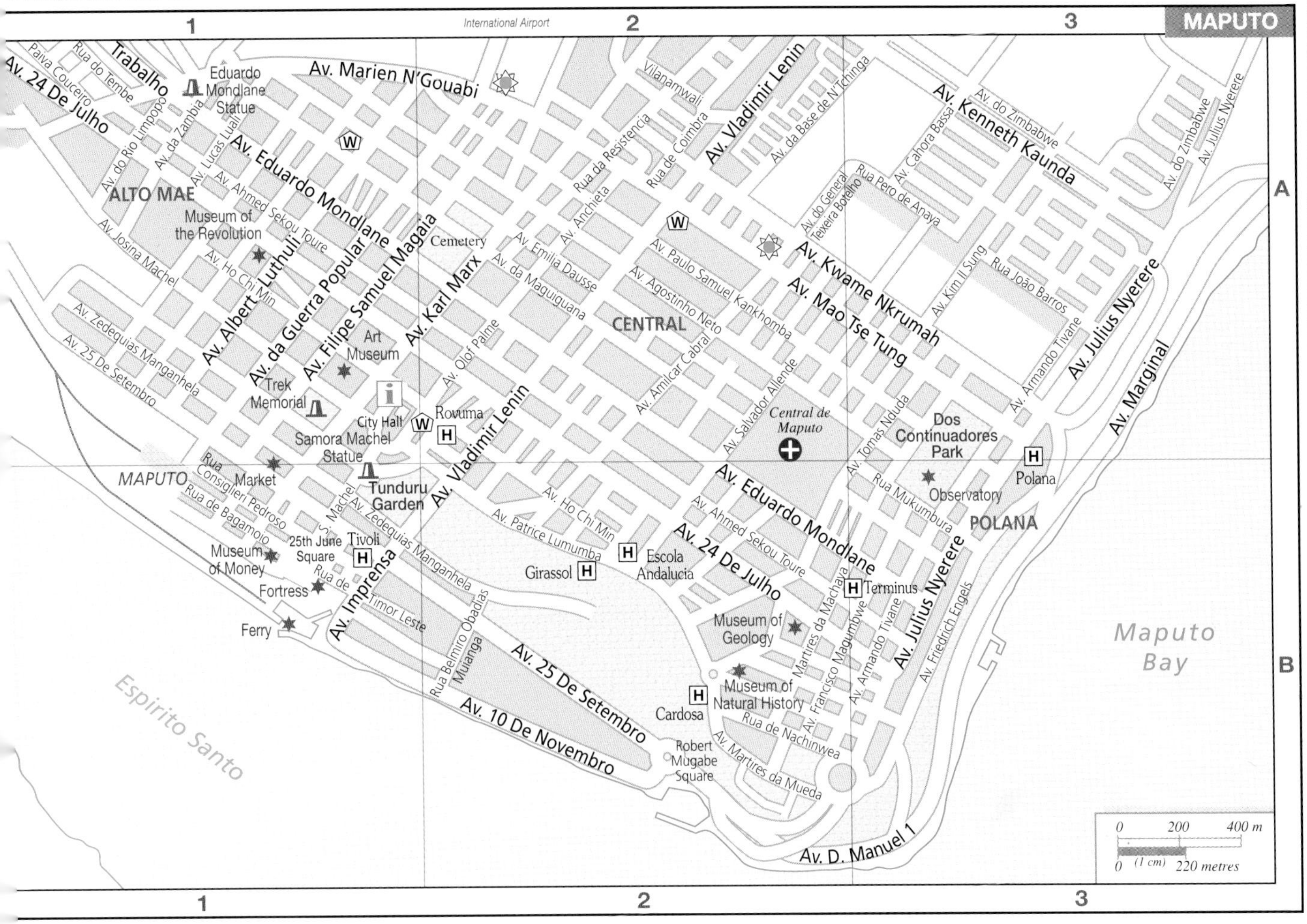
MAPUTO
1
2
3
A
B
International Airport
Av. Marien N'Gouabi
Av. 24 De Julho
Trabalho
Eduardo Mondlane Statue
Av. Eduardo Mondlane
ALTO MAE
Museum of the Revolution
Av. Albert Luthuli
Av. da Guerra Popular
Av. Filipe Samuel Magaia
Av. Karl Marx
Cemetery
Art Museum
Trek Memorial
City Hall
Rovuma
Samora Machel Statue
Market
Tunduru Garden
Av. Vladimir Lenin
MAPUTO
Rua Consigliere Pedroso
Rua de Bagamoio
25th June Square
Tivoli
Museum of Money
Fortress
Ferry
Av. Imprensa
Rua de Timor Leste
Av. Zedequias Manganhela
Av. Josina Machel
Av. Ho Chi Min
Av. Ahmed Sekou Toure
Av. Zedequias Manganhela
Av. 25 De Setembro
Espirito Santo
Av. Patrice Lumumba
Girassol
Escola Andalucia
Av. 24 De Julho
Rua Belmiro Obadias Muianga
Av. 25 De Setembro
Av. 10 De Novembro
Robert Mugabe Square
Cardosa
Museum of Natural History
Museum of Geology
Rua de Nachinwea
Av. Martires da Mueda
Av. D. Manuel 1
CENTRAL
Central de Maputo
Av. Salvador Allende
Av. Amilcar Cabral
Av. Agostinho Neto
Av. Paulo Samuel Kankhomba
Av. Vladimir Lenin
Av. Kwame Nkrumah
Av. Mao Tse Tung
Av. Eduardo Mondlane
Terminus
Av. Julius Nyerere
Av. Friedrich Engels
Dos Continuadores Park
Observatory
Polana
POLANA
Av. Kenneth Kaunda
Av. Marginal
Av. Julius Nyerere
Maputo Bay
Rua Mukumbura
Av. Tomas Nduda
Av. Armando Tivane
Av. Kim Il Sung
Rua João Barros
Av. Cahora Bassa
Av. do Zimbabwe
Av. Julius Nyerere
Av. da Base de N'Tchinga
Vilanamwali
Rua de Coimbra
Rua da Resistencia
Av. Anchieta
Av. Emilia Dausse
Av. da Maguiguana
Av. Olof Palme
0 200 400 m
0 (1 cm) 220 metres

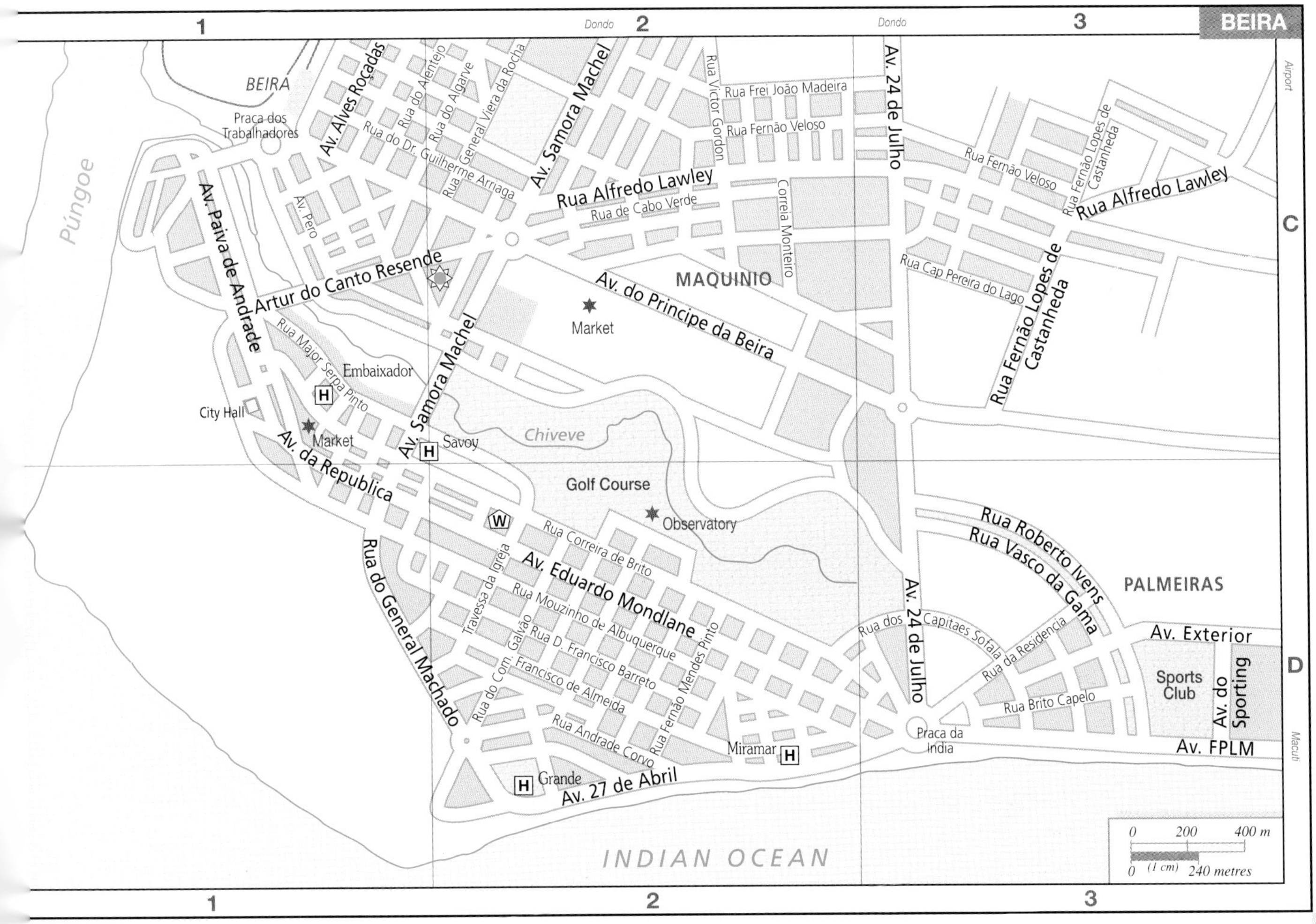
BEIRA
1
2
3
C
D
Dondo
Dondo
Airport
BEIRA
Praca dos Trabalhadores
Púngoe
Av. Alves Roçadas
Av. Paiva de Andrade
Av. Pero
Artur do Canto Resende
Av. Samora Machel
Rua Alfredo Lawley
Rua de Cabo Verde
Rua Victor Gordon
Rua Frei João Madeira
Rua Fernão Veloso
Correia Monteiro
Av. 24 de Julho
MAQUINIO
Av. do Principe da Beira
Market
Embaixador
City Hall
Market
Av. Samora Machel
Savoy
Av. da Republica
Chiveve
Golf Course
Observatory
Rua Correira de Brito
Av. Eduardo Mondlane
Rua do General Machado
Travessa da Igreja
Rua Mouzinho de Albuquerque
Rua D. Francisco Barreto
Francisco de Almeida
Rua Andrade Corvo
Rua Fernão Mendes Pinto
Miramar
Grande
Av. 27 de Abril
INDIAN OCEAN
Rua Fernão Veloso
Rua Alfredo Lawley
Rua Cap Pereira do Lago
Rua Fernão Lopes de Castanheda
Rua Roberto Ivens
Rua Vasco da Gama
PALMEIRAS
Av. 24 de Julho
Rua dos Capitaes Sofala
Rua da Residencia
Rua Brito Capelo
Praca da India
Av. Exterior
Sports Club
Av. do Sporting
Av. FPLM
Macuti
0 200 400 m
0 (1 cm) 240 metres

PLACE NAMES INDEX

Page

42nd Hill 18 D 2

A

Abbotsdale 4 C 1
Abbotspoort 20 B 2
Abercorn Drift 19 C 6
Aberdeen 6 B 1
Aberdeen Road 6 B 1
Aberfeldy 18 D 2
Acacia 5 A 5
Acornhoek 21 C 5
Addo 6 C 2
Adelaide 6 B 3
Adendorp 6 A 1
Afguns 20 C 2
Afrikaskop 18 D 2
Aggeneys 9 B 4
Agtergang 11 C 5
Ahrens 13 A 4
Ai-Ais 14 D 3
Airlie 19 A 4
Albert Falls 13 B 4
Albertinia 5 D 4
Alberton 18 B 2
Alcockspruit 18 D 3
Aldam 12 A 1
Alexander Bay 8 A 1
Alexandria 6 C 3
Algeria 4 A 2
Algiers 16 B 3
Alheit 9 A 5
Alice 7 B 4
Alicedale 6 C 3
Aliwal North 11 C 6
Allandale 12 A 1
Allanridge 17 D 6
Alldays 20 A 3
Alma 20 C 2
Amalia 17 C 4
Amanzimtoti 13 C 5
aMatikulu 13 A 5
Amerika 18 D 1
Amersfoort 18 C 3
Ammerville 5 A 4
Amsterdam 19 B 4
Andrieskraal 6 C 1
Andriesvale 15 C 6
Ann's Villa 6 B 3
Anysspruit 19 C 4
Arboretum 13 A 6
Argent 18 B 2
Ariamsvlei 15 D 5
Ariesfontein 10 A 3
Arlington 18 D 1
Aroab 15 C 5
Arundel 11 D 4
Asab 14 A 3
Asbospan 14 C 2
Ascent 18 C 2
Ashburton 13 B 4
Ashton 4 C 3
Askeaton 12 D 1
Askham 15 C 6
Assegaaibos 6 C 1
Assen 18 A 1
Aston Bay 6 C 2
Atamelang 17 C 5
Atlanta Sta. 20 D 2
Atlanta 18 A 1
Atlantis 4 C 1
Atteridgeville 18 A 1
Attie 18 C 1
Augrabies 9 A 5
Aukam 14 C 2
Aurora 4 B 1
Aurus 14 A 3
Aus 14 C 1
Ausnek 14 C 2
Aussenkehr 8 A 2
Austin's Post 11 B 5
Ausweiche 14 C 1
Avondrus 4 C 3
Avondster 17 C 5
Avontuur 5 C 6

B

Baardskeerdersbos 4 D 2
Babanango 13 A 5
Badplaas 19 B 4
Baikhutso 17 B 5
Bailey 6 A 3
Baines Drift 20 A 3
Bakenberg 20 C 3
Bakenklip 10 D 1
Bakerville 17 B 5
Balfour 18 C 2
Balfour 6 B 3
Balgowan 13 B 4
Balkfontein 17 C 6
Ballengeich 18 D 3
Ballito 13 B 5
Balmoral 18 B 2
Baltimore 20 B 3
Bandelierkop 21 B 4
Bandur 21 A 4
Bankies 11 D 6
Banksvlei 9 A 5
Banner's Rest 13 D 4
Bapong 18 A 1
Bapong 20 D 1
Bapsfontein 18 B 2
Barandas 5 C 6
Barberspan 17 B 5
Barberton 19 B 4
Barkly East 12 D 1
Barkly Pass 12 D 2
Barkly West 11 A 4
Baroda 6 A 2
Baroe 6 B 1
Barrington 5 C 6
Barrydale 4 C 3
Bashee 7 A 5
Bashibisi 13 A 6
Bathurst 7 C 4
Batlharo 16 C 3
Baviaanskrans 17 C 6
Bayala 19 D 6
Baynesfield 13 B 4
Baziya 7 A 5
Beacon Bay 7 B 5
Beaufort West 5 A 5
Beauty 20 B 2
Beauvallon 8 A 1
Bede 7 A 4
Bedford 6 B 3
Beesbank 8 A 2
Beeshoek 10 A 2
Beeshoek 16 D 2
Beestekraal 18 A 1
Beeswater 8 D 3
Beitbridge 21 A 4
Bela Vista 19 B 6
Bela-Bela 20 D 3
Bela-Bela (Les.) 12 A 2
Belfast 18 A 3
Belfast 21 D 6
Belgrave 12 C 2
Bell 7 C 4
Bellsbank Mine 17 D 4
Bellville 4 C 1
Belmont 11 B 4
Bendell 16 C 3
Benoni 18 B 2
Bensonvale 12 C 1
Berbice 19 C 5
Bergnek 21 C 4
Bergplaas 5 C 5
Berg River 4 B 1
Bergsig 18 C 2
Bergsig 8 B 3
Bergville 12 A 3
Berlin 7 B 4
Bermolli 10 A 2
Berseba 14 B 3
Besters 12 A 3
Bethal East 18 B 3
Bethal 18 B 3
Bethanie, Namibia 14 B 2
Bethanie 18 A 1
Bethelsdorp 6 C 2
Bethesda Road 6 A 2
Bethlehem 12 A 2
Bethulie 11 C 5
Betta 14 A 2
Betty's Bay 4 D 2
Bewaarkloof 21 C 4
Bhadeni 19 C 4
Bhalekane 19 B 5
Bhekuzulu 19 D 4
Bhunya 19 B 4
Bidiza 12 D 3
Bierspruit 20 D 1
Biesiesfontein 8 D 3
Biesiespoort 5 A 6
Biesiesvlei 17 B 5
Big Bend 19 C 5
Biggersberg 13 A 4
Bisho 7 B 4
Bisi 13 C 4
Bitterfontein 8 D 3
Bityi 7 A 5
Bizana 13 D 4
Black Rock 16 C 2
Blackheath 17 B 4
Bladgrond 9 A 5
Blanco 5 C 5
Blandsdrift 5 D 4
Bleakmoor 7 B 4
Bleskop 18 A 1
Blesmanspos 17 D 4
Bletterman 11 C 4
Blikfontein 16 D 3
Blinkpan 18 B 3
Blinkwater 21 B 4
Bloekomspruit 18 C 2
Bloemfontein 11 A 6
Bloemhof 17 D 5
Blood River 19 D 4
Blouberg 20 B 3
Bloubergstrand 4 C 1
Bloudrif 17 D 6
Bluegums 12 C 1
Bluewater Bay 6 C 2
Blydskap 18 D 2
Blythedale Beach 13 B 5
Blyvoortsig 9 B 4
Boane 19 B 6
Bochum 20 B 3
Bodenstein 17 B 6
Boegoeberg 10 A 2
Boerboonfontein 4 C 3
Boesmanskop 11 C 6
Boetsap 17 D 4
Bogogobo 16 C 1
Bogwasa 21 C 5
Bohlokong 18 D 2
Boipelo 17 D 4
Boitshoko 10 A 3
Boitumelong 17 D 5
Bokaa 20 A 1
Bokkoppie 16 D 2
Bokkraal 17 B 6
Boknes 6 C 3
Boksburg 18 B 2
Bokspits 15 C 6
Bolahlakgomo 21 C 4
Bollantlokwe 18 A 1
Bolo 7 A 4
Bolokaneng 11 B 5
Bolotwa 7 A 4
Bon Accord 18 A 2
Bongolethu 5 C 5
Bonnievale 4 C 3
Bonteheuwel 10 D 2
Bontrug 6 C 3
Bonwapitse 20 B 1
Boomplaas 12 D 1
Boons 18 B 1
Boord 18 A 3
Borolelo 17 A 6
Bosbult 21 B 4
Boshoek 17 A 6
Boshof 11 A 5
Boskop 17 B 6
Boskuil 17 C 5
Bospoort 17 B 5
Bossies 17 B 5
Bossiesvlei 14 A 2
Bosterlea 11 D 6
Boston 13 B 4
Bothaspas 18 D 3
Bothaville 17 C 6
Bothithong 16 C 3
Botleng 18 B 2
Bot River 4 D 2
Botshabelo 11 B 6
Bourke's Luck 21 C 5
Bo-Wadrif 4 B 3
Boyateng 18 A 1
Braemar 13 C 4
Brakbos 10 B 1
Brakpan 18 B 2
Brakpoort 10 D 3
Brakspruit 17 C 6
Brandfort 11 A 6
Brandkop 9 D 5
Brandrivier 5 C 4
Brandvlei 9 C 5
Brandwag 5 C 5
Braunschweig 19 C 4
Bray 16 A 3
Breakfast Vlei 7 B 4
Bredasdorp 4 D 3
Breipaal 11 C 6
Brent Park 18 D 1
Breyten 18 B 3
Bridgewater 21 A 4
Brits 20 D 2
Britstown 10 C 3
Britten 17 D 5
Broedersput 17 C 4
Broederstroom 18 A 1
Brombeek 21 A 4
Brondal 21 D 5
Bronkhorstspruit 18 B 2
Brooks Nek 12 C 3
Brospan 9 C 6
Brukkaros 14 A 3
Bruntville 13 B 4
Bruyns Hill 13 B 4
Buckingham 17 B 6
Bucklands 10 A 3
Buffeljags Bay 4 D 2
Buffeljags River 4 C 3
Buffels Bay 5 C 6
Buffelsbank 8 B 2
Buffelsdoorn 20 C 1
Buffelsdoring 12 D 1
Buffelsdrifhek 20 B 1
Buffelsfontein 17 C 6
Buffelsfontein 6 B 2
Buffelsvlei 21 D 5
Buitenzorg 19 C 4
Bukwana 7 A 4
Bulembu 19 B 5
Bulge River 20 C 2
Bulletrap 8 B 3
Bulpan 18 A 2
Bultfontein 17 D 5
Bulwana 15 A 4
Bulwer 13 B 4
Burgersdorp 11 D 6
Burgersfort 21 C 5
Burgervilleweg 11 D 4
Burnshill 7 B 4
Bushbuckridge 21 D 5
Bushlands 19 D 6
Bushman's Nek 12 B 3
Bushmans River Mouth 6 C 3
Butha-Buthe 12 A 2
Butterworth 7 A 5
Buysdorp 21 B 4
Bylsteel 21 B 4

C

Cacadu 7 A 4
Cala Road 12 D 1
Cala 12 D 1
Caledon 4 D 2
Calitzdorp Spa 5 C 4
Calitzdorp 5 C 4
Calvert 19 D 4
Calvinia 9 D 5
Cambria 6 C 1
Cameron's Glen 6 B 3
Campbell 10 A 3
Camperdown 13 B 4
Cannon Rocks 6 C 3
Cannonvale 6 C 3
Cape Agulhas 4 D 3
Cape St Francis 6 D 2
Cape Town 4 C 1
Carletonville 18 B 1
Carlisle Bridge 6 B 3
Carlisonia 17 B 6
Carlow 21 A 4
Carlton 11 D 4
Carnarvon 10 D 2
Carolina 19 B 4
Carolusberg 8 B 3
Casteel 21 D 5
Catembe 19 B 6
Cathcart 7 A 4
Cathedral Peak 12 A 3
Cato Ridge 13 B 4
Catuane 19 C 6
Cebe 7 B 5
Cedarville 12 C 3
Cederberg 4 B 2
Centuli 7 B 5
Centurion 18 B 2
Ceres 4 C 2
Chalumna 7 B 4
Chamchawib 14 A 2
Chamieites 14 C 3
Champagne Castle 12 A 3
Chamunange 21 A 4
Charl Cilliers 18 C 3
Charlestown 18 C 3
Charlesville 11 B 5
Chatsworth 13 B 5
Chicualacuala 21 A 6
Chidima 17 B 6
Chieveley 13 A 4
Chikwarakwara 21 A 5
Christiana 17 D 5
Chromedale 20 D 2
Churchhaven 4 B 1
Cintsa Mouth 7 B 5
Cintsa West 7 B 5
Citrusdal 4 B 2
Clansthal 13 C 5
Clanville 12 D 1
Clanwilliam 4 A 2
Clarens 12 A 2
Clarkebury 7 A 5
Clarkson 6 C 1
Clewer 18 B 3
Clifford 12 D 1
Clocolan 12 A 1
Clydesdale 18 C 1
Coalville 18 B 3
Coega 6 C 2
Coenbult 14 C 3
Coerney 6 C 2
Coetzersdam 17 C 4
Coffee Bay 7 A 6
Cofimvaba 7 A 4
Coghlan 7 A 5
Colchester 6 C 3
Coleford 12 C 3
Colenso 13 A 4
Colesberg 11 C 5
Coligny 17 B 6
Committees Drift 7 B 4
Concordia 16 B 2
Concordia 8 B 3
Content 17 D 4
Conway 6 A 2
Cookhouse 6 B 3
Copperton 10 B 2
Cornelia 18 C 2
Cottage 21 C 4
Cottondale 21 C 5
Cradock 6 A 2
Cramond 16 C 1
Crecy 20 C 3
Crocodile Bridge Gate 19 A 5
Crooks Corner 21 A 6
Cross Roads 7 B 4
Croydon 19 B 5
Cullinan 18 A 2
Curia 21 A 6
Curry's Post 13 B 4

D

Dadane 12 C 3
Dagab 9 B 5
Dagbreek 10 A 1
Daleside 18 B 1
Dalmanutha 19 A 4
Dalton 13 B 4
Dan 21 C 5
Daniëlskuil 16 D 3
Daniëlsrus 18 D 2
Daninge 7 C 4
Dannhauser 18 D 3
Dansters 12 C 1
Dargle 13 B 4
Darling 4 C 1
Darnall 13 B 5
Dassen Island 4 C 1
Dassiefontein 6 A 1
Davel 18 B 3
Daveyton 18 B 2
Davignab Süd 15 D 5
De Aar 10 C 3
De Beers 17 C 4
De Bos 4 A 2
De Brug 11 B 5
De Doorns 4 C 2
De Gracht 20 A 3
De Hoek 4 B 1
De Hoek 5 C 4
De Kelders 4 D 2
De Klerk 10 D 3
De Kol 6 C 3
De Kop 9 C 4
De Kuilen 18 C 3
De Langesdrif 18 C 3
De Rust 5 C 5
De Wildt 20 D 2
Dealesville 11 A 5
Dedeben 16 C 2
Deelfontein 10 D 3
Deelpan 17 B 5
Deetlefsville 10 C 3
Delareyville 17 C 5
Delfkom 19 C 5
Delmas 18 B 2
Delportshoop 11 A 4
Dendron 21 B 4
Deneysville 18 C 1
Dennilton 21 D 4
Deorham 16 C 3
Derby 17 B 6
Derdepoort 20 C 1
Despatch 6 C 2
Devenishputs 15 C 5
Devon 18 B 2
Devondale 17 C 4
Dewar 16 C 3
Dewetsdorp 11 B 6
Dibeng 16 D 2
Dibeng 20 B 3
Dibete 20 B 1
Die Dam 4 D 2
Die Hoek 5 C 6
Die Vlug 5 C 6
Diemansput 9 B 6
Diepdal 19 B 4
Diepdrif 9 D 5
Diepkloof 5 C 5
Diepwalle 5 C 6
Dikabeya 20 A 2
Dikgale 21 B 4
Dimbaza 7 B 4
Dindela 18 A 3
Dingapong 21 C 5
Dingleton 16 D 2
Dinokana 17 A 5
Dinokwe 20 B 1
Dinopeng 16 C 3
Dinuzulu 13 A 5
Diphuti 21 C 5
Dirkiesdorp 19 C 4
Dirkiesrus 17 B 4
Dithakong 16 C 3
Dithakong 17 B 5
Diti 21 A 5
Ditlhake 11 B 4
Ditloung 16 D 2
Ditshipeng 16 C 3
Dkoyi 12 D 2
Dlowana 13 A 5
Dominionville 17 C 6
Dondotsha 13 A 6
Donkerpoort 11 C 5
Donnybrook 13 B 4
Doornfontein 20 D 2
Doornkraal 13 A 4
Dordrecht 12 D 1
Doring Bay 4 A 1
Doringbos 4 A 2
Doringbult 17 B 5
Doringkop 13 B 5
Dorset 20 C 3
Douglas 10 A 3
Douglas 18 B 3
Dover 18 C 1
Downes 9 D 5
Draaiberg 6 B 1
Draaikraal 18 A 3
Draghoender 10 B 2
Drakensberg Garden 12 B 3
Drakensberg Sun 12 A 3
Draycott 12 A 3
Drayton 4 D 2
Driebad 11 C 5
Driefontein 12 A 3
Driefontein 16 B 3
Driefontein 19 C 4
Driekop Mine 21 C 4
Driekoppies 19 A 5
Driver's Drift 7 A 4
Droëputs 10 D 1
Droërivier 5 A 5
Droëspruit 16 D 2
Droëvlakte 5 D 4
Droëvlei 5 C 4
Drummondlea 20 C 3
Dry Harts 17 C 4
Dudfield 17 B 5
Dududu 13 C 4
Duikersdal 10 A 2
Duiwelskloof 21 B 4
Dukathole 11 C 6
Dullstroom 21 D 4
Dumbe 19 C 4
Dumisa 13 C 4
Dundee 19 D 4
Dundonald 19 B 4
Dupleston 11 C 6
Dupperspos 17 B 6
Durban North 13 B 5
Durban 13 B 5
Durbanville 4 C 1
Dwaal 11 D 4
Dwaalboom 20 D 1
Dwaalhoek 16 D 1
Dwaleni 19 C 5
Dwarsberg 17 A 6
Dwarskersbos 4 B 1
Dwesa 7 A 6
Dweshula 13 C 4
Dwyka 5 B 4
Dysselsdorp 5 C 5
Dzanani 21 A 4

E

East London 7 B 5
Eastpoort 6 B 3
Eastwolds 13 C 4
Ebenhaeser 8 D 3
eBhuga 19 A 5
Edenburg 11 B 5
Edendale 13 B 4
Edengrove 13 B 4
Edenvale 18 B 2
Edenville 18 D 1
Eendekuil 4 B 2
Eensgevonden 11 A 6
Eeram 18 D 2
Eerste River 4 C 1
Egham 16 B 3
Eidsamub 14 A 3
Eindpaal 15 A 4
Ekangala 18 A 2
Eksteenfontein 8 A 2
eKulindeni 19 B 4

Page
eKuvukeni 13 A 4
Elands Bay 4 A 1
Elands Heights 12 D 2
Elandsdrift 11 A 4
Elandshoek 19 A 4
Elandskop 13 B 4
Elandslaagte 13 A 4
Elandsputte 17 B 5
Elangeni 13 B 4
Eldorado 20 A 3
Eleasar 17 C 6
Elgin 4 D 2
Elim 21 B 4
Elim 4 D 2
Elliot 12 D 2
Elliotdale 7 A 5
Ellisras 20 B 2
Elmeston 20 C 2
Eloff 18 B 2
eMahlubini 7 B 4
Emantuma 19 D 6
eManzini 19 A 5
eMbalenhle 18 B 2
Embotyi 12 D 3
eMjindini 19 B 4
eMondlo 19 D 4
Empangeni 13 A 6
eMzinoni 18 B 3
Endicott 18 B 2
Engcobo 7 A 5
eNhlalakahle 13 A 4
Ennerdale 18 B 1
Enselspruit 18 B 1
Enselsrus 17 B 5
Enterprise 20 B 2
eNtshatshongo 7 A 5
eNtsimekweni 12 C 1
Entumeni 13 A 5
Enzelsberg 17 A 6
E'Thembeni 10 B 2
Erasmia 18 B 1
Ermelo 18 B 3
Erts 16 D 2
Erts 21 D 4
Eshowe 13 A 5
Esigodini 19 D 4
eSikhawini 13 A 6
eSizameleni 19 C 4
Eskdale 16 C 3
Espagsdrif 17 D 4
Estancia 18 B 3
Estcourt 13 A 4
Eston 13 B 4
eThandakukhanya 19 C 4
Etwatwa 18 B 2
Eureka 16 C 3
Evander 18 B 2
Evaton 18 B 1
Excelsior 12 A 1
eXwili 7 A 5
eZamokuhle 18 C 3
eZibeleni 7 A 4
eZitandini 7 A 5
Ezulwini 19 B 5

F

Fafung 18 A 1
Falkenhorst 14 A 3
Fallodon 7 C 4
Fanie's Island 19 D 6
Fateng-Tse-Ntsho 18 D 1
Fauresmith 11 B 5
Fawn-Leas 13 B 4
Feldschuhhorn 14 C 3
Felixton 13 A 6
Ferndale 12 C 3
Fernie 19 B 4
Ferreira 11 B 6
Ficksburg 12 A 2
Firgrove 4 C 2
Fisantekraal 4 C 3
Fish Hoek 4 D 1
Fish River 6 A 2
Flagstaff 12 D 3
Florisbad 11 A 5
Floukraal 12 D 1
Fochville 18 B 1

Page
Forbes Reef 19 B 5
Fort Beaufort 6 B 3
Fort Brown 6 B 3
Fort Donald 12 C 3
Fort Jackson 7 B 4
Fort Mistake 18 D 3
Fort Nottingham 13 B 4
Fountain Head 6 B 3
Fouriesburg 12 A 2
Frankfort 18 C 2
Frankfort 7 B 4
Franklin 12 C 3
Franschhoek 4 C 2
Fransenhof 10 B 2
Franskraalstrand 4 D 2
Fraserburg 5 A 4
Fraser's Camp 7 C 4
Frederickshoek 17 D 6
Frere 13 A 4
Friedenau 13 C 4
Frisgewaagd 14 B 2
Frylinckspan 16 C 2

G

Gabane 20 A 1
Gaborone 20 A 1
GaDikgale 20 B 3
Gainachas 14 A 3
GaKomape 21 B 4
Ga-Luka 20 D 2
GaMabelebele 20 A 3
GaMabitsela 20 B 3
GaMabotsa 21 C 4
GaMaja 21 C 4
Ga-Malwane 21 C 5
Ga-Mamatlhola 21 C 5
GaMametsa 21 C 5
GaMankgodi 20 B 3
GaMankopane 21 C 4
GaMantlhodi 20 B 3
GaMasemola 21 C 4
GaMathiba 21 C 4
GaMathule 21 B 4
GaMatlala 21 D 4
Ga-Matshogo 17 A 5
GaMatswe 21 B 5
GaMmakola 18 A 2
GaModipana 20 C 3
Gamoep 8 B 3
Ga-Mogopa 17 B 6
GaMolekwa 20 B 3
GaMolepo 21 C 4
GaMonyebodi 20 B 3
Ga-Mopedi 16 C 3
Gamoswaana 17 A 5
GaMotlana 20 C 3
Ga-Motlatla 17 B 6
Ga-Motlhware 16 C 3
Gans Bay 4 D 2
Gansfontein 4 B 2
Ganspan 17 D 4
Ganyesa 17 B 4
GaPhahla 21 C 4
Ga-Ramatale 16 C 3
Ga-Ramodingwana 17 B 6
GaRamokgopa 21 B 4
Ga-Rankuwa 20 D 2
Gariep Dam 11 C 5
Garies 8 C 3
Garinals 15 B 4
Garub 14 C 1
GaSeleka 20 B 2
GaSetshaba 20 B 3
Gatberg 12 D 2
Ga-Tlhose 16 D 3
Gawachab 14 C 3
Gcina 7 A 4
Geelwal 4 A 2
Gege 19 C 4
Geluksburg 12 A 3
Gelukspruit 15 D 6
Gemsbokvlakte 17 B 4
Gemsvlakte 15 D 4
Gemvale 12 D 3
Genadendal 4 C 2
Geneva 18 D 1
Gengqe 7 A 5

Page
George 5 C 5
Gerdau 17 B 5
Germiston 18 B 2
Geysdorp 17 B 5
Gibeon Station 14 A 3
Gibeon 14 A 3
Gilead 20 B 3
Gingindlovu 13 A 5
Giyani 21 B 5
Glaudina 17 C 5
Glen Cowie 21 D 4
Glen Echo 13 C 4
Glen Harmony 17 D 6
Glen Mill 13 B 5
Glen Muir 7 B 5
Glen Thorn 6 B 3
Glen 11 A 6
Glencoe 19 D 4
Glenconnor 6 C 2
Glenmore Beach 13 D 4
Glenmore 19 B 4
Glenside 13 B 5
Glosam Park 16 D 2
Glückstadt 19 D 4
Goageb 14 C 2
Goba 19 B 6
Gobas 14 C 3
Goedemoed 11 C 6
Goedverwacht 4 B 1
Golden Fleece 17 D 6
Golden Valley 6 B 3
Golela 19 C 5
Gonubie 7 B 5
Goodhope 17 A 5
Goodhouse 8 A 3
Goodwood 4 C 1
Gordon's Bay 4 D 2
Gorges 14 D 3
Gottenburg 18 C 1
Gouda 4 C 2
Goudini 4 D 2
Gouldville 21 A 5
Gourits 5 D 4
Gouritsmond 5 D 5
Graaff-Reinet 6 A 1
Graafwater 4 A 1
Grabouw 4 D 2
Grabwasser 14 D 3
Grahamstown 6 C 3
Granaatboskolk 9 C 5
Granite 21 B 4
Graskop 21 D 5
Grasmere 18 B 1
Graspan 11 B 4
Grasplatz 14 C 1
Grass Valley Mine 21 C 4
Grauwater 15 A 4
Gravelotte 21 C 5
Great Brak River 5 C 5
Great Vaalkop Island 9 A 5
Greenlands 18 C 1
Gregory 20 A 3
Greylingstad 18 C 2
Greyton 4 C 2
Greytown 13 A 4
Griquatown 10 A 3
Groblersdal 18 A 3
Groblershoop 10 A 1
Groenberg Suid 9 C 5
Groenebloem 17 C 6
Groenkop 6 B 3
Groenpunt 18 C 1
Groenriviersmond 8 D 2
Groenvlei 19 C 4
Groot Marico 20 D 1
Groot Mier 15 C 6
Groot Waterval 5 C 4
Grootdraai 20 B 3
Grootdrink 10 A 1
Grootfontein 14 A 2
Grootgeluk 20 B 2
Grootkloof 4 A 2
Grootkraal 5 C 5
Grootmis 8 B 2
Grootpan 17 B 6
Grootvlei 18 C 2
Groveput 10 B 2
Gruisdrif 11 A 6
Grunau 15 D 4

Page
Gründorner 14 A 3
Guibes 14 C 2
Gujini 13 A 4
Gumtree 12 A 1
Gunab 14 B 3
Gwadana 7 A 5
Gwiligwili 7 B 4

H

Ha Makoae 12 C 2
Haakdoring 20 C 3
Haakdoringdraai 18 A 3
Haalenberg 14 C 1
Haarlem 5 C 6
Hackney 6 A 3
HaDavhana 21 B 5
Haenertsburg 21 C 4
Haga-Haga 7 B 5
Hagesdam 11 B 5
Halane 7 A 5
Halcyon Drift 12 D 2
Halfmanshof 4 B 2
Hali 7 A 4
Hallatt's Hope 17 C 5
Hamab 15 D 5
Ha-Magoro 21 B 5
HaMakuya 21 A 5
Hamburg 7 C 4
Hammanshof 4 C 2
Hammanskraal 18 A 2
Hanaus 14 A 3
Hange 7 A 4
Hankey 6 C 2
Hanover Road 11 D 4
Hanover 11 D 4
Happy Valley 4 C 3
Ha-Rasebei 11 B 5
Hardekraaltjie 20 B 2
Harding 13 C 4
Hardup 12 D 1
Harefield 6 B 2
Harkerville 5 C 6
Harrisburg 17 C 6
Harrismith 12 A 3
Hartbeesfontein 17 C 6
Hartbeespoort 18 A 1
Hartebeeskop 19 B 4
Hartenbos 5 D 5
Hartswater 17 D 4
Haruchas 15 A 4
Hattingspruit 19 D 4
Hawerklip 18 B 2
Hawston 4 D 2
Hayfield 11 B 4
Hazel 5 A 6
Hazyview 19 A 5
Heatonville 13 A 6
Hectorspruit 19 A 5
Heidelberg 18 B 2
Heidelberg 5 C 4
Heilbron 18 C 1
Hekpoort 18 B 1
Helmeringhausen 14 B 2
Helpmekaar 13 A 4
Helvetia 11 B 6
Hendriksdal 19 A 4
Hendrina 18 B 3
Hendrinakrag 18 B 3
Hennenman 17 D 6
Henning 11 D 6
Herbertsdale 5 C 4
Herefords 19 B 5
Hermanus 4 D 2
Hermanusdorings 20 C 2
Hermon 4 C 2
Herold 5 C 5
Herolds Bay 5 C 5
Herschel 12 C 1
Hertzogville 17 D 5
Het Kruis 4 B 1
Heuningneskloof 11 B 4
Heuningspruit 18 C 1
Hex River Tunnel 4 C 2
Heydon 6 A 1
Hibberdene 13 C 4
Hibernia 12 A 1
Highflats 13 C 4
Highlands 6 C 3

Page
Himeville 12 B 3
Hlabisa 19 D 5
Hlathikhulu 19 C 5
Hlatikulu 12 B 3
Hleoheng 12 A 2
Hlobane 19 D 4
Hlobo 7 A 5
Hlogotlou 18 A 3
Hlohlo 19 A 5
Hlotse (Leribe) 12 A 2
Hluhluwe 19 D 6
Hluleka 7 A 6
Hluti 19 C 5
Hobeni 7 A 6
Hobhouse 12 B 1
Hoedjies 9 D 5
Hoedspruit 21 C 5
Hoekwil 5 C 5
Hofmeyr 6 A 3
Hogsback 7 B 4
Hohane 12 D 3
Hole in the Wall 7 A 6
Holmdene 18 C 2
Holme Park 20 D 3
Holoog 14 C 3
Holy Cross 12 D 3
Hondefontein 5 A 4
Hondeklip Bay 8 C 2
Hoogte 18 C 1
Hoopstad 17 D 5
Hope 14 C 2
Hopefield 4 B 1
Hopetown 11 B 4
Hotazel 16 C 2
Houmoed 9 B 4
Hout Bay 4 C 1
Houtbosdorp 21 C 4
Houtkop 19 C 4
Houtkraal 11 C 4
Houtnek 11 A 6
Houtnek 12 A 1
Houw Hoek 4 D 2
Howick 13 B 4
Huams 14 A 2
Huhudi 17 C 4
Hukuwa 6 A 3
Humansdorp 6 C 2
Huns 14 C 2
Huntleigh 21 A 4
Hutchinson 10 D 3

I

Ibika 7 A 5
Idutywa 7 A 5
Ifafa Beach 13 C 4
Ifafa 13 C 4
Ikageleng 17 A 5
Ikageng 17 C 6
Ikhutseng 17 D 4
iLangakazi 13 A 5
Ilinge 7 A 4
Illovo Beach 13 C 5
iMbali 13 B 4
Immerpan 21 C 4
Impendle 13 B 4
Inachab 14 C 3
Inanda 13 B 5
Indwe 12 D 1
Infanta 5 D 4
iNgogo 18 D 3
Ingwavuma 19 C 5
Inhaca 19 B 6
Inkbospan 15 C 6
Inverdoorn 4 B 3
Ipelegeng 17 C 5
Ipopeng 11 B 5
Isipingo Beach 13 C 5
Isithebe 13 B 5
Iswepe 19 C 4
Itsoseng 17 B 5
Ixopo 13 C 4
Izingolweni 13 D 4

J

Jacobsdal 11 B 4
Jagersfontein 11 B 5

Page
Jamela 21 B 5
Jameson's Drift 13 A 5
Jamestown 12 D 1
Jammerdrif 12 B 1
Jan Kempdorp 17 D 4
Jane Furse 21 D 4
Jansenville 6 B 1
Jeffreys Bay 6 C 2
Jeppe's Reef 19 A 5
Jericho 18 A 1
Johannesburg 18 B 1
Johnson's Post 5 D 5
Jojweni 7 A 5
Josling 10 A 1
Joubertina 6 C 1
Jouberton 17 C 6
Jozana's Hoek 12 C 1
Jozini 19 C 6
Jujura 7 A 5
Jurgen 14 C 3

K

Kaallaagte 18 D 1
Kaapmuiden 19 A 5
Kaapsehoop 21 D 5
Kabeana 20 C 3
KaDinga 21 B 5
Kagiso 16 B 3
KaJilongo 21 B 5
Kakamas 9 A 5
Kalbaskraal 4 C 1
Kalkbank 21 B 4
Kalkmond 9 A 5
Kalkwerf 10 A 1
KaMadonsi 21 B 5
Kamagams 14 A 2
KaMapuva 21 B 5
Kamassies 8 C 3
KaMatsakali 21 B 5
KaMavele 21 B 5
KaMbokota 21 B 4
Kameel 17 B 4
KaMhinga 21 A 5
Kamieskroon 8 C 3
Kamkusi 21 A 4
Kammiebos 6 C 1
KaMphambo 21 B 5
Kamsogwaba 19 A 5
Kana 18 A 1
Kanakies 9 D 4
Kanana 17 C 6
KaNkomo 21 B 5
KaNkuzani 21 B 5
Kanoneiland 10 A 1
Kanus 15 D 4
KaNyamazane 19 A 5
Kanye 17 A 5
Karaam 15 A 4
Karasburg 15 D 4
Karatara 5 C 5
Karee 11 A 6
Kareedouw 6 C 1
Kareefontein 11 A 6
Kareekloof 10 B 3
KaRhangani 21 B 5
Karino 19 A 5
Karos 10 A 1
KaSabulane 21 B 5
Kasouga 6 C 3
Katberg 6 B 3
Kathu 16 D 2
Katikati 7 A 4
Katkop 9 C 5
Katlehong 18 B 2
Katse 12 B 2
Katsibane 20 D 3
Kauletsi 20 B 2
Kaya se Put 20 D 1
Kayser's Beach 7 B 4
Keate's Drift 13 A 4
Keetmanshoop 14 B 3
Kei Mouth 7 B 5
Kei Road 7 B 4
Keimoes 9 A 6
Keiskammahoek 7 B 4
Kelso 13 C 4
Kemp 19 C 4
Kempton Park 18 B 2

Page
Kendal 18 B 2
Kendrew 6 B 1
Kenhardt Sta. 9 B 6
Kenhardt 10 B 1
Kenilworth 11 A 4
Kennedy's Vale 21 D 4
Kennoway 6 A 3
Kentani 7 B 5
Kenton on Sea 6 C 3
Kerkraad 5 C 5
Kestell 12 A 2
Ketane 12 C 2
Kgagodi 20 A 2
Kgalala 11 A 6
Kgoroshi 21 B 4
Kgotsong 17 C 6
Khabo 12 A 2
Khadubeng 18 A 2
Khanyane 12 A 2
Khanyiso 6 B 2
Kharkams 8 C 3
Khayakhulu 20 D 1
Khayamnandi 11 D 5
Khayelitsha 4 C 1
Khubvi 21 A 5
Khudutlou 17 D 4
Khuis 16 C 1
Khukhune 12 A 2
Khuma 17 C 6
Khureng 21 C 4
Khutsong 18 B 1
Khyayakhulu 17 A 6
Kidd's Beach 7 B 4
Kiepersol 19 A 4
Kiesel 20 C 2
Kieserville 17 B 5
Kilmun 12 B 3
Kimberley 11 A 4
Kinana 20 B 3
King William's Town 7 B 4
Kingsburgh 13 C 5
Kingscote 12 C 3
Kingsley 19 D 4
Kingswood 17 C 5
Kinkelbos 6 C 3
Kinross 18 B 2
Kirkwood 6 C 2
Klaarstroom 5 C 5
Klaserie 21 C 5
Klawer 4 A 1
Klein Bay 4 D 2
Klein Karas 14 D 3
Klein Sleutelfontein 5 B 5
Klein Tshipise 21 A 5
Kleinbegin 9 A 6
Kleinberg 5 D 5
Kleinemonde 7 C 4
Kleinmond 4 D 2
Kleinood 20 C 3
Kleinplaat 5 C 5
Kleinpoort 6 C 2
Kleinsee 8 B 2
Klerksdorp 17 C 6
Klerkskraal 17 B 6
Klipdale 4 D 3
Klipdam 15 C 5
Klipdrif 18 B 1
Klipfontein 12 B 1
Klipfontein 6 B 3
Klipplaat 6 B 1
Klipplaatdrift 17 B 6
Klippunt 10 A 1
Kliprand 9 C 4
Kliprivier 13 A 4
Klip River 18 B 1
Klipskool 19 A 4
Klipwerf 9 D 5
Knapdaar 11 C 6
Koës 15 B 4
Kobe 9 D 4
Kochena 15 C 4
Koegasbrug 10 B 2
Koegrabie 10 A 1
Koekenaap 8 D 3
Koekoeskop 20 D 2
Koelemansrus 20 C 3
Koffiefontein 11 B 4
Kokerboom 15 D 5
Kokosi 18 B 1

PLACE NAMES INDEX

Kokstad 12 C 3
Kokwaneng 21 D 4
Kolke 9 B 6
Koloni 12 D 3
Komaggas 8 B 2
Komatipoort 19 A 5
Komga 7 B 5
Komkans 8 D 3
Komkhulu 7 A 5
Kommadagga 6 B 3
Kommandodrif 17 D 6
Kommetjie 4 D 1
Kommissiedrif 11 B 6
Kommissiepoort 12 B 1
Koningnaas 8 C 2
Konstabel 4 C 3
Koolbank 19 B 4
Koopan-Suid 15 C 6
Koopmansfontein Sta. 16 D 3
Koopmansfontein 10 A 3
Koornplaats 5 B 4
Kootjieskolk 9 D 5
Kopong 20 A 1
Koppies 18 C 1
Koringberg 4 B 1
Kosmos 18 A 1
Koster 17 B 6
Kotakala 17 C 6
Kotzeshoop 8 A 2
Kotzesrus 8 D 3
Koup 5 B 4
Koutjie 5 C 5
Kraaibrug 12 C 1
Kraaifontein 4 C 1
Kraaipan 17 B 5
Kraaldoom 5 C 4
Kraankuil 11 B 4
Krakeel River 5 C 6
Kransfontein 18 D 2
Kransfontein 19 B 4
Kranshoek 5 C 6
Kranskop 13 A 5
Kranspoort Dorp 18 A 3
Kriel 18 B 3
Kromdraai 21 D 4
Kromellenboog 21 C 5
Kromrivier 5 A 6
Kroomie 6 B 3
Kroondal 18 A 1
Kroonstad 18 D 1
Krugersdorp 18 B 1
Krugerspos 19 A 4
Kruidfontein 5 B 5
Kruisfontein 6 C 1
Kruispad 18 D 2
Kruispad 4 B 3
Kruis River 5 C 5
KuBhonxa 12 D 3
Kuboes 8 A 2
Kubuta 19 C 5
KuMbaxa 7 A 4
Kums 15 D 5
Ku-Ndeyingana 13 C 4
Kuruman 16 C 3
Kutenhuas 14 A 3
Kutlwano 11 A 4
Kutlwanono 17 D 6
Kuyasa 11 C 5
Kwa Magwaza 13 A 5
KwaBhubesi 12 C 2
KwaBityi 7 A 5
KwaDinda 12 D 3
KwaDukuza 13 B 5
KwaDungu 12 D 3
KwaFanti 7 A 4
Kwaggafontein 20 D 3
Kwaggaskloofdam 4 C 2
Kwa-Guqa 18 B 3
Kwakwatsi 18 C 1
KwaLupindo 12 C 2
KwaMadikana 7 A 4
KwaMafunze 13 B 4
KwaMagoda 13 B 4
Kwamahlathi 19 D 5
KwaMahomba 7 B 5
Kwamakhutha 13 C 5
KwaMangati 7 B 4
KwaMashu 13 B 5
KwaMbonambi 13 A 6
KwaMhlanga 18 A 2
Kwa-Mkhize 12 B 3
KwaMoseja 18 A 1
KwaMpeko 7 C 4
KwaMzola 7 A 4
KwaNdelane 7 A 5
KwaNgwanase 19 C 6
KwaNobuhle 6 C 2
KwaNojoli 6 B 2
KwaNokatana 7 A 5
KwaNonzame 11 D 4
KwaNonzwakazi 6 C 3
KwaNtlola 12 C 3
KwaThandeka 19 C 4
Kwa-Thema 18 B 2
KwaZamokuhle 18 B 3
KwaZamukucinga 6 B 1
KwaZamuxolo 11 D 4
KwaZanele 18 B 3
KwaZenzele 6 C 3
KwaZulu 7 A 6
Kwezi 13 A 4

L

La Cotte 21 B 5
La Lucia 13 B 5
La Mercy 13 B 5
Laaiplek 4 B 1
Ladismith 5 C 4
Lady Frere 7 A 4
Lady Grey 12 C 1
Ladybrand 12 B 1
Ladysmith 12 A 3
Laersdrif 21 D 4
Lahlangubo 12 D 2
Laing's Nek 18 C 3
Laingsburg 5 B 4
Lakalakala 20 C 3
Lake Eric 6 C 3
Lake Chrissie 19 B 4
Lambert's Bay 4 A 1
Lammerkop 21 D 4
Landplaas 8 D 3
Langberg 16 D 2
Langebaan Road 4 B 1
Langebaan 4 B 1
Langholm 6 C 3
Langklip 15 D 6
Langkrans 19 D 4
Lavumisa 19 C 5
Laxey 16 C 3
Leandra 18 B 2
Lebaneng 17 C 5
Lebohang 18 B 2
Lebotloane 18 A 1
Lebowakgomo 21 C 4
Ledig 20 D 1
Leeudoringstad 17 C 6
Leeufontein 18 A 2
Leeu-Gamka 5 B 5
Leeupoort 20 D 2
Lefurutshane 17 A 6
Legkraal 21 B 4
Legonyane 20 D 2
Lehurutshe 17 A 5
Leipoldtville 4 A 1
Lejone 12 B 2
Lekgophung 20 A 1
Lekkersing 8 A 2
Lekoko 17 B 5
Lekokoaneng 12 B 1
Leliefontein 8 C 3
Lemoenshoek 5 C 4
Lenasia 18 B 1
Lentsweletau 20 A 1
Lephalale 20 B 2
Lerala 20 A 2
Lesseyton 7 A 4
Letaba 21 C 5
Letjiesbos 5 B 5
Letlhabile 18 A 1
Letshana 20 A 2
Letsitele 21 C 5
Letswatla 20 B 3
Levubu 21 B 5
Leybank 15 A 4
Leydsdorp 21 C 5
Libertas 18 D 1
Libode 12 D 3
Lichtenburg 17 B 5
Lidgetton 13 B 4
Likalaneng 12 B 2
Likhetlane 12 C 2
Limburg 20 B 3
Lime Acres 10 A 3
Linakeng 12 B 3
Lindequesdrif 18 C 1
Lindeshof 4 D 2
Lindley 18 D 1
Lindleyspoort 17 A 6
Line Drift 7 B 4
Linton 21 A 4
Lionelton 18 B 2
Little Brak River 5 C 5
Little Switzerland 12 A 3
Livingstone 17 A 5
L'Agulhas 4 D 3
Lobamba 19 B 5
Lobatse 17 A 5
Lochiel 19 B 4
Loerie 6 C 2
Loeriesfontein 9 D 4
Logagane 17 B 4
Logageng 17 B 4
Lohatlha 16 D 2
Lokweni 12 D 3
Longlands 11 A 4
Longvale 6 C 3
Lorraine 21 C 5
Losdorings 17 D 6
Lose 20 B 1
Lotana 12 D 3
Lothair 19 B 4
Lotlhakane 17 B 5
Loubad 20 C 3
Louis Trichardt 21 B 4
Louisvale 10 A 1
Lourdes 12 C 3
Lourensbeen 17 C 4
Louwna 17 C 4
Louw's Creek 19 A 5
Louwsburg 19 D 5
Lower Blinkwater 6 B 3
Loxton 10 D 2
Lubbeskolk 9 B 5
Lubhuku 19 B 5
Luckhoff 11 B 4
Ludeke 12 D 3
Lukhanyisweni 11 C 4
Lulekani 21 C 5
Lundin's Nek 12 C 1
Lundzi 19 B 4
Lunsklip 20 C 3
Lusikisiki 12 D 3
Lusizi 7 B 5
Lutsheko 7 A 6
Luttig 5 B 5
Lutzburg 9 A 5
Lutzputs 9 A 5
Lutzville 8 D 3
Luxeni 7 A 4
Luyengo 19 B 5
Lydenburg 21 D 5
Lykso 16 C 3
Lüneburg 19 C 4

M

Maake 21 C 5
Maanhaarrand 18 B 1
Maartenshoop 19 A 4
Maasstroom 20 A 3
Mabaalstad 17 A 6
Mabede 12 D 3
Mabehana 7 A 6
Mabeskraal 17 A 6
Mabibi 19 C 6
Maboloko 18 A 1
Mabopane 18 A 1
Mabula 20 D 2
Mabule 17 A 4
Mabvuka Jazz 21 A 4
Macaene 21 D 6
Machadodorp 19 A 4
Machaneng 20 B 2
Machangulo 19 B 6
Macia 19 A 6
Macleantown 7 B 4
Maclear 12 D 2
Madadeni 18 D 3
Madadeni 19 B 5
Madibogo 17 B 5
Madietane 20 C 3
Madikgetla 11 C 5
Madipelesa 17 D 4
Mafahaneng 18 D 2
Mafeteng 12 B 1
Mafikeng 17 B 5
Mafube 12 C 2
Mafukani 21 A 5
Mafutseni 19 B 5
Magabeni 13 C 5
Magagane 21 B 6
Magaliesburg 18 B 1
Magatle 21 C 4
Magdala 6 A 3
Magogeni 19 A 5
Magonya 21 B 5
Magoriapitse 17 A 5
Magude 19 A 6
Magudu 19 D 5
Mahalapye 20 B 1
Mahehle 13 C 4
Mahetlwe 20 A 1
Mahlabatini 19 D 5
Mahlangasi 19 D 5
Mahlatswetsa 12 A 1
Mahlutshini 12 B 3
Mahobong 12 A 2
Mahwelereng 20 C 3
Maidstone 13 B 5
Maile 18 A 1
Maipeing 17 B 5
Majwemasweu 11 A 6
Makapanstad 20 D 2
Makeleketia 12 A 1
Makgaung 21 C 5
Makgobistad 17 A 4
Makgori 17 D 4
Makhado 21 B 4
Makhwezini 13 A 6
Makobeng 20 B 2
Makokskraal 17 B 6
Makonde 21 A 5
Makopong 16 A 2
Makoppa 20 C 1
Makoseni 13 A 5
Makubung 21 C 4
Makuleni 21 A 5
Makwassie 17 C 5
Makwate 20 B 2
Malaita 21 D 4
Malealea 12 B 1
Malebogo 17 D 5
Maleketla 21 B 5
Malelane Gate 21 D 6
Maleshe 16 B 2
Malgas 4 D 3
Malingoaneng 12 B 3
Malkerns 19 B 5
Malmesbury 4 C 1
Malomo 19 C 5
Malotwana 20 A 1
Mamafubeda 18 D 2
Mamaila 21 B 5
Mamathwane 16 C 2
Mamelodi 18 A 2
Mammutla 17 D 4
Mamre 4 C 1
Manamakgoteng 20 D 2
Mandala 21 A 5
Mangaung 11 B 6
Mangeni 13 A 5
Mangobomvu 7 A 5
Mangoloaneng 12 C 2
Mangwane 7 A 5
Mangwaneni 12 D 3
Manhiça 19 A 6
Mankayane 19 C 4
Mankurwane 11 A 4
Mankweng 21 C 4
Mannamead 21 B 4
Mansfield 17 B 4
Manthestad 17 D 4
Mantsho 20 D 1
Mantsonyane 12 B 2
Manubi 7 B 5
Manyana 20 A 1
Manzi 7 A 6
Manzini 19 B 5
Maokeng 18 D 1
Mapai 21 A 6
Maphalong 21 C 4
Maphodi 11 C 5
Mapholaneng 12 B 3
Mapoleseng 12 C 2
Mapoteng 12 A 2
Mapulanguene 21 C 6
Mapumulo 13 B 5
Maputo 19 B 6
Maputsoe 12 A 2
Maqabaqabeni 12 A 3
Mara Sta. 21 B 4
Mara 21 B 4
Maraisvlei 9 A 5
Marakabei 12 B 2
Marakaneng 12 C 1
Marambane 19 A 4
Marapjane 20 D 3
Marble Hall 21 D 4
Marburg 13 C 4
Marchand 9 A 5
Mareetsane 17 B 5
Maremane 16 D 3
Margate 13 D 4
Maricodraai 20 C 1
Marievale 18 B 2
Marikana 18 A 1
Marina Beach 13 D 4
Marite 21 D 5
Marken 20 B 3
Markramsdraai 16 D 2
Marlow 6 A 2
Marnitz 20 B 3
Marokolong 20 D 3
Marquard 12 A 1
Marracuene 19 A 6
Marsala 18 D 2
Marydale 10 B 2
Masakhane 12 D 1
Masama 20 C 1
Maseru 12 B 1
Masham 12 C 1
Masibekela 19 B 5
Masibi 17 B 5
Masikhwa 21 A 5
Masinda Lodge 13 A 6
Masinyusane 10 D 3
Masisi 21 A 5
Masobe 18 A 2
Massingir 21 B 6
Mataleng 11 A 4
Matandele 19 C 5
Matatiele 12 C 3
Matato 19 C 5
Matebeng Ha Lelingoana 12 B 3
Matelile 12 B 1
Matenteng 20 D 3
Mathathane 20 A 3
Mathopestad 18 B 1
Matiwane 13 A 4
Matjiesfontein 4 B 3
Matjies River 5 C 5
Matlabas 20 C 2
Matlakeng 12 C 1
Matlala 20 D 3
Matlapaneng 17 C 4
Matlerekeng 20 D 3
Matloding 17 B 4
Matlomola 10 A 3
Matlope 20 B 2
Matlwangtlwang 18 D 1
Matola 19 B 6
Matroosberg 4 C 3
Matsa 21 A 4
Matsap 10 A 2
Matsapha 19 B 5
Matshona 12 D 3
Matsieng 12 B 1
Matsulu 19 A 5
Matukeng 12 B 1
Maunatlala 20 A 2
Mavhulani 21 B 5
Mayireni 7 A 4
Mazenod 12 B 1
Mazeppa Bay 7 B 5
Mazista 17 A 6
Mbabane 19 B 5
Mbalakweza 7 A 4
Mbazwana 19 C 6
Mbhawula 21 B 5
Mbhongo 18 A 2
Mbulungwane 19 C 5
McCarthy's Rest 16 B 2
McGregor 4 C 3
Mdantsane 7 B 4
Mdzonga 7 A 5
Meadows 11 B 6
Mecklenburg 21 C 4
Mekaling 12 C 1
Melinda 20 B 3
Melk 12 D 1
Melkbosstrand 4 C 1
Melk River 20 C 3
Melmoth 13 A 5
Meloding 17 D 6
Meltonwold 10 D 2
Melville 13 B 5
Memel 18 D 3
Merriman 10 D 3
Merrivale 13 B 4
Merry Pebble Stream 21 D 6
Merweville 5 B 4
Mesitsaneng 12 C 1
Messina 21 A 4
Metsimaholo 18 C 2
Meyerton 18 B 1
Meyerville 18 C 3
Mgobode 19 B 5
Mgwali 7 B 4
Mhlambanyatsi 19 B 4
Mhlambanyatsi 19 A 5
Mhlosheni 19 C 5
Mhlume 19 B 5
Mhluzi 18 A 3
Mica 21 C 5
Michausdal 6 A 2
Mid Illovo 13 C 4
Middel Koegas 10 B 2
Middelburg 11 D 4
Middelburg 18 A 3
Middeldrift 20 D 2
Middelfontein 20 C 3
Middelplaats Mine 16 C 2
Middelpos 4 A 3
Middelputs 16 C 1
Middelrus 13 A 4
Middelwit 20 D 1
Middledrift 7 B 4
Middleton 4 D 2
Middleton 6 B 3
Middlewater 6 B 2
Midros 11 D 4
Miershoopholte 16 D 1
Migdol 17 C 5
Milford 19 D 4
Miller 6 B 1
Milnerton 4 C 1
Minera 18 C 3
Mirage 17 C 6
Misgund 5 C 6
Mitchell's Plain 4 C 1
Mjaliswa 12 D 3
Mjanyana 7 A 5
Mjula 7 A 5
Mkambati 13 D 4
Mkhazane 13 A 5
Mkhuhlu 21 D 6
Mkhulu 19 A 5
Mkondeni 13 B 4
Mkuze 19 D 5
Mliba 19 B 5
Mlungisi 7 B 4
Mmakgori 17 B 4
Mmamabula 20 B 1
Mmamahabane 18 D 1
Mmamatlakala 20 C 3
Mmanethlake 18 A 2
Mmankgodi 20 A 1
Mmatau 17 A 6
Mmathethe 17 A 5
Mmopyane 17 A 6
Mnyani 17 C 4
Moamba 19 A 6
Mochudi 20 A 1
Modder River 11 A 4
Modimolle 20 C 3
Modimong 20 D 1
Modipane 20 A 1
Modutung 17 D 4
Moebani 21 B 4
Moedig 19 B 4
Moedwil 17 A 6
Moemaneng 12 A 1
Moeng 20 A 2
Moeswal 16 D 2
Mofulatshepe 11 C 6
Mogapi 20 A 2
Mogapinyana 20 A 2
Mogoditshane 20 A 1
Mogologola 21 C 4
Mogoto 21 C 4
Mogwase 18 A 1
Mohale's Hoek 12 C 1
Mohlakeng 18 B 1
Mohlamonyane 18 A 2
Mohlonong 20 C 3
Mokasa 17 D 4
Mokgalwaneng 20 D 1
Mokgareng 17 D 4
Mokgola 17 A 5
Mokgomane 17 A 5
Mokgosi 20 A 1
Mokhotlong 12 B 3
Mokopane 20 C 3
Mokopung Ha Nkau 12 C 2
Mokwalio 18 C 1
Molapole Maseko 18 A 1
Molatedi 20 D 1
Molenrivier 5 C 5
Molepolole 20 A 1
Moletsane 12 B 2
Molimo Nthuse 12 B 2
Molopo River 17 A 4
Moloto 20 D 3
Molshoop 4 D 3
Molteno 11 D 6
Molumong 12 B 3
Mononono 18 A 1
Monontsha 12 A 2
Mont Pelaan 18 D 3
Montagu 4 C 3
Mont-aux-Sources 12 A 3
Monte Christo 20 B 2
Montebello 13 B 5
Montrose 21 D 5
Monyakeng 17 D 6
Monzi 13 A 6
Mooi River 13 B 4
Mooifontein 14 B 2
Mooiplaas 7 B 5
Mookane 20 B 1
Mooketsi 21 B 4
Mookgophong 20 C 3
Moolman 19 C 4
Moorreesburg 4 B 1
Mopane 21 A 4
Moretele 18 A 1
Morgan's Bay 7 B 5
Morgenzon 18 C 1
Morgenzon 18 C 3
Morija 12 B 1
Morojaneng 11 B 6
Morokweng 16 B 3
Morone 21 D 5
Morristown 12 D 1
Mortimer 6 A 2
Morupule 20 A 1
Moses Mabida 6 C 2
Moshesh's Ford 12 D 2
Mosita 17 B 4
Mosomane 20 C 1
Mossel Bay 5 D 5
Motetema 21 D 4
Moteti 20 D 3
Mothibistad 16 C 3
Motjane 19 B 4
Motlhabe 17 A 6
Motlolo 21 C 5
Motsekuoa 12 B 1
Motsweding 17 D 4
Mount Alida 13 B 4
Mount Ayliff 12 D 3
Mount Carmel 16 D 3

Page
Mount Elias 13 B 5
Mount Fletcher 12 C 2
Mount Frere 12 D 3
Mount Moorosi 12 C 2
Mount Stewart 6 B 1
Moyeni (Quthing) 12 C 1
Mpafane 12 D 2
Mpaka 19 B 5
Mpemvana 19 D 4
Mpetu 7 B 5
Mphahlele 21 C 4
Mphakane 21 B 4
Mphaki 12 C 2
Mphelelo 20 B 3
Mpheleng 20 D 3
Mpila Lodge 13 A 6
Mpolweni 13 B 4
Mposa 13 A 6
Mpumalanga 13 B 4
Mpungamhlophe 19 D 5
Mqanduli 7 A 5
Msjaing 12 A 2
Mtombeni 13 A 5
Mtonjaneni 13 A 5
Mtubatuba 13 A 6
Mtunzini 13 A 6
Mtwalume 13 C 4
Muden 13 A 4
Muizenberg 4 C 1
Mukhomi 21 B 5
Muldersdrif 18 B 1
Munnik 21 B 4
Munster 13 D 4
Munyu 7 A 5
Murchison 21 C 5
Murraysburg 6 A 1
Musina 21 A 4
Mushithe 21 A 5
Muswodi 21 A 5
Mutale 21 A 5
Mvumane 12 C 2
Myfontein 10 D 3
Mzamba Beach 13 D 4
Mzamomhle 11 D 6
Mzinti 19 A 5

N

Nababeep 8 B 3
Nabas 15 D 5
Nabes 15 D 4
Nabies 9 A 5
Naboomspruit 20 C 3
Nadi 13 A 4
Nakop 15 D 5
Namaacha 19 B 5
Namahadi 18 C 2
Namakgale 21 C 5
Namies 9 B 4
Nanzes 15 D 4
Napier 4 D 3
Nariep 8 C 3
Narubis 15 C 4
Natal Spa 19 D 4
Nature's Valley 5 C 6
Ncwadi 13 B 4
Ndabakazi 7 A 5
Ndakeni 12 D 3
Ndaleni 13 B 4
Ndevana 7 B 4
NdlunKulu 7 A 5
Ndumu 19 C 6
Ndundulu 13 A 5
Ndwedwe 13 B 5
Ndzingeni 19 B 5
Neilersdrif 9 A 6
Neisip 14 B 2
Nekina 12 D 2
Nelsdrif 17 D 6
Nelshoogte 19 B 4
Nelspoort 5 A 6
Nelspruit 21 D 5
Netherby 12 B 3
Nevada 12 B 1
New Amalfi 12 C 3
New England 12 D 1
New Hanover 13 B 4
New Largo 18 B 2
New Machavie 17 C 6

Page
Newcastle 18 D 3
Newington 21 D 6
Newtown 9 D 5
Ngagane 18 D 3
Ngangelizwe 12 D 2
Ngcabasa 7 B 4
Ngobi 20 D 2
Ngodwana 21 D 5
Ngomane 19 B 5
Ngome 19 D 5
Ngqeleni 7 A 6
Ngubevu 13 A 4
Ngwathe 18 D 1
Ngwenya 19 B 4
Ngwenyeni 19 A 5
Ngxanga 12 D 3
Nhlangano 19 C 5
Nhlazatje 19 B 4
Nhlazatshe 19 D 5
Niekerkshoop 10 B 2
Nietverdiend 17 A 5
Nieu-Bethesda 6 A 1
Nieuwoudtville 9 D 4
Nigel 18 B 2
Nigramoep 8 B 2
Nkande 19 D 4
Nkandla 13 A 5
Nkonjane 13 A 6
Nkumandeni 7 A 6
Nkumba 13 B 4
Nkungwini 12 D 3
Nkwalini 13 A 5
Nkwe 20 B 3
Nkwenkwezi 7 C 4
Nobumba 7 C 4
Nocwane 7 A 5
Noenieput 15 D 5
Noetzie 5 C 6
Nokaneng 18 A 2
Nomonde 11 D 6
Nondweni 19 D 4
Nongoma 19 D 5
Nonzwakazi 10 C 3
Nooitgedacht 11 A 4
Nooitgedacht 5 C 5
Noordhoek 4 C 1
Noordkaap 19 A 4
Noordoewer 8 A 2
Normandien 18 D 3
Northam 20 D 2
Norvalspont 11 C 5
Nossob Lodge 15 A 6
Notintsila 7 A 6
Nottingham Road 13 B 4
Noupoort 11 D 4
Nous 9 A 5
Nqabeni 13 C 4
Nqalweni 12 C 3
Nqutu 19 D 4
Nseleni 13 A 6
Nshongweni 13 B 4
Nsikazi 19 A 4
Nsoko 19 C 5
Ntambanana 13 A 5
Ntha 18 D 1
Nthorwane 18 C 2
Ntibane 7 A 6
Ntlhantlhe 20 A 1
Ntlhaveni 21 A 5
Ntsundwane 7 A 6
Ntunjambili 13 A 5
Ntwane 21 D 4
Ntywenka 12 D 2
Numbi Gate 21 D 6
Nutfield 20 D 3
Nuwefontein 15 D 4
Nuwerus 8 D 3
Nuy 4 C 2
Nxaxo Mouth 7 B 5
Nyakallong 17 D 6
Nyalasa 7 A 4
Nyalazi River 19 D 6
Nyandeni 12 D 3
Nyanyadu 19 D 4
Nyara 6 B 3
Nyezane 13 A 5
Nylstroom 20 C 3
Nzhelele 21 A 4
Nzwakazi 7 A 6

Page

O

Oatlands 6 B 1
Oberholzer 18 B 1
Obobogorob 15 C 5
Odendaalsrus 17 D 6
Oetting 13 C 4
Ofcolaco 21 C 5
Ogies 18 B 2
Ohrigstad 21 D 5
Okiep 8 B 3
Old Bunting 7 A 6
Old Morley 7 A 6
Olifants Drift 20 C 1
Olifantshoek 16 D 2
Olyfberg 21 B 4
Omdraaisvlei 10 C 3
Onder-Wadrif 4 A 3
Ongers 10 C 3
Onrus River 4 D 2
Onseepkans 9 A 4
Oorlogspoort 11 D 5
Op die Berg 4 B 2
Opperman 11 B 4
Opuzane 19 C 4
Orangeville 18 C 2
Orania 11 B 4
Oranjemund 8 A 1
Orange River 11 B 4
Oranjevallei 10 A 1
Orkney 17 C 6
Orpen Gate 21 C 6
oSizweni 19 D 4
Otimati 13 B 5
Otse 17 A 5
Ottosdal 17 C 5
Ottoshoop 17 A 5
Oudekraalfontein 4 B 1
Oudtshoorn 5 C 5
Ouhoutdraai 18 C 2
Oukraal 4 D 2
Ouplaas 4 D 3
Oven 5 B 6
Overwacht 20 B 2
Overyssel 20 B 3
Oviston 11 C 5
Owendale 16 D 3
Owen's Cutting 13 A 5
Oxbow 12 A 2
Oyster Bay 6 D 1

P

Paarl 4 C 2
Paballelo 10 A 1
Pachsdraai 17 A 6
Paddock 13 C 4
Paddon 16 A 3
Padstow 16 C 3
Pafuri Gate 21 A 5
Palala 20 C 3
Palapye 20 A 1
Paleisheuwel 4 B 1
Palm Beach 13 D 4
Palmerton 12 D 3
Palmietfontein 17 C 5
Pampierstad 17 D 4
Pampoenpoort 10 D 2
Panbult 19 C 4
Papendorp 4 A 1
Papkuil 10 A 3
Paradise Beach 6 C 2
Paradise 17 C 4
Park Rynie 13 C 4
Parow 4 C 1
Parr's Halt 20 B 2
Parys 18 C 1
Patensie 6 C 2
Paternoster 4 B 1
Paterson 6 C 3
Paul Kruger Gate 21 D 6
Paul Roux 18 D 1
Paulpietersburg 19 C 4
Peace Town 12 A 3
Pearly Beach 4 D 2
Pearson's Hunt 16 D 1
Pearston 6 B 2
Peddie 7 B 4

Page
Peka 12 A 2
Pelindaba 18 B 1
Pella 17 A 6
Pella 9 A 4
Penge 21 C 5
Pennington 13 C 4
Penryn 16 C 2
Pepworth 13 A 4
Perdeberg 11 A 5
Perdekop 18 C 3
Persip 15 A 4
Perth 16 B 2
Petersburg 6 A 2
Petrus Steyn 18 D 2
Petrusburg 11 B 5
Petrusville 11 C 4
Petsana 18 D 2
Pevensey 12 B 3
Pfolz 14 B 3
Phahameng 11 A 6
Phahameng 20 C 3
Phalaborwa Gate 21 C 6
Phalaborwa 21 C 5
Phamong 12 C 2
Phelandaba 19 C 6
Phelindaba 10 A 3
Phepheng 16 A 2
Philadelphia 4 C 1
Philippolis 11 C 5
Philipstown 11 C 4
Phiritona 18 C 1
Phoenix 18 B 3
Phokeng 18 A 1
Phokwane 21 D 4
Phola 18 B 2
Phomolong 17 D 6
Phuthaditjhaba 12 A 3
Pienaar's River 20 D 3
Piet Plessis 17 B 4
Piet Retief 19 C 4
Pietermaritzburg 13 B 4
Pietersburg 21 C 4
Piggs Peak 19 B 5
Pigott's Bridge 6 B 3
Piketberg 4 B 1
Pilgrim's Rest 19 A 4
Pilikwe 20 A 2
Pinetown 13 B 5
Pitsane 17 A 5
Pitseng 12 A 2
Pitsi's Nek 12 A 2
Platbakkies 8 C 3
Platjan 20 A 3
Platkoppiesdrif 12 D 1
Platrand 18 C 3
Plettenberg Bay 5 C 6
Plooysburg 11 A 4
Poding-tse-Rolo 11 C 5
Pofadder 9 B 4
Politsi 21 B 4
Polokwane 21 C 4
Pomeroy 13 A 4
Pomfret 16 B 3
Pomona 14 C 1
Pongola 19 C 5
Ponta do Ouro 19 C 6
Pontdrif 20 A 3
Pools 4 B 2
Port Alfred 7 C 4
Port Beaufort 4 D 3
Port Durnford 13 A 6
Port Edward 13 D 4
Port Henrique 19 B 6
Port Nolloth 8 B 2
Port Shepstone 13 C 4
Port St Johns 12 D 3
Porterville 4 B 2
Post Chalmers 6 A 2
Postmasburg 10 A 3
Potchefstroom 18 C 1
Potfontein 11 C 4
Potgietersrus 20 C 3
Poupan 11 C 4
Pretoria North 18 A 2
Pretoria 18 A 2
Prieska 10 B 2
Prince Albert Road 5 B 4
Prince Albert 5 B 5
Prince Alfred Hamlet 4 C 2

Page
Pringle Bay 4 D 2
Priors 11 C 5
Protem 4 D 3
Protest 19 C 4
Providence 11 C 5
Pudimoe 17 C 4
Pudumong 17 C 4
Punda Maria Gate 21 A 5
Putsonderwater 10 B 1
Pyramid 18 A 2

Q

Qacha's Nek 12 C 2
Qalabotiha 18 C 2
Qalo 12 A 2
Qaqane 12 D 1
Qarnata 7 A 4
Qawukeni 7 B 4
Qedusizi 19 D 4
Qhoweng 11 B 6
Qibing 11 B 6
Qobong Ha Tsiu 12 C 1
Qokama 7 A 5
Qolora Mouth 7 B 5
Qomoqomong 12 C 1
Qora Mouth 7 B 5
Qota 7 A 5
Qudeni 13 A 5
Queensberry Bay 7 B 5
Queensburgh 13 B 5
Queenstown 7 A 4
Quiba 12 D 2
Qumbu 12 D 3
Qwaninga 7 A 5

R

Radisele 20 A 1
Raditshaba 20 A 3
Radium 20 D 3
Railton 4 C 3
Ramabanta 12 B 2
Ramatlabama 17 A 5
Rammulotsi 17 C 6
Ramohlakoana 12 C 3
Ramokgonami 20 A 2
Ramokokastad 18 A 1
Ramotswa 20 A 1
Ramsgate 13 D 4
Randburg 18 B 1
Randfontein 18 B 1
Rankin's Pass 20 C 2
Rantebeng 20 D 2
Raphahlelo 21 B 4
Rapitsi 20 B 3
Rasesa 20 A 1
Ratanang 11 B 4
Ratelfontein 4 A 1
Rawsonville 4 C 2
Rayton 18 A 2
Reagile 17 B 6
Rebone 20 B 3
Reddersburg 11 B 6
Redelinghuys 4 B 1
Redhouse 6 C 2
Redlands 10 B 2
Redoubt 13 D 4
Reedstream Park 18 B 3
Refengkgotso 18 C 1
Regina 17 C 6
Reitz 18 D 2
Reivilo 17 D 4
Renosterkop 5 A 6
Rensburgdorp 18 B 2
Ressano Garcia 21 D 6
Rhadhopololo 20 A 3
Rhenosterspruit 17 C 6
Rhodes 12 D 2
Richards Bay 13 A 6
Richmond 10 D 3
Richmond 13 B 4
Riebeek West 4 C 2
Riebeek-East 6 B 3
Riebeeckstad 17 D 6
Riebeek-Kasteel 4 C 2
Riemvasmaak 9 A 5
Rietbron 5 B 6

Page
Rietfontein 15 C 5
Rietfontein 21 C 5
Rietkuil 18 B 3
Rietpan 17 C 5
Rietpoel 4 D 2
Rietpoort 8 D 3
Rietspruit 12 A 1
Rietvlei 13 C 4
Ringane 21 C 6
Rini 6 C 3
Ritchie 11 A 4
Rite 21 D 4
River View 13 A 6
Riversdale 18 B 1
Riversdale 5 C 4
Riverside 12 C 3
Riverton 11 A 4
Riviersonderend 4 D 3
Roadside 18 D 2
Robben Island 4 C 1
Roberts Drift 18 C 2
Robertson 4 C 3
Roedtan 20 C 3
Roleleathunya 11 C 6
Rolle 21 D 6
Roma 12 B 1
Romanslaagte 6 A 3
Roodepan 11 B 4
Roodepoort 18 B 1
Roodewal 19 B 4
Rooiberg 20 D 2
Rooibokkraal 20 C 1
Rooibosbult 20 C 2
Rooiels 4 D 2
Rooifontein 8 C 3
Rooigrond 17 B 5
Rooihoogte 6 A 2
Rooikraal 18 C 1
Rooikraal 21 D 4
Rooilyf 10 A 1
Rooirivier 5 C 5
Rooiwal 18 C 1
Rookdale 12 A 3
Roosboom 12 A 3
Roossenekal 21 D 4
Rorke's Drift 13 A 4
Rosebank 13 B 4
Rosedene 5 A 5
Rosendal 12 A 2
Rosetta 13 B 4
Rosh Pinah 14 D 2
Rosmead 11 D 5
Ross Mission 12 D 2
Rossouw 12 D 1
Rothe 12 B 1
Rothmere 7 A 6
Rotkop 14 C 1
Rouxpos 5 C 4
Rouxville 12 C 1
Royal Kraal 19 D 5
Rugseer 10 B 1
Ruitersbos 5 C 5
Rusplaas 21 D 5
Rust 4 C 1
Rustenburg 18 A 1
Rustfontein 12 C 3
Rustig 18 C 1
Rusverby 20 D 1
Rutland 19 D 4
Rwantsana 7 A 4
Rydal 13 C 4
Ryno 12 D 2

S

Saaibult 12 A 1
Saaifontein 5 A 5
Sabelo 10 D 3
Sabie 21 D 5
Sada 7 A 4
Saggiesberg 9 D 4
Sakhile 18 C 3
Sakrivier 9 D 5
Salamanga 19 B 6
Saldanha 4 B 1
Salem 6 C 3
Salitje 19 C 5
Salpeterpan 17 C 4
Salt Lake 10 B 3

Page
Salt Rock 13 B 5
Sand Bay 4 D 2
Sandberg 4 A 1
Sandlane 19 B 4
Sandspruit 18 C 3
Sandton 18 B 1
Sandverhaar 14 C 3
Sandvlakte 6 C 1
Sani Pass 12 B 3
Sannaspos 11 B 6
Sannieshof 17 B 5
Santa Maria 19 B 6
Sasolburg 18 C 1
Satco 15 D 4
Sauer 4 B 1
Saulspoort 18 A 1
Scarborough 4 D 1
Schlechtgenoeg 6 A 2
Schmidtsdrif 10 A 3
Schoemansdal 19 A 5
Schoemanshoek 5 C 5
Schoemansville 18 A 1
Scholtz 5 C 5
Schoombee 11 D 5
Schoongelegen 20 A 3
Schoongezicht 6 B 3
Schwarzkuppe 14 A 2
Schweizer-Reneke 17 C 5
Scottburgh 13 C 5
Sea Park 13 C 4
Sea View 6 C 2
Sebapala 12 C 2
Seboche 12 A 2
Sebokeng 18 B 1
Secunda 18 B 3
Sedgefield 5 C 5
Sediba 12 A 1
Seeheim 14 C 3
Seekoegat 5 B 5
Sefare 20 B 2
Sefikeng 12 B 2
Sefophe 20 A 2
Seforong 12 C 2
Segole 20 B 3
Sehlabathebe 12 B 3
Sehlakwane 18 A 3
Sehonghong 12 B 3
Sekake 12 C 2
Sekhing 17 D 4
Sekhukhune 21 D 4
Sekwati 21 D 4
Selatirivier 21 C 5
Seleka 20 A 2
Selokolela 17 A 4
Selonsrivier 21 D 4
Semonkong 12 B 2
Sendelingsdrif 14 D 2
Sendelingsplaas 20 D 1
Senekal 18 D 1
Senlac 16 B 3
Senotlelo 20 D 3
Sentrum 20 C 2
Seoding 16 C 3
Sephaku 18 A 3
Sepharane 20 C 3
Serake 17 A 5
Seretse 11 A 5
Serfontein 18 C 1
Seru 7 A 5
Sesesehu 21 C 4
Seshego 21 C 4
Seshote 12 B 2
Sesobe 20 D 1
Setateng 20 B 2
Setlagole 17 B 4
Settlers 20 D 3
Seven Fountains 6 C 3
Seven Oaks 13 B 4
Severn 16 B 2
Seymour 7 B 4
Sezela 13 C 4
Shaka's Rock 13 B 5
Shakaskraal 13 B 5
Shakung 20 D 2
Shannon 11 B 6
Sharpeville 18 C 1
Shaw Park 7 C 4
Shayandima 21 B 5
Sheepmoor 19 C 4

PLACE NAMES INDEX

Sheffield Beach 13 B 5
Shelly Beach 13 D 4
Sherborne 11 D 4
Sheridan 12 A 2
Sherwood 20 A 2
Shigalo 21 A 5
Shirley 15 B 4
Sibasa 21 A 5
Sibayeni 19 A 5
Sicunusa 19 C 4
Sidbury 6 C 3
Sidney-on-Vaal 11 A 4
Sidvokodvo 19 B 5
Sidwadweni 12 D 3
Sigangeni 19 B 4
Signalberg 14 D 3
Sigundwaneni 12 D 3
Sihhoye 19 B 5
Sihlabeni 7 A 5
Sijungqwini 7 A 6
Sikobeni 7 A 5
Silaka 7 A 6
Silent Valley 20 C 1
Silkaatskop 20 D 1
Silobela 19 B 4
Silutshana 13 A 5
Silver Streams 10 A 3
Simlangetja 19 C 4
Simon's Town 4 D 1
Simuma 13 C 4
Simunye 19 B 5
Sinakho 11 D 6
Siphofaneni 19 C 5
Sir Lowry's Pass 4 D 2
Sishen Mine 16 D 2
Siteki 19 B 5
Sithobela 19 C 5
Sittingbourne 7 B 4
Sivukile 18 C 3
Siyabuswa 20 D 3
Siyathemba 18 C 2
Siyathuthuka 18 A 3
Sizanani Village 18 A 2
Skaapvlei 8 D 3
Skandinawiëdrif 17 C 6
Skeerpoort 18 B 1
Skelmwater 21 A 4
Skietfontein 10 D 2
Skipskop 4 D 3
Skoenmakerskop 6 C 2
Skoonspruit 17 D 6
Skuinsdrif 20 D 1
Skukuza 21 D 6
Slabberts 12 A 2
Slangfontein 5 A 5
Slangrivier 5 D 4
Slurry 17 B 5
Smithfield 11 C 6
Smitskraal 6 C 1
Sneeukraal 5 A 5
Sobabili 12 A 3
Sodium 10 C 3
Soebatsfontein 8 C 2
Soekmekaar 21 B 4
Somerset East 6 B 2
Somerset West 4 C 2
Somerset 20 C 1
Sondagsloop 20 C 3
Sonop 11 B 6
Sonop 18 A 1
Sonskyn 11 C 6
Sonstraal 16 C 2
Sorgvliet 11 B 5
Soshanguve 20 D 2
Sotong 21 B 5
Soutfontein 8 C 2
Southbroom 13 D 4
Southey 16 C 3
Southport 13 C 4
Southwell 6 C 3
Soutkuil 4 B 1
Soutpan 11 A 5
Soweto 18 B 1
Spanwerk 20 C 1
Speelmanskraal 5 C 6
Spes Bona 14 A 1
Spitskopvlei 6 A 2
Spoegrivier 8 C 3
Spring Valley 6 A 3
Springbok 8 B 3
Springfontein 11 C 5
Springs 18 B 2
Spytfontein 11 A 4
St Faith's 13 C 4
St George's Strand 6 C 2
St Helena Bay 4 B 1
St Lucia Estuary 13 A 6
St Mark's 7 A 4
St Matthews 19 D 4
Stafford's Post 12 C 3
Standerton 18 C 3
Stanford 4 D 2
Stanford's Cove 4 D 2
Steel's Drift 18 C 3
Steelpoort 21 D 5
Steenbokpan 20 B 2
Steilloopbrug 20 B 3
Steinkop 8 B 3
Stella 17 B 4
Stellenbosch 4 C 2
Sterkrivier 20 C 3
Sterkspruit 12 C 1
Sterkstroom 11 D 6
Sterling 10 D 1
Steynsburg 11 D 5
Steynsrus 18 D 1
Steynville 11 B 4
Steytlerville 6 C 1
Stilfontein 17 C 6
Still Bay 5 D 4
Stockpoort 20 B 2
Stoffberg 21 D 4
Stofvlei 9 C 4
Stompneus Bay 4 B 1
Stormberg 11 D 6
Storms River 6 C 1
Storms River Mouth 6 C 1
Stormsvlei 4 C 3
Straatsdrif 20 D 1
Strand 4 C 2
Strandfontein 4 A 1
Straussburg 10 A 1
Struis Bay 4 D 3
Strydenburg 10 C 3
Strydomsvlei 5 B 6
Strydpoort 17 C 5
Studtis 6 C 1
Stutterheim 7 B 4
Sukkelaar 18 B 3
Summerstrand 6 C 2
Sundra 18 B 2
Sundumbili 13 B 5
Sunland 6 C 2
Susannahspos 12 A 1
Susannaskop 18 D 2
Sutherland 4 A 3
Sutton 16 C 2
Suurberg 6 C 2
Suurbraak 4 C 3
Swartberg 12 C 3
Swartkop 10 C 1
Swartkops 6 C 2
Swart-Mfolozi 19 D 5
Swartmodder 15 D 6
Swartputs 16 D 3
Swartruggens 17 A 6
Swartwater 20 A 3
Swawel 9 D 5
Swellendam 4 C 3
Swempoort 12 D 1
Swinburne 12 A 3
Süderecke 14 A 2
Syferfontein 17 B 6
Syfergat 11 D 6

T

Taaiboschgroet 20 A 3
Tabankulu 12 D 3
Table Mountain 13 B 4
Table View 4 C 1
Tafelberg 11 D 5
Tamasane 20 A 2
Tarka Bridge 6 A 3
Tarkastad 6 A 3
Taung 17 D 4
Taupye 20 A 2
Tebellong 12 C 2
Teebus 11 D 5
Tellebrug 12 C 1
Temba 20 D 3
Tembinkosi 11 C 4
Tembisa 18 B 2
Terra Firma 16 A 3
Tevoit 6 A 2
Teyateyaneng 12 B 1
Teza 13 A 6
Thaba Bosiu 12 B 1
Thaba Nchu 12 B 1
Thaba Phatshwa 12 B 1
Thabana Morena 12 C 1
Thabana 20 D 3
Thabankulu 19 B 5
Thaba-Tseka 12 B 2
Thabazimbi 20 C 2
Thabong 17 D 6
Thakazele 19 D 4
Thamaga 20 A 1
Thambokhulu 19 B 5
The Brook 19 B 4
The Cavern 12 A 3
The Crags 5 C 6
The Haven 7 A 6
The Nest 12 A 3
The Willows 6 C 2
Thembalesizwe 6 B 1
Thembalihle 18 C 3
Thengwe 21 A 5
Theron 17 D 6
Theunissen 11 A 6
Thixwadza 21 A 5
Thlakalatlou 16 D 3
Thohoyandou 21 B 5
Thokazi 19 D 5
Tholeni 13 A 4
Thomas River 7 B 4
Thomeng 17 D 4
Thomo 21 B 5
Thornham 6 C 1
Thornhill 6 A 3
Thornville 13 B 4
Three Sisters 5 A 6
Tidbury's Toll 6 B 3
Tidimalo 11 A 4
Tierfontein 17 D 6
Tierkloof 17 C 4
Tigane 17 C 6
Tikwana 17 D 5
Timbavati Gate 21 C 5
Tina Bridge 12 D 3
Tinley Manor Beach 13 B 5
Tinmyne 20 C 3
Tiptree 6 C 2
Tjakastad 19 B 4
Tlapeng 16 C 3
Tlaseng 20 D 2
Tlhabane 18 A 1
Tlhabologang 17 B 6
Tlhakgameng 17 B 4
Tlholong 12 A 2
Tlokoeng 12 B 3
Tlokweng 17 A 6
Tlokweng 20 A 1
Toeslaan 9 A 5
Togo 6 C 2
Toleni Head 7 A 5
Tolse 7 B 4
Tolwe 20 B 3
Tom Burke 20 B 2
Tombo 7 A 6
Tongaat Beach 13 B 5
Tongaat 13 B 5
Tontelbos 9 D 5
Tooseng 21 C 4
Tosca 16 B 3
Touws River 4 C 3
Trawal 4 A 1
Treves 20 B 3
Trichardt 18 B 3
Trichardtsdal 21 C 5
Trompsburg 11 C 5
Trooilapspan 10 A 1
Tsakane 18 B 2
Tsa-Kholo 12 B 1
Tsatsane 21 C 4
Tsatsaneng 21 C 4
Tsaukaib 14 C 1
Tsawisis 14 B 3
Tses 14 B 3
Tsetsebjwe 20 A 3
Tshabong 16 B 2
Tshakhuma 21 B 5
Tshamahansi 20 C 3
Tshaneni 19 B 5
Tshani 7 A 6
Tshatshu 7 A 4
Tshiame 12 A 3
Tshidilamolomo 17 B 4
Tshing 17 B 6
Tshiozwi 21 B 4
Tshipise 21 A 5
Tsilwana 16 B 3
Tsineng 16 C 2
Tsitsa Bridge 12 D 3
Tsitsing 18 A 1
Tsoelike 12 C 2
Tsolo 12 D 2
Tsomo 7 A 5
Tswaing 21 C 4
Tswaraganang 11 A 5
Tswatago 21 C 4
Tswelelang 17 C 5
Tugela Ferry 13 A 4
Tugela Mouth 13 B 5
Tugela 13 B 5
Tuinplaas 20 D 3
Tulbagh 4 C 2
Tumahole 18 C 1
Turfbult 20 C 3
Turton 13 C 4
Tutuka 18 C 3
Twee Rivier 15 A 5
Twee Rivieren 15 B 6
Tweebuffels 17 B 6
Tweefontein 12 B 1
Tweefontein 20 D 3
Tweefontein 4 A 2
Tweeling 18 D 2
Tweespruit 12 B 1
Twenty Four Rivers 20 C 3
Tyinindini 12 C 1
Tylden 7 A 4
Tzaneen 21 C 4

U

Ubombo 19 D 6
Ugie 12 D 2
Uitenhage 6 C 2
Uitkeer 6 B 2
Uitkomst 6 B 1
Uitsig 15 D 5
Uitspankraal 4 A 2
Uitspanning 18 C 3
Uitvlug 10 B 2
Uitvlugte 20 D 3
Uitweg 9 D 6
Uitzicht 20 B 3
Ulco 11 A 4
Ulundi 13 A 5
Umbumbulu 13 C 4
Umdloti Beach 13 B 5
Umgababa 13 C 5
Umgazi Mouth 7 A 6
uMhlali 13 B 5
Umhlanga Rocks 13 B 5
Umkomaas 13 C 5
Umlazi 13 C 5
Umtata Mouth 7 A 6
Umtata 7 A 5
Umtentweni 13 C 4
uMunywana 13 A 5
Umzamomhle 6 C 2
uMzimkulu 13 C 4
uMzinto 13 C 4
uMzumbe 13 C 4
Underberg 12 B 3
Uniondale 5 C 6
Upington 10 A 1
Upper Chilton 7 A 4
Upper Telle 12 C 1
Urionskraal 4 A 2
Urionskraal 9 D 4
Usutu 20 A 3
Utlwanang 17 D 4
Utrecht 19 D 4
Uvongo 13 D 4

V

Vaalboshoek 17 D 4
Vaalhoek 21 D 5
Vaalplaats 17 B 5
Vaalwater 20 C 2
Val 18 C 2
Valspan 17 D 4
Valsrivier 18 D 2
Van Dyks 18 B 3
Van Reenen 12 A 3
Van Stadens 6 C 2
Van Stadensrus 12 C 1
Van Wyksdorp 5 C 4
Van Wyksrus 17 C 6
Van Wyksvlei 10 C 1
Van Zylsrus 16 C 1
Vanderbijlpark 18 C 1
Vanderkloof 11 C 4
Vanrhynsdorp 4 A 1
Vant's Drift 19 D 4
Veekraal 21 C 4
Velddrif 4 B 1
Velloor 9 A 4
Ventersburg 18 D 1
Ventersdorp 17 B 6
Venterspos 18 B 1
Venterstad 11 D 5
Vereeniging 18 B 1
Verena 20 D 3
Vergeleë 17 A 4
Vergesig 16 C 1
Verkeerdevlei 12 A 1
Verkykerskop 18 D 3
Vermaaklikheid 5 D 4
Vermaas 17 B 5
Vermont 4 D 2
Verulam 13 B 5
Victoria Bay 5 C 5
Victoria West 10 D 3
Vierfontein 17 C 6
Viljoensdrif 18 C 1
Viljoenshof 4 D 2
Viljoenskroon 17 C 6
Viljoenspos 19 D 4
Villa Nora 20 B 2
Villiers 18 C 2
Villiersdorp 4 C 2
Vioolsdrif 8 A 2
Virginia 17 D 6
Visgat 20 C 2
Vivo 21 B 4
Vlakdrif 18 B 1
Vlaklaagte 20 D 3
Vlakplaas 18 C 2
Vlakpoort 18 C 3
Vlakteplaas 5 C 5
Vlees Bay 5 D 5
Vleidam 5 D 4
Vleiland 5 C 4
Vleirivier 5 C 5
Vlieëkraal 17 D 5
Vlieëkraal 4 A 3
Voëlgeraas 10 C 3
Volksrust 18 C 3
Volmoed 5 C 5
Volop 10 A 2
Volstruisleegte 5 B 6
Volstruispan 18 A 2
Vondeling 5 C 6
Voorbaat 5 C 4
Voorreg 20 D 3
Voorspoed 16 B 3
Vorstershoop 16 B 2
Vosburg 10 C 2
Vouga 21 A 6
Vrede 18 C 3
Vredefort 18 C 1
Vredenburg 4 B 1
Vredendal 4 A 1
Vredeshoop 15 C 5
Vroenspan 15 D 6
Vryburg 17 C 4
Vryheid 19 D 4
Vukusakhe 18 C 3
Vuyolwethu 6 C 1
Vyandsvlei 18 C 1
Vyeboom 21 B 5
Vyeboom 4 C 2

W

Waenhuiskrans (Arniston) 4 D 3
Wag 'n Bietjie 19 C 4
Wagenaarskraal 5 A 5
Wakefield 18 B 2
Wakkerstroom 19 C 4
Walkerville 18 B 1
Wallekraal 8 C 2
Wanda 11 B 4
Waqu 7 A 4
Warburton 19 B 4
Warden 18 D 2
Warmbad Noord 9 A 4
Warmbad 9 A 4
Warmbaths 20 D 3
Warmfontein 15 C 4
Warmwaterberg 5 C 4
Warrenton 17 D 4
Wartburg 13 B 4
Wasbank 19 D 4
Wasser 14 B 3
Waterford 6 B 2
Waterkloof 11 C 5
Waterpoort 21 A 4
Watersend 16 A 2
Waterval Boven 19 A 4
Waterval Onder 19 A 4
Waverley 6 A 3
Weenen 13 A 4
Wegdraai 10 A 1
Wegdraai 15 A 5
Weiveld 18 C 1
Welbedagtdam 11 B 6
Welgeleë 17 D 6
Welkom 17 D 6
Wellington 4 C 2
Welverdiend 15 A 5
Welverdiend 16 C 1
Welverdiend 18 B 1
Wepener 12 B 1
Werda 16 A 3
Wesley 7 C 4
Wesselsbron 17 D 6
Wesselton 18 B 3
Westerberg 10 B 2
Westminster 12 B 1
Westonaria 18 B 1
Weza 12 C 3
White Mountain 12 B 3
White River 21 D 5
Whites 17 D 6
Whitesands 5 D 4
Whitmore 12 D 2
Whittlesea 7 A 4
Wiegnaarspoort 5 B 6
Wilderness 5 C 5
Wilgenhoutsdrif 10 A 1
Willemsdal 18 C 2
Williston 9 D 6
Willowmore 5 C 6
Willowvale 7 A 5
Winburg 12 A 1
Wincanton 16 D 2
Wind Mill 4 C 2
Windfield 18 C 2
Windsorton Road 11 A 4
Windsorton 17 D 4
Winterstrand 7 B 5
Winterton 12 A 3
Wirsing 17 B 4
Witbank 18 B 3
Witbank 8 A 3
Witbooisvlei 15 A 4
Witdraai 15 C 6
Witfontein 20 C 2
Withoogte 12 D 1
Witkleigat 17 A 5
Witkop 11 D 6
Witmos 6 B 3
Witpan 10 A 2
Witpoort 17 C 5
Witput 11 B 4
Witpütz 14 D 2
Witrand 18 B 3
Witrandsfontein 17 B 6
Wittenberg 19 C 4
Witwater 4 B 1
Witwater 8 C 3
Wolmaransstad 17 C 5
Wolplaas 15 D 4
Wolseley 4 C 2
Wolwefontein 5 C 4
Wolwefontein 6 C 2
Wolwehoek 18 C 1
Wolwespruit 11 A 5
Wonderfontein 18 B 3
Wonderheuwel 18 C 1
Wonderkop 18 D 1
Wondermere 17 A 6
Wongalethu 6 B 1
Woodbine 20 D 1
Woodford 12 A 3
Woodlands 6 C 1
Woodlands 7 B 4
Worcester 4 C 2
Wrenchville 16 C 3
Wuppertal 4 A 2
Wurasoord 11 B 5
Wyongwana 7 A 4

X

Xalanga 12 D 1
Xawela 21 B 5
Xinavane 19 A 6
Xolobe 7 A 4

Y

York 13 B 4
Ypres 20 C 3
Yzerfontein 4 C 1

Z

Zaaimansdal 5 C 6
Zadungweni 12 D 2
Zamani 18 D 3
Zamdela 18 C 1
Zanzibar 20 A 3
Zaris 14 A 1
Zastron 12 C 1
Zebediela Sta. 21 C 4
Zebediela 21 C 4
Zebra 5 C 5
Zeekoegat 21 C 4
Zeerust 17 A 5
Zenzeleni 18 D 2
Zinkwazi Beach 13 B 5
Zion City Moria 21 C 4
Zitapaleni 7 A 4
Zitende 19 C 5
Zithabiseni 18 A 2
Zithobeni 18 A 2
Zitundo 19 C 6
Zoar 5 C 4
Zola 6 A 3
Zolani 4 C 3
Zunckels 12 A 3
Zwelitsha 7 B 4

ACKNOWLEDGEMENTS:

We would like to thank all the relavent authorities for their help, information and material which enabled John Hall to compile and produce the cartography for this atlas. The Survey and Land Information office with their maps, aeronautical charts, aerial photography and Orthophoto maps were as always a great help.